D1571577

Yellowstone

and the Biology of Time

Yellowstone and the Biology of Time

PHOTOGRAPHS ACROSS A CENTURY

Mary Meagher &
Douglas B. Houston

UNIVERSITY OF OKLAHOMA PRESS

Norman

Published with the generous assistance of the United States Geological Survey and the National Park Service–Yellowstone National Park, and of Edith Gaylord Harper.

Library of Congress Cataloging-in-Publication Data

Meagher, Margaret Mary.
   Yellowstone and the biology of time: photographs across a century /
Mary Meagher & Douglas B. Houston.
       p.   cm.
   Includes bibliographical references (p.   ) and index.
   ISBN 0-8061-2996-4
   1. Natural history—Yellowstone National Park. 2. Natural history
—Yellowstone National Park—Pictorial works.   I. Houston, Douglas B.
II. Title.
QH105.W6M435 1998
508.787'52—dc21   97-40591
                                                          CIP

Book design and composition by Wesley B. Tanner/Passim Editions

The paper in this book meets the guidelines for permanence and durability of the Committee on Production Guidelines for Book Longevity of the Council on Library Resources, Inc. ☉

1 2 3 4 5 6 7 8 9 10

For Jack K. Anderson

Superintendent of Yellowstone National Park 1967–75;

Glen F. Cole

Supervisory Research Biologist of Yellowstone National Park 1967–76;

Nathaniel P. Reed

Assistant Secretary of Interior for Fish, Wildlife and Parks 1971–77.

Their time marked an exceptional period for the natural resources of Yellowstone National Park. The sum was more than the parts.

For Graeme Caughley

Truly a Renaissance ecologist. We are in your debt.

Contents

Illustrations

PLATES

FIGURES

Preface

HOW THIS BOOK CAME TO BE

Twenty-five years ago we set about compiling a collection of comparative photographs of Yellowstone National Park. The idea was generated initially by Doug Houston's studies of the northern Yellowstone elk. After he came to Yellowstone in 1970, we began to talk about the need for perspective on the vegetation changes that had occurred historically on ungulate winter ranges in the park—a subject of considerable controversy and speculation. We decided to try using repeat photographs. Biologist George Gruell had used this technique with great success on the Bridger-Teton National Forest, which abuts the park's south boundary. Mary had a long-standing interest in the biological information to be gleaned from the early years of park history, an interest fostered by nearly a decade of working as a naturalist-curator. She was personally familiar with the Yellowstone photo collections and with the work of many early photographers. Her interest in what is now the field of environmental history intensified during her studies of bison because of the need for information on vegetation trends for their winter ranges.

From the beginning we collaborated; between 1971 and 1973 we built a collection of some 320 sets of photographs. Ours was a project of discovery and adventure. Searches through the various collections for scenes of Yellowstone were akin to treasure hunts. We would think a view interesting and useful and would set out to locate the site. From our collective years of beating around Yellowstone's backcountry, we usually had a good idea of where to look, but sometimes not. Sometimes an early photo point no longer existed, having been removed by erosion acting as an agent of geological time. Trees would grow; views would be obscured. Our cameras and lens lengths were different from those first used, so perspectives were not exact. We could not always find early views that we would like to have had for some parts of the park. As with any form of historical record, what you see is what you get. Early photographers did not take scenes for the likes of us to use later; they took what interested them at the time.

The sets of photographs were captioned, mounted somewhat casually on large sheets of heavy paper, and then stored in proper archival boxes. The repeat sets were intended as working tools for a couple of research biologists, so it did not matter too much that early views were sometimes of poor quality for reproduction purposes. We still could discern useful details. The totality of the collection was important, because we could consider patterns on a parkwide scale. This helped our thinking greatly.

Doug used 51 sets of repeat photographs in the *Northern Yellowstone Elk* monograph published by Macmillan in 1982. Sam McNaughton, of Syracuse University, one of Doug's technical reviewers for that publication, remarked that the photo comparisons were much too valuable to provide only selected views for a monograph about elk. This jogged our thinking, and we began to talk about publishing more of the collection. But Doug transferred to another assignment; Mary's workload changed. And changes came also, of course, to the natural scene and the inhabitants thereof. The collection was stored as a part of the park's photo archives, although selected views sometimes provided insight for someone's particular interest. Occasionally we talked long distance about Sam's comment.

Then came the fires of 1988. It seemed to us a not-to-be-missed opportunity to retake all the scenes that had burned, and so for part of the collection there is now a series of three views. We also retook some that did not burn, because the comparisons with the views taken just 20 years earlier did much for our perspective on rates of change. We realized we had not yet seen the full expression of fire's effects on some sites; in forested areas burned trees may take some years to die. In contrast, fire effects on meadow grasslands were sometimes quite transient, and so were waning by 1990 when we began the rephotography. The scale of the fires gave us an opportunity to test many of our earlier ideas about the forces that shape plant communities in the park. And we benefited from a wealth of recent research in many disciplines.

The book is divided into three parts. First are the photographs, the visual presentation of the topics to be discussed, and of interest in their own right. The first repeat photographs span roughly 100 years, the second series a 20-year interval, for a total perspective of 120 years. The photographs are captioned to stand on their own. They have plate numbers and are referenced in sections of the topical discussions that comprise parts 2 and 3. Part 2 presents the physical and biological framework for the photographs and part 3 is our synthesis of the lessons they have given us. We offer our interpretations of the forces driving biological change in the park. We share with you our perspective on the changes that we regard as natural and those we interpret as caused by the actions of present-day humans. Extensive endnotes elaborate on points raised in the text, provide information, and supply references. In those, we provide our operational definition of *natural ecosystems* and tackle that much abused term, *natural regulation.* Our effort would not be complete without offering an epilogue, a discussion of the management of ecosystems of Yellowstone and other parks set aside as natural areas.

In presenting this book, we hope to reach a broad audience. Yellowstone is a place special to many people, for many reasons. We assume that some readers will want to look mostly at photographs, perhaps focusing on places they have visited. Others will be interested in the text but not necessarily all of it. We have not tried to synthesize all current biological research information; rather we present our best shot at appraising the biological state of the park. A technical synthesis is needed, but this is not it; this is an overview and a lead-in to the literature. This is our way of saying that for us, Yellowstone is a special place, a fascinating place. We have learned a lot, we've had fun, and we now want to share with you the best of the collection.

Enjoy!

Acknowledgments

We could not have produced this book without the contributions of many people. The early photographers provided the cornerstone that made the project possible; all are acknowledged with their photographs. W. H. Jackson and J. P. Iddings of the U.S. Geological Survey, and F. J. and J. E. Haynes of Haynes, Inc., stand out.

All the negatives of our own retake photographs are part of the Yellowstone National Park photo archives, as is the complete collection. The Yellowstone National Park Archives are a branch of the National Archives in Washington, D.C. Other National Park Service (NPS) collections from which photos are drawn are either within Yellowstone, which includes photographic prints obtained from many sources since the time the park was established, or within the Washington, D.C., office of the NPS. Additional federal agencies supplying photos are the United States Forest Service and U.S. Geological Survey, which has a photographic collection housed at their Denver library. Some photos came from universities.

Abbreviations used in the photo captions for the collections are:

MHS	*Montana Historical Society, Helena*
NPS-YNP	*National Park Service, Yellowstone National Park*
NA	*National Archives, Washington, D.C.*
NPS-WASO	*National Park Service, Washington office*
SUNY ESF	*Terence J. Hoverter College Archives at F. Franklin Moon Library, College of Environmental Science and Forestry, State University of New York, Syracuse*
UA	*University of Arizona, Tucson*
USFS	*U.S. Forest Service*
USGS	*U.S. Geological Survey*
UW	*University of Wyoming, Laramie*

Janis Burger (Olympic National Park) did a magnificent job of processing negatives and printing photographs and helped with innumerable and essential details. She also applied her editorial eye with skill.

Thanks to J. Larson, Pacific Northwest Region, National Park Service, and to S. Coleman, Yellowstone National Park, for facilitating Doug Houston's trips to Yellowstone to work on photo retakes and other details of the project. M. Finley, superintendent, R. Smith, acting superintendent, and E. Williams, landscape architect, all of Yellowstone National Park, supported financially the manuscript review copies. J. D. Varley, Yellowstone National Park, funded helicopter costs for some of Doug Houston's retakes. The National Park Service supported our work as research biologists until our reassignments in 1993 to a newly formed research agency, now the Biological Resources Division of the U.S. Geological Survey. That agency has supported us since.

We also wish to acknowledge J. Agee, R. Bahr, M. Boyce, S. Coleman, T. Danforth, D. Despain, J. Donaldson, M. Gracz, K. Gunther, T. Hudson, J. Houston, J. Mack, S. McNaughton, C. and J. Mernin, A. Mitchell and his helicopter operations crew; photo curators E. Kortge and J. Peaco (Yellowstone National Park), J. MacGregor (U.S. Geological Survey), and F. Nyland (State University of New York); P. Perkins; pilots C. Rogers, D. Stradley, and C. Wainwright; R. Renkin, T. Tankersley, and N. Ward. We thank the support staffs of the Yellowstone National Park ranger office, corral operations, data processing, and the equipment repair garage. The Yellowstone Association kindly helped with replacement photo prints. We remember also that others helped us with the original project of retakes in the early 1970s.

Researchers W. Romme, L. Wallace, and C. Whitlock generously provided unpublished manuscripts and publications unknown to us. C. White, assistant chief warden at Banff National Park, was equally generous in providing access to a draft manuscript of photographic comparisons for that park.

R. Evanoff and L. Wilkinson produced graphics. R. Renkin drafted maps from a Geographic Information System. U. Weltman, with cheer and care, made the review copies of the original photographs. S. Broadbent and P. Schullery provided insight into nuances of the publication process. L. Wallace facilitated our initial contact with our publisher.

We benefited from topical reviews by D. Frank (herbivory), J. Good (geology), A. Johnson (early humans), L. Wallace (herbivory), and J. Whipple (plant taxonomy and photo captions). R. Gresswell, D. Knight, W. Romme, L. Wallace, and C. Whitlock shared their experiences and insights with reviews in entirety. J. Houston reviewed the manuscript for typographical errors, and P. Schullery assessed our ability to communicate.

We thank the University of Oklahoma Press, particularly Alice Stanton and Colleen Waggoner. Copy editor Sally Antrobus was especially helpful.

Our families and friends were always there for us, with interest, patience, forbearance, and support. There is no price.

For us all, this is *our* book.

Yellowstone
and the Biology of Time

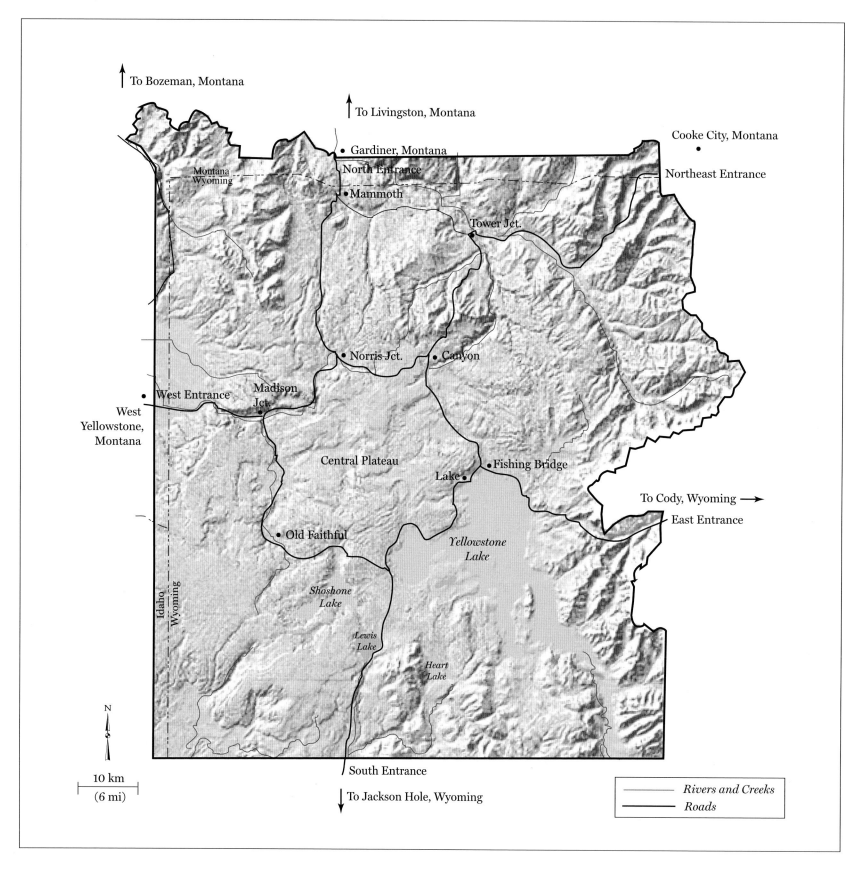

Fig. 1. *Map of Yellowstone National Park showing roads, development locations,*
and major lakes and rivers. Topography shaded in. Yellowstone GIS.

Prologue

Time, and changes that occur with time, seem to be among the most difficult concepts for people to grasp. Today is today; we sometimes have difficulty thinking about tomorrow, let alone next year. We give little reality to potential events that are beyond our control. For instance, we know intellectually that earthquakes occur, but we usually regard them as abstractions that happen to someone else in some other place and time. Perhaps our evolutionary heritage has given us little sense of time; if we did not make it through today, there would be no tomorrow. If we accepted clearly and realistically the many negative things that could happen to us, it would be difficult to function today. We live in the present moment and our individual life spans are relatively short.

However, to protect and preserve a place such as Yellowstone National Park as a natural area to the extent possible, we must find ways to alter and expand our perspective on time. Otherwise, how can we possibly know whether a biological change occurs because of the activities of modern humans, or because such change is a function of the natural processes and events that are a part of any ecosystem?[1] Some changes may represent influences of both kinds. But we seem prone to assume that modern humans have had the dominant role in causing change.

Here, our need was to try to separate factors driving change, to distinguish symptoms from causes, and then to attempt to synthesize and relate these factors into a whole. To the extent that we were successful, we progressed from some understanding of biological change and the ecological relationships involved to eventually gaining some insight into ecosystem processes. For our purposes we approached the first as a subset of the second, recognizing that there is not always a clear demarcation between the two. The natural world rarely seems to fit our definitions neatly.

Biological change may be slow in pace and small in scale, as when ponds gradually fill in to become meadows, or change may be rapid and occur on a grand scale, as underscored by the Yellowstone fires. Few people seem to grasp the amount of change that may occur in natural systems over relatively short spans of time. Large-scale changes brought about by events such as the wildfires of 1988 seem particularly difficult to accept and recognize as a natural force. Perhaps this is because we are accustomed to controlling smaller fires. In the experience of modern peoples fire is usually a destroyer, but wildfire in Yellowstone is a natural agent of change and renewal. Fire simply alters the biological characters on the stage, for a time.

Our starting point for addressing changes within "biological time" in Yellowstone is necessarily arbitrary. We consider biological time for Yellowstone as the Holocene epoch of geological time, roughly the last 10,000 years since the Pleistocene ice vanished from this locale. In particular, we focus on the biological changes during historic time and shortly before, which happen to equate generally with Yellowstone's history as a national park. Indeed, Yellowstone is the first *national* park, established in 1872. The photographs are the images of historic time.

The Yellowstone we see and try to know today is a visible representation of geological, climatological, and biological forces and events. As such it is complex; indeed we have learned that if the "answer" or analysis is simple, as in elk browsing aspen and cottonwood, the reality is likely to be much more complex. Not only are there diverse forces and influences involved, but the relative role of these forces will vary and sometimes reverse over time, occurring on a continuum from specific events to gradual processes. *If it's simple, be careful* became our guiding principle. We may not understand or even identify all the complexities, but nothing we have learned about Yellowstone's biological world is simple.

The complexities that shaped Yellowstone are myriad. Mountain building, volcanism, and ice provided the foundation and formed the surface expression of much that we see. These forces dictated the soils that developed, derived from the parent bedrock and the surface deposits left by glacial activity. In turn, soils together with long-term climatic influences and prevailing weather patterns produced kinds, distributions, and the relative abundance of vegetation that grows here.

Even as the last vestiges of the ice disappeared a mere 10,000 years ago, soils began to develop and plants to colonize. Those plants that already occupied adjacent areas had the best opportunity. Those with wind-borne seeds or seeds carried by travelers such as birds had an additional edge for colonization. So too the animals, not just those of major interest—what we jokingly call the charismatic megafauna—but all the smaller creatures, including those of the soil and the air. These colonizers also must have been living relatively nearby, although their greater mobility would have aided many of the mammals, birds, and insects.

Opportunity to colonize would have been important, but so would the inherent characteristics of the colonizing life, derived from their evolutionary heritage. Some plants need more moisture, some more sun. Temperatures dictate the growing season available to plants. Some plants are able to grow on acidic soils that preclude other forms. Animal life also has particular needs, governed by the kinds of plants and climates that prevail. The colonizers that could become seasonal or permanent residents in Yellowstone did so because conditions were right for their kind.

Most biological inhabitants of Yellowstone arrived long before European humans. There were no greater or lesser inhabitants among them, all were components of the scene. Accordingly, we reason that they existed with some kinds of interrelationships, but the relative abundance among them undoubtedly varied over time even as the environment itself varied. Just as the many forms of plants and animals colonized the area after the ice, so too some forms disappeared as the conditions allowing their presence changed, long before the arrival of explorers and tourists, bureaucrats and biologists. We should expect change; it has been the only constant since the ice. Nor, as we shall see, could we prevent change if we wished. The natural forces that shaped the area we call Yellowstone and the variations in these forces over time are beyond the will of humankind, and are indeed indifferent to our presence.

PART 1
The Photographs

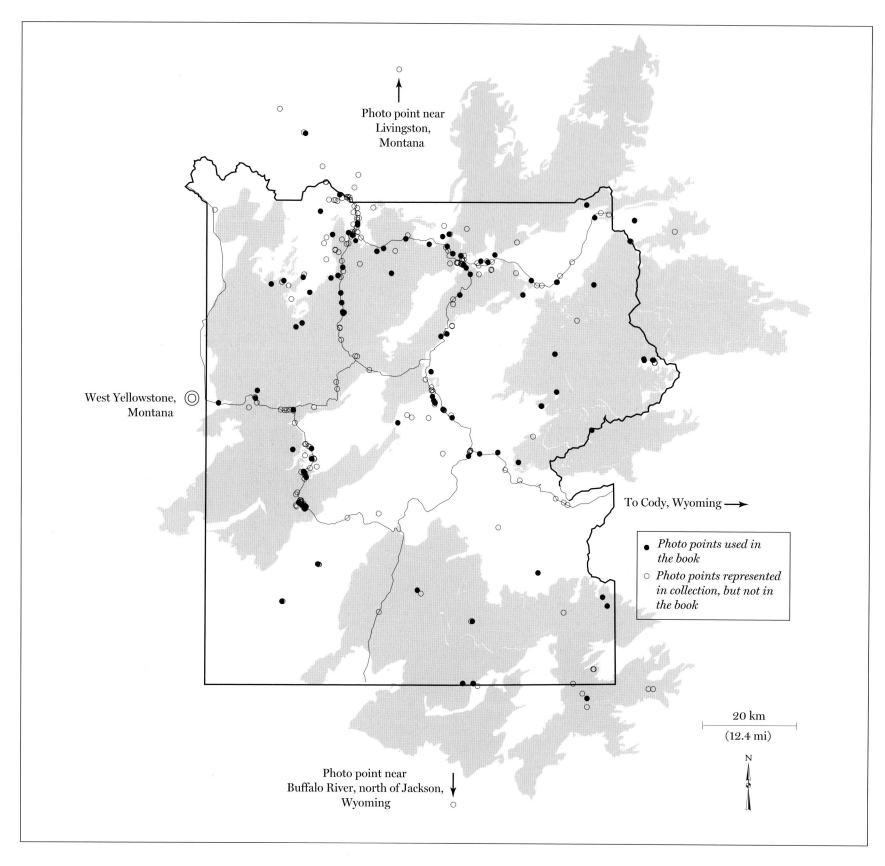

Photo point near
Livingston,
Montana

West Yellowstone,
Montana ◎

To Cody, Wyoming ⟶

● *Photo points used in
the book*

○ *Photo points represented
in collection, but not in
the book*

20 km
(12.4 mi)

N

Photo point near
Buffalo River, north of Jackson,
Wyoming

Fig. 2. *Map showing the distribution of all photographic points represented in the comparative photo collection. Some circles overlap because photo points cluster at popular locations. Also, many are located near the park road system because these were the travel routes most often used by early photographers. Shading indicates the extent of the forest fires of 1988, often driven from southwest to northeast by prevailing winds. Yellowstone GIS.*

Introduction

THE ART OF REPEAT PHOTOGRAPHY

Repeat photography has been used throughout the world to document landscape change over time.[1] In essence, the procedure is simple enough: locate the camera position used by the original photographer and rephotograph the scene as close to the same date and time of day as circumstances permit. But this brief statement fails to convey the excitement and frustrations involved. For example, the locations noted on many of the original photographs in the collections we searched were labeled simply "Yellowstone Park," and some did not provide even that much information; we assumed they had been taken in the park from the subject matter or context of the original collection.

Fortunately, Yellowstone's dramatic skylines and abundant geologic features usually provided clues to location. When our own earlier travels in the backcountry failed to suggest a starting point for the search, we showed unidentified photos to colleagues. It was not unusual for our pilot, Dave Stradley, to have the print of a particularly troublesome scene taped up in the cockpit of his Supercub while flying parkwide wildlife surveys. In retrospect, we were remarkably fortunate in finding most of the sites we set out to rephotograph. There remained, however, an exasperating few scenes that eluded us, and these haunted us. We have each awakened from sound sleep with thoughts akin to: "That 'lost' Iddings photo of the spring surrounded by aspen and subalpine fir might have been taken at . . ." Reluctantly, we leave these for future landscape detectives.

The timing necessary for a good retake photograph required some educated guessing on our part. Usually the original photographers indicated the year a scene was taken. We often inferred approximate seasonal dates from knowledge of an expedition itinerary, the stage of growth of the vegetation, volume of water in streams, size and shape of snowbanks, etc. Shadows in the photograph usually indicated the approximate time of day. Locating the camera point was sometimes difficult unless the foreground contained a convenient stone, unusually shaped tree, or some other unique feature. In a few instances we could not stand where our predecessors had; the viewpoint had eroded away. Perspectives occasionally were confusing because of differences in camera lenses. All these conditions meant that two or more trips (usually hiking or on horseback) were required to some sites before we were satisfied with the match.[2]

In the field, we marked the locations of camera points on maps, described the existing vegetation, and noted similarities to and differences from past conditions. We also noted the extent of grazing and the animal species involved, evidence of past fires, amount of human disturbance to the site, and any other information that would help interpret the scene.

This stark description of the field work does not convey the underlying sense of excitement we often felt when the early camera points were first rediscovered. Part of this was simply opening a window into the past: many retakes showed virtually no change—the pioneer photographer would have been perfectly at home looking through the viewfinders of our cameras. Other scenes provided such stunning contrast that even we at first doubted that the replication was correct. But there was more to it, including such personal thoughts as: Why did you, my photographer predecessor, select this particular scene? Did you too hear elk bugling in the distance or note grizzly bear tracks in the meadow?[3]

We were constantly amazed at the efforts the early photographers must have made to haul cumbersome camera equipment into difficult locations—these were truly dedicated photographers.[4] Early cameras were often handsome but large objects of varnished wood, glass, and metal, of a size needed to take the desired view, because enlargements were a technique of the future. Moreover, the early cameras often used fragile wet-plate glass negatives, which—fortunately for us—produced photos with exquisite detail.

The original photographs were not random scenes of the landscape, because each photographer was biased toward particular subjects of interest. We enjoyed the good fortune of being able to use photos from collections assembled by many different early photographers, each with varying interests. Even so, the original scenes were biased in favor of geological features, especially geysers and spectacular waterfalls that attracted tourists. Ease of access dictated that more of the original photographs were taken near early travel routes and roads than in remote backcountry areas. Our selection of scenes to rephotograph was also biased to a degree by our interest in vegetation, particularly grasslands. We were further limited to those early scenes containing enough recognizable features for us to relocate the camera points. However, because of the large number of photographs available, we are comfortable that the scenes represent general conditions and provide reasonable perspective on the extent of change or lack of it (stasis) that has occurred throughout the park.

Criticisms have been leveled at the repeat photography technique, especially as regards having too few scenes from which to draw conclusions about the extent of a particular change. A related criticism we have encountered is the idea that we simply have two points in time (the photos) separated by unknown events and activities; we do not know what happened at the site during the intervening years. These concerns seem minimal in Yellowstone for several reasons. First, the amount of material available was large. The likelihood that we were dealing with the odd, unrepresentative scene was greatly reduced whenever patterns of similar change occurred among comparisons drawn from widely separated sites. Second, the wealth of narrative material and land use records available for Yellowstone provided considerable insight into the events that occurred at particular sites. And finally, we have had the great advantage of working in the world's first national park (fig. 1), a land dedicated to the conservation of nature, where change has been driven, to a great extent, by natural forces.

To give perspective on the scope of our repeat photograph project: By August 1992 the collection contained 345 sets of comparisons (fig 2; see also appendix 2). Of these, 323 scenes were taken in the park; 22 were outside but nearby.[5] Of the in-park sets, 212 contained three photographs each: an original, a retake from the early 1970s, and a third view taken between 1990 and 1993. The remaining 111 comparisons taken in the park consisted of only two photos, either because the sites did not burn in 1988 and were not rephotographed or because we obtained the originals only recently (25 views). One hundred and eighty-five comparative sets taken within the park show effects from the 1988 fires. No repeat photographs were taken outside the park after the fires of 1988, because few of those sites were affected.

We were fortunate to document conditions for 104 sites over intervals of 100 years or more. W. H. Jackson first photographed Yellowstone in 1871, giving us the longest time spans for the project, 120 to 121 years. Nearly half of the original photos were taken before 1901.

When captioning the photographs, we followed accepted scientific practice and used metric units but added English units in parentheses. Park maps and other reference materials may be available only in English units.

Scenes selected for this book represent the sharpest images available from the earliest views and the most widely distributed locations. We also chose originals of later dates for sites of particular interest and when

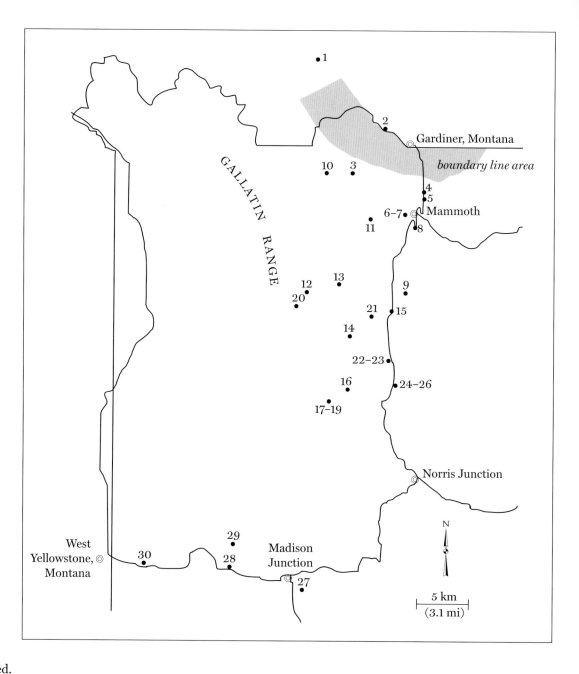

Fig. 3. *The northwest quarter of Yellowstone National Park, showing photo point locations of plates 1–30. This represents a topographic and ecological unit lying between the park's boundary and the road from West Yellowstone to Gardiner, Montana. The shaded part near Gardiner is referred to as the boundary line area, an ecological and geographical unit.*

detailed vegetation change was the focus of the comparison. For instance, some originals taken in the 1930s and 1940s were chosen because they showed dominant plant species in grasslands.

The photographs are presented geographically, with area maps (figs. 3–7) preceding them to show the locations for plate numbers of photo sets. We begin our visual tour near the north boundary of Yellowstone

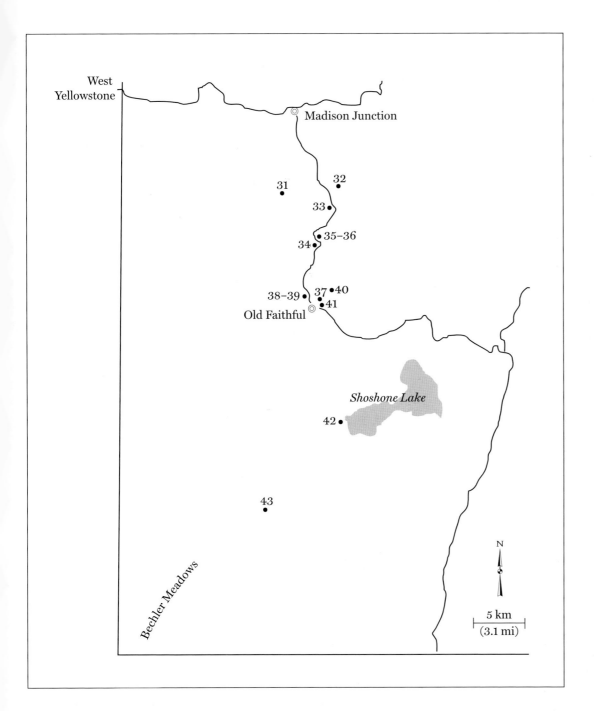

Fig. 4. *The southwest quarter of Yellowstone National Park, showing photo point locations of plates 31–43. This topographic unit lies between the southwestern park boundary and the roads accessing the Old Faithful area from the west and south.*

National Park. We then go south to headquarters at Mammoth, and on south to Norris, with views of the Gallatin Mountain Range. Further south we reach Madison Junction and make a short detour west toward West Yellowstone (fig. 3). Returning to Madison Junction, we travel south to Old Faithful, and touch on the Shoshone and Bechler areas of back-country (fig. 4). We then return to Mammoth and travel eastward and upcountry, following the rising topography of the Yellowstone River across the northern part of the park, including the Absaroka Mountains

(fig. 5). Then we return to Tower Junction and head south across Mount Washburn and down through Hayden Valley, swinging eastward at Fishing Bridge to Pelican Valley and associated higher country (Fig. 6). Our tour terminates in the southeast quadrant of the park (Fig. 7), with sites in the backcountry of the Heart Lake area, the south boundary, Mountain Creek, and the Southeast Arm of Yellowstone Lake.

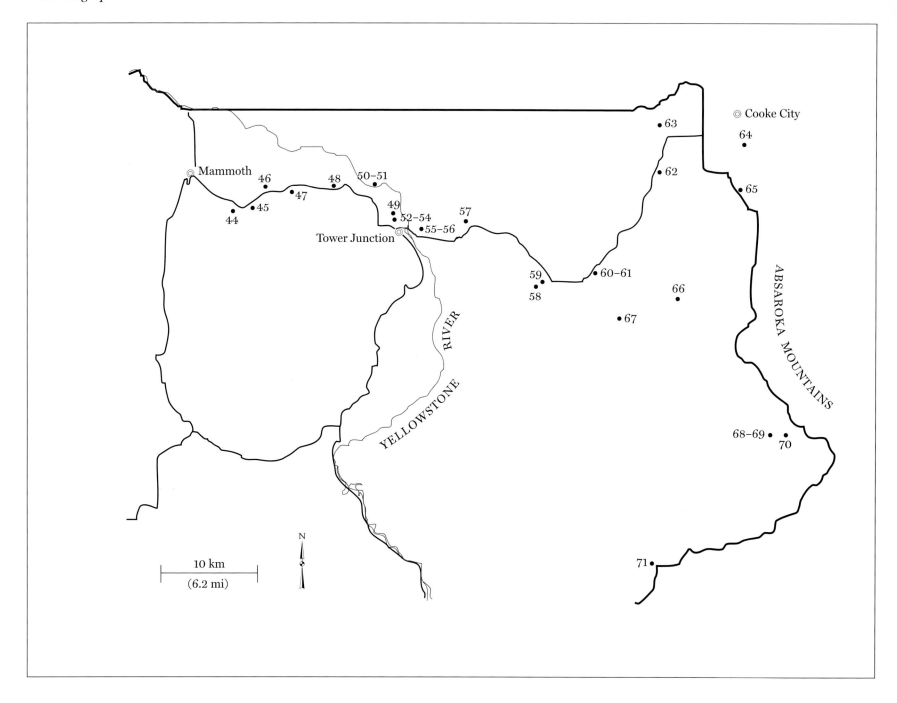

Fig. 5. *The area of Yellowstone National Park called the northern winter range and associated summer range, showing photo point locations of plates 44–71. This is an important topographic and ecological unit lying along the drainage of the Yellowstone River and transected by the road from Mammoth to the northeast corner.*

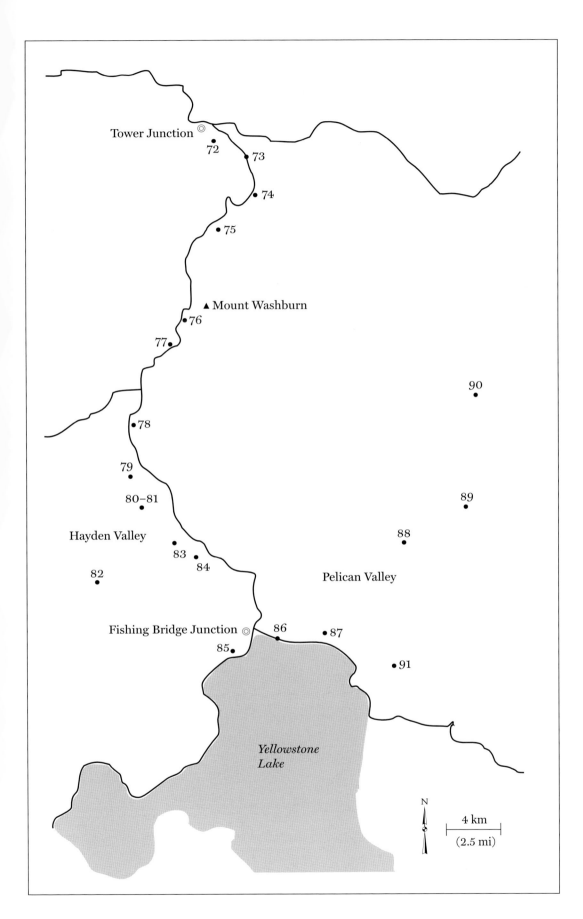

Fig. 6. *The eastern side of Yellowstone National Park, Tower to Pelican Valley, showing photo point locations of plates 72–91. The road crosses Mount Washburn from the northern range to the central part of the park.*

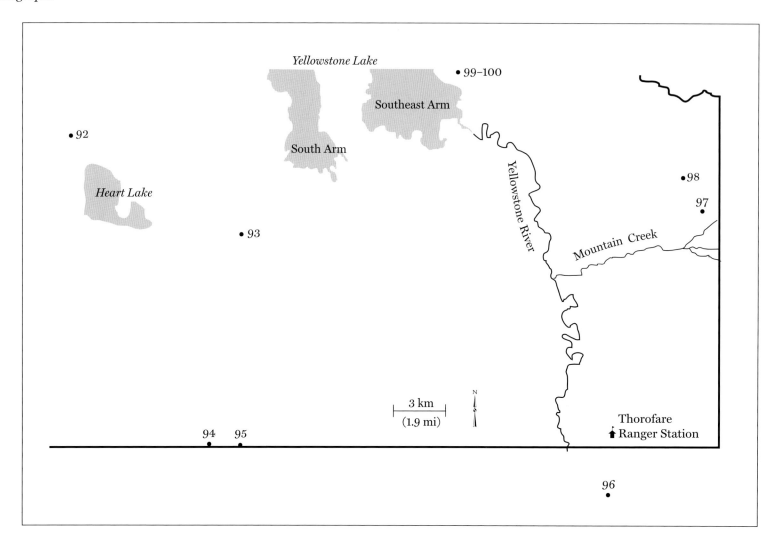

Fig. 7. *The southeast part of Yellowstone National Park, showing photo point locations of plates 92–100. This is a roadless wilderness area, sometimes referred to as the Thorofare.*

Plates

1.1

Plates 1.1–2

Cutler Lake, view south to Cinnabar Mountain

Location: 513.4 E, 4999.8 N; elev. 1,590 m/5,215 ft

Dates and Photographers: 1.1, 1871—W. H. Jackson (NPS-YNP); 1.2, 18 July 1971—D. B. Houston

Interval: 100 years. Camera point moved about 5 m (5.5 yd) south.

Vegetation Changes: *Foreground* shows a bunchgrass community in the original (probably bluebunch wheatgrass and needle-and-thread) with scattered big sagebrush. Winterfat and fringed sagebrush also were present in the original. Vegetation in 1971 was dominated by needle-and-thread, bluegrasses, Indian ricegrass, and phlox. *Middleground* supports a bluebunch wheatgrass–sagebrush steppe. Other grasses present in 1971 were needle-and-thread, bluegrasses, and nonnative cheatgrass. Big sagebrush and common rabbitbrush were more abundant in the retake. Intensive year-round livestock grazing has occurred for decades (note livestock trails, arrow). *Background* increases are apparent in Douglas-fir and big sagebrush.

Cutler Lake was the site of an ice-cutting operation to supply the residents of Gardiner, Montana, before electric refrigerators became common. Ice cutting and the use of ice houses continued in this area into the late 1950s. Such activities were often light on the land, leaving few traces other than the road.

This site is outside Yellowstone Park, about 10 km (6.25 mi) north of the boundary, and serves as winter range for mule deer, elk, and pronghorn. Before Euroamerican settlement, which began in the 1870s, wildfires were more common in south-central Montana (Gruell 1983). Fires have been suppressed since. Despite the long history of livestock grazing, the site appears much the same, except for subtle shifts in the composition of grass species and the increases in big sagebrush and conifers.

We rephotographed seven early scenes taken in 1871 by W. H. Jackson of sites north down the Yellowstone River between the park and Livingston, Montana (about 80 km or 50 mi). The major vegetation changes noted were increased coniferous forest and big sagebrush, changes that are illustrated also in many of the comparisons from inside the park. Other photo comparison studies in the Rocky Mountains have shown similar patterns of vegetation change. This means that the forces driving the changes were not unique to the park but were common across a much larger area. A reduction in frequency of fires seems to be a plausible explanation for the changes.

1.2

2.1

PLATES 2.1–3

View southwest to Electric Peak from the Gardiner–Reese Creek road

LOCATION: 520.7 E, 4987.2 N; elev. 1,620 m/5,313 ft

DATES AND PHOTOGRAPHERS: 2.1, ca. 1893—Photographer unknown (NPS-YNP); 2.2, 17 June 1971—D. B. Houston; 2.3, 12 August 1990—D. B. Houston

INTERVAL: Approximately 78 and 97 years. Camera points similar.

VEGETATION CHANGES: *Foreground* substrate is a mudflow with clay soils. By 1990 there had been some decrease in greasewood, but vegetation in the swale was still primarily greasewood with scattered big sagebrush, bluegrasses, cheatgrass, and foxtail barley. Vegetation on the slopes was dominated by Sandberg's bluegrass and junegrass, with scattered bluebunch wheatgrass and phlox. A decline in shrubs, probably big sagebrush, occurred. An increase in grass cover occurred by 1971, but annual variations in the cover of grasses are spectacular at this low elevation. The 1990 retake was taken later in the summer, hence the vegetation was cured and the standing crop of grasses was greater. The site receives intensive grazing by native ungulates in winter. This area did not burn in 1988. *Background* shows an increase in Douglas-fir on the lower slopes.

This represents our earliest photo of vegetation in the north boundary area of the park near Gardiner, Montana. It is a very complex site. The appearance of the vegetation and soil surface in the original suggests that the bentonite clay soils (note the "pavement" of small stones on the soil surface) have low potential for supporting vegetation. Accounts of early travelers reinforce this interpretation. Military explorer Lieutenant Gustavus Doane of the U.S. Army (Bonney and Bonney 1970:236) described the general area in August 1870 as "passing from a dead level alkali plain to a succession of plateaus covered with a sterile soil,"—almost certainly a reference to the mudflows shown here.

Terraces in the retake and other information on human occupancy suggest that intensive livestock grazing occurred year-round from the 1870s until the area was added to the park in 1932. The vegetation is also intensively used by native ungulates each winter (elk, mule deer, pronghorn) and may have supported unnaturally high concentrations of elk because of conditioned avoidance behavior resulting from hunting outside the park boundary. A reduction in frequency of natural fires has probably further influenced plant composition, especially on the slope where Douglas-fir increased.

2.2

2.3

3.1

Plates 3.1–3

View southeast to summit of Sepulcher Mountain across the headwaters of Stephens Creek

Location: 516.6 E, 4983.8 N; elev. 2,530 m/8,298 ft

Dates and Photographers: 3.1, ca. 1885—J. P. Iddings (USGS); 3.2, 1 September 1972—D. B. Houston; 3.3, 11 August 1991—D. B. Houston

Interval: Approximately 87 and 106 years. Camera points similar.

Vegetation Changes: *Foreground* at left shows a decrease in big and silver sagebrush. No portion of this scene burned during 1988. *Middleground* shows increased size and density of whitebark pine and subalpine fir. Grassland in both retakes was dominated by slender wheatgrass and Idaho fescue, with bluebunch wheatgrass, junegrass, and bluegrasses increasingly important on the sparsely vegetated ridgetops. Several poorly vegetated snowbank sites in retakes were dominated by herbs such as mountain dandelion. *Background* of coniferous forest increased; otherwise, there is little change. The poorly vegetated ridgetop and snowbank swale sites visible in the original were present in the retakes (they are more pronounced in the original because the photo probably was taken in July, judging from the

remaining snowbanks). A major elk migration trail crosses the hydrographic divide in the foreground but is not visible in the photographs. The highlined appearance of several conifers suggests ungulate browsing.

Scattered antlers and aerial surveys indicated that these windblown ridgetops are winter range for bull elk, and the area receives spring, summer, and autumn use by elk. Sepulcher Mountain is also summer range for bighorn ewes and lambs from the Cinnabar winter range just north of the park.

The scalloped appearance of the ridgetop resulted from glacial scour, as Pinedale age glaciers flowed north (left) across Sepulcher Mountain as recently as 15,000 years ago. The mountain was named in 1871 by Captain J. W. Barlow of the U.S. Army's Barlow-Heap Expedition.

4.1

Plates 4.1–2

Gardner River Canyon near Eagle's Nest Rock

Location: 524.2 E, 4983.5 N; elev. 1,680 m/5,510 ft

Dates and Photographers: 4.1, 1912—U.S. Army Engineers (NPS-YNP); 4.2, 14 July 1971—D. B. Houston

Interval: 59 years. Camera points similar.

Vegetation Changes: *Foreground* on both sides of the river has been altered by road construction. The combination of the movement of the extensive mudflow at left and the channel changes in the river completely obliterated the road shown in 1912. Conifers present in the mudflow gully, just above the middle of the original, fell following movement of the mudflow. The site has been colonized by willows, as has other suitable substrate on both sides of the river bank. *Background* shows relatively little change in herbaceous vegetation patterns; sagebrush may have declined in the swale. Cottonwoods and willows colonized the lower slopes above the river.

The site is mainly a mudflow that contains large amounts of clay. Clearly, the engineers did not anticipate the dynamics of this particular flow. Mudflows of various ages and levels of activity occur along much of the north boundary of the park from the Gardner River to Stephens Creek. As shown here, vegetation on the flows is often sparse. This area was grazed by livestock through at least 1905, and winter feedgrounds for native ungulates were located in the vicinity. Elk and mule deer winter here at present. Even so, there appears to be relatively little change in the herbaceous vegetation on the slopes.

Army engineers and subsequent builders have tried various road alignments in the Gardner Canyon. However, the area is geologically very unstable. Such instability and the tremendous force of the river when it is swollen with snowmelt dictates how long a road will last in this location. Traces of the army-built road in the first view can still be seen elsewhere in the canyon. The Gardner River, Canyon, and Hole were named for fur trapper Johnson Gardner. An "i" crept into the official name of Gardiner, Montana.

4.2

5.1

PLATES 5.1–3

Approximately 1.6 km (1 mi) north of Mammoth Hot Springs on the Mammoth-Gardiner road

LOCATION: 524.2 E, 4981.4 N; elev. 1,800 m/5,904 ft)

DATES AND PHOTOGRAPHERS: 5.1, ca. 1900—Photographer unknown (NPS-YNP); 5.2, 29 June 1971—D. B. Houston; 5.3, 31 August 1992—D. B. Houston

INTERVAL: Approximately 71 and 92 years. Camera points similar.

VEGETATION CHANGES: *Foreground* had been altered by 1992 by a new roadside turnout and guardrail. *Middle* and *background* bunchgrass community in both 1971 and 1992 was dominated by bluebunch wheatgrass but also contained junegrass, Indian ricegrass, needle-and-thread, and Sandberg's bluegrass. Grass cover was greater in 1971, but this could reflect differences in growing conditions or timing of the photo. Big sagebrush declined on the slopes. In contrast, the sagebrush stands in the swales contained all size classes and were in excellent condition. The site did not burn in 1988. There appears to be a lower standing crop of vegetation in 1992 and an increase in ungulate trails (or they were more conspicuous). Plants on the slopes are heavily grazed each winter and spring by native ungulates. At the time of the original view, there may have been limited livestock use by travelers and park personnel, but trespass use by local citizens seems not to have been tolerated by the army administration.

This area is winter range for elk and mule deer. Pronghorn occur during spring, summer, and autumn.

Although the first automobile entered the park in 1902, private automobiles were not admitted until 1 August 1915 (Haines 1977). Horses and mules were used for everything: tourists, park administration, and freight.

5.2

5.3

6.1

PLATES 6.1–3

Minerva Terrace, Mammoth Hot Springs, view northwest to Sepulcher Mountain

LOCATION: 523.1 E, 4979.4 N; elev. 1,950 m/6,396 ft

DATES AND PHOTOGRAPHERS: 6.1, 1878—W. H. Jackson (NPS-YNP); 6.2, 25 July 1971—D. B. Houston; 6.3, 12 August 1990—D. B. Houston

INTERVAL: 93 and 112 years. Camera points similar.

VEGETATION CHANGES: *Foreground* shows striking changes in hot spring deposits. Note that Minerva Terrace is quite similar in the 1878 and 1990 views. *Middleground* behind the hot spring terraces demonstrates little change in the sagebrush grassland. Ridgetop and upper south slopes show sparse vegetation in all three photographs. Douglas-fir increased on upper slopes. A trail into the Mammoth Hot Springs basin shows clearly in the original. *Background* suggests an increase in coniferous forest on Sepulcher Mountain. Spot burns from 1988 fires killed some Douglas-fir at upper left, but Douglas-fir has continued to invade unburned areas.

This area is elk and mule deer winter range. Jackson's 1878 photo is one of a series taken around Mammoth Hot Springs showing sparse herbaceous vegetation on upper slopes and ridgecrests. The upper slopes are intensively grazed each winter and probably were used in much the same way when the original was taken.

Although the total amount of water flowing on the Mammoth terraces is relatively constant, the flow patterns of the springs change from year to year and sometimes within a season. When the flow changes, the newly exposed calcium carbonate deposits quickly crumble and erode. The combination of changes in water flow and erosion constantly alters the appearance of the terraces. Hot spring activity has persisted here for thousands of years. There are glacial deposits atop the much older hot spring deposits of Terrace Mountain.

6.2

6.3

7.1

Plates 7.1–3

Mammoth Hot Springs, view east to Mount Everts

Location: 523.1 E, 4979.4 N; elev. 1,950 m/6,396 ft

Dates and Photographers: 7.1, 1871—W. H. Jackson (NPS-YNP); 7.2, 19 July 1971—D. B. Houston; 7.3, 12 August 1990—D. B. Houston

Interval: 100 and 119 years. Camera points similar.

Vegetation Changes: *Foreground* shows substantial changes in the pattern of the hot spring deposits. *Middleground* has been altered by human activities. Note the double-track dirt road at right center in 1971 and the degree to which it had revegetated naturally by 1990. Unfortunately, many of the herbaceous plants on this flat are nonnative, such as mullein, toadflax, hound's tongue, and cheatgrass. The pond to the right in the 1971 and 1990 views is an old reservoir constructed in 1901 (Battle and Thompson 1972). Vegetation in the retakes was primarily bluebunch wheatgrass grassland with stands of big sagebrush in swales. Dark areas in the 1871 photo are marshes, which show no change. Other early Jackson photos suggest no change in the character of the sagebrush grassland and show sagebrush and common rabbitbrush as dominant shrubs in swales. The area did not burn in 1988. *Background* patterns of herbaceous vegetation have changed little on the west and southwest slopes of Mount Everts. Erosion rills and channels appear similar over the 119 years. Vegetation on bare south slopes was Indian ricegrass, greasewood, and saltbush, with 60–80 percent bare ground. Some increase in conifers, mostly Douglas-fir, had occurred on upper slopes and atop Mount Everts. The 1990 image shows scattered mortality of Douglas-fir trees resulting from attacks during the 1980s by a native insect, the spruce budworm.

Mount Everts is winter range for bighorn sheep, mule deer, and elk. Soils on the steep slopes have developed from Cretaceous sedimentary rocks and contain high amounts of clay. Vegetative cover on the slopes is considered to be the result of unusual soil conditions and grazing by native ungulates.

The mountain rises about 487 m (1,600 ft) above the plain. The face exposes gently tilted Cretaceous deposits that erode readily; a summer thunderstorm can close the Gardner Canyon road temporarily or put new point bars in the Gardner River overnight. The conspicuous hard, protective rimrock that caps the mountain on the right half of the view is Huckleberry Ridge tuff, deposited about 2 million years ago during the eruption of the first Yellowstone caldera (Fritz 1985).

8.1

PLATES 8.1–3

Mammoth Hot Springs, view south to Bunsen Peak

LOCATION: 523.1 E, 4978.6 N; elev. 1,950 m/6,396 ft

DATES AND PHOTOGRAPHERS: 8.1, 1907—H. Shantz (UA); 8.2, 7 July 1972—D. B. Houston; 8.3, 8 August 1991—D. B. Houston

INTERVAL: 65 and 84 years. Camera points similar.

VEGETATION CHANGES: *Foreground* swale shows an increase in big sagebrush. The conspicuous large clumps in the original were probably wildrye. This grass was still present in the retakes (closed arrow, 1907). *Middleground* has changed markedly. The sagebrush grassland of 1907, created when an earlier forest burned, by 1972 supported a substantial overstory of Douglas-fir, which continued to increase in density and extent. The lower arrow marks the same tree as a point of reference. The low, shrubby-appearing vegetation beyond the conspicuous dead tree at left-center of the original was a combination of aspen and willow, mainly gone at the time of the retakes. *Background* arrow marks an 1886 fire boundary on Bunsen Peak. The photo shows the influence of past fire, and much of the original scene may have burned during two fires, in 1882 and 1886. By 1972, the burned area had reforested with lodgepole pine as the dominant conifer. Douglas-fir and subalpine fir also occurred on this north slope. Forests on Bunsen Peak burned extensively during 1988. Note that the 1886 fire boundary is still visible in the 1991 retake. The 1991 image was deliberately taken later in the day than the older photographs to highlight the recent burn.

This area is part of the northern winter range; elk, mule deer, and occasional moose forage throughout. In 1988 Bunsen Peak burned mostly after dark; watching the fire travel through the tree crowns was awesome. Fire in these circumstances is as much an unalterable natural force as is a volcano or an earthquake.

8.2

8.3

9.1

Plates 9.1–3

Gardner's Hole, view northeast to Bunsen Peak

Location: 521.4 E, 4972.3 N; elev. 2,200 m/7,215 ft)

Dates and Photographers: 9.1, 1907—H. Shantz (UA); 9.2, 7 July 1972—D. B. Houston; 9.3, 9 August 1990—D. B. Houston

Interval: 65 and 83 years. Camera points approximate.

Vegetation Changes: *Foreground* grasses dominant at the retakes were bluebunch wheatgrass and Idaho fescue. A slight reduction in the density of big sagebrush was evident in 1972. Big sagebrush and scattered silver sagebrush burned in 1988. *Middleground* shows a reduction in willow in the sedge meadow (primarily beaked sedge). Scattered Wolf's willow occurred in the meadow at the time of the 1972 retake. These willows were largely killed by the 1988 fire, which burned down through their root crowns. The sedge meadow also burned intensely; the dark bare patches are where fire burned through accumulated organic (peat) layers to mineral soil. Beaked sedge was eliminated for the time being from these areas; elsewhere in the meadow the sedge resprouted following the fire. *Background* forest of lodgepole pine at the base of Bunsen Peak increased on the slopes by 1972, with smaller increases in Douglas-fir. Note that in 1972, a reduction in trees and shrubs had occurred in the small drainage on the center slopes; the remaining shrubs suggested that the plants in the original included willows, aspen, and chokecherry. Forests and grasslands at the base of Bunsen Peak burned extensively in 1988, as did the peak. Big sagebrush was eliminated temporarily, and most conifers were killed.

The area is summer range for elk and mule deer. A few moose occur year-round. Bunsen Peak is c1omposed of intrusive igneous rock that may be the eroded remnant of an Absaroka volcano from the Eocene. It was named in 1872 to honor Robert Wilhelm Eberhard von Bunsen, an eminent German physicist who studied geysers in Iceland (Whittlesey 1988). The Bunsen burner, familiar to chemistry students the world over, was also named for him. The m-stick (divided into 10 cm blocks) supplies scale for height of ground cover.

9.2

9.3

10.1

Plates 10.1–3

Upper Glen Creek, view northwest to Electric Peak

Location: 517.6 E, 4979.8 N; elev. 2,348 m/7,700 ft

Dates and Photographers: 10.1, ca. 1885—J. P. Iddings (USGS); 10.2, 1 September 1971—D. B. Houston; 10.3, 11 August 1991—D. B. Houston

Interval: Approximately 87 and 106 years. Camera points similar.

Vegetation Changes: *Foreground* changed from a sagebrush-dominated grassland to an open grassland by 1971, containing Idaho fescue, mountain brome, and slender wheatgrass. The few silver sagebrush shrubs of 1971 increased by 1991. No portion of the scene burned during 1988. *Middleground* shows a decrease in willows in the meadow (arrow, 1971). Vegetation at the retake was dominated by sedges, reedgrass, and hairgrass, with Idaho fescue in drier sites. The extensive stand of aspen at right in the original has been nearly completely replaced by lodgepole pine (open arrow, 1885). *Background* of coniferous forest (whitebark pine, subalpine fir, lodgepole pine) increased on the lower slopes of Electric Peak. Mortality of individual conifers visible in 1991 probably resulted from attacks by native insects.

The area receives relatively light grazing from migratory groups of elk and other ungulates during spring, summer, and autumn. Upper Glen Creek was once the site of corrals and sheds for an early dairy cattle summer operation that supplied the Mammoth Hotel. Lumber remnants persisted into the 1970s and the established hiking trail (not visible) has faint traces of an early road. The nonnative eastern brook trout planted in Glen Creek in 1889 represent a longer-lasting biological effect.

The peak's name dates back to 1892 when members of the Hayden expedition experienced an electrical storm on its summit. Expedition member Gannet wrote, "I attached the name of 'Electric Peak' to the mountain . . . because at that time and on this summit I first acted as a lightning rod" (Whittlesey 1988: 51).

10.2

10.3

11.1

Plates 11.1–3

Gardner's Hole area, view southwest across Glen Creek to the Gallatin Range

Location: 519.2 E, 4979.0 N; elev. 2,380 m/7,806 ft

Dates and Photographers: 11.1, ca. 1885—J. P. Iddings (USGS); 11.2, 23 August 1971—D. B. Houston; 11.3, 10 August 1990—D. B. Houston

Interval: Approximately 86 and 105 years. Camera points for retakes about 50 m (164 ft) west of original because of increase in conifers.

Vegetation Changes: *Foreground* of big sagebrush has increased and aspen has decreased on the slopes. A small decrease in willow occurred in the Glen Creek bottom. The foreground did not burn. *Middleground* presence of big sagebrush increased by 1971 such that glacial erratic boulders visible on the ridge in the original (open arrow) are obscured by sagebrush in the retakes. A small increase in forested area and a definite change in species composition occurred. Aspen declined (solid arrow) and Douglas-fir, lodgepole pine, and subalpine fir increased by 1971. Idaho fescue was the dominant grass in 1971 and 1990. Dead conifers at left in the original suggest a fire or insect attack. Trees along the forest-grassland boundary

(ecotone) had multiple fire scars. Fires in 1988 killed sagebrush in the steppe on the right and left of the 1990 image. Also, spot fires occurred throughout the forest, killing small groups of trees. *Background*, which did not burn, shows an increase in area and density of forest on the high elevation mountain slopes.

This area is on the periphery of the northern winter range and receives some use by elk year-round. Small groups of elk and a few bison and moose may spend the entire winter in the area, depending on snow depths. The changes in vegetation documented in the first comparison are likely the result of reduced fire frequency.

The mountains in the background are the Mount Holmes complex and Antler Peak.

12.1

PLATES 12.1–3

Bighorn Pass from the west, across the Gallatin River

LOCATION: 508.9 E, 4969.5 N; elev. 2,560 m/8,396 ft

DATES AND PHOTOGRAPHERS: 12.1, ca. 1885—J. P. Iddings (USGS); 12.2, 30 August 1972—D. B. Houston; 12.3, 9 August 1991—D. B. Houston

INTERVAL: Approximately 87 and 106 years. Camera points similar.

VEGETATION CHANGES: *Foreground* shows little change in the subalpine fir-whitebark pine forest from 1885 to 1972. The original photo hints that a willow community (arrow) occurred along the Gallatin River. Willows were essentially gone at the time of the retakes. The forest burned extensively during 1988 in an extremely hot crown fire; rocks at the bases of trees were cracked by the heat. Note that the trees had increased substantially in height from 1972 to 1988. *Middleground* of subalpine herbland was dominated in 1972 by slender wheatgrass, mountain brome, mountain dandelion, larkspur, clematis, and many-flowered stickseed. Swale vegetation was dominated by cow-parsnip and western coneflower. The light-colored areas of sparse vegetation in the original were in similar condition in 1972, with 70–80 percent bare ground due to pocket gopher burrowing. The areas are not as conspicuous in the retakes because of differences in lighting and stage of plant growth (abundant gopher mounds supported a sparse cover of Douglas knotweed in 1972). The subalpine fir groves increased slightly in size and height by 1972. The herbland and subalpine fir stands experienced hot fires in 1988, and most of the trees were killed. Note the standing dead trees in the 1885 view; these suggest a fire not long before. Composition of the herbaceous vegetation in 1991 was similar to that described in 1972. Moderate elk use occurred during 1991, but gophers seemed somewhat less abundant than earlier. *Background* changes were slight from 1885 to 1972 in the distribution of subalpine fir on the talus and cliff areas of Madison limestone. The subalpine fir burned in 1988, even though continuous ground fuels appear to have been absent.

The entire area of the upper Gallatin River is important elk summer range and habitat for grizzly bears. A road was surveyed across Bighorn Pass in 1907 because of pressure from local interests, but the idea was dropped after costs were compared to the expected public benefit (Haines 1977).

12.2

12.3

13.1

Plates 13.1–3

Panther Creek, view northwest to Bannock Peak

LOCATION 513.0 E, 4970.2 N; elev. 2,440 m/8,003 ft

DATES AND PHOTOGRAPHERS: 13.1, ca. 1885—J. P. Iddings (USGS); 13.2, 23 July 1974—D. B. Houston; 13.3, 14 August 1990—D. B. Houston

INTERVAL: Approximately 89 and 105 years. Camera points approximate, but the adjustment makes the valley bottom appear flatter. Boulder (arrow) in meadow confirms accuracy of photopoint.

VEGETATION CHANGES: *Foreground* channel of Panther Creek shifted by 1974 to an area 50 m (55 yd) farther north, to the right. The original photo suggests abundant willows along the stream. These were absent along both the former stream bed and the new channel by the time of the 1974 retake. At that time, and in 1990, the meadow was dominated by alpine timothy, slender wheatgrass, oniongrass, and mountain brome, with stickseed, mountain dandelion, and western coneflower. The only change apparent in 1990 was an increase in vegetation density along the intermittent stream course. *Middleground* shows a decline in big sagebrush and an increase in subalpine fir, whitebark pine, and scattered lodgepole pine. Meadow vege-

tation was dominated by slender wheatgrass, arnica, mountain brome, and oniongrass, with scattered big sagebrush at both retakes. Portions of the middleground meadow appeared to have burned in 1988 (right); sagebrush was eliminated temporarily from burned sites. *Background* subalpine fir thickets show little change on Bannock Peak. Spot fires occurred in the subalpine fir and whitebark pine forest during 1988, causing mortality of some stands at left.

Stream channels are well known for making natural changes in their courses. Minor changes occurred in this one between 1885 and 1974, but by 1990 the stream had become intermittent and it is barely visible in the photograph.

This area is elk summer range. A low-density moose population also occurs throughout the Gallatin Range.

Bannock Peak was named in 1885 for the Bannock Indian tribe. The travel route that became known as the Bannock Trail crossed the Gallatin Range to the south. The Bannocks, a Shoshone group, traversed the area en route from what is now Idaho to bison hunting lands east of the park area after intermountain groups of bison disappeared about 1840 due to overhunting, probably combined with climatic change. The trail was used for about 40 years, ending in 1878 with the military defeat of dissident Bannocks by General N. A. Miles (Haines 1977).

13.2

13.3

14.1

PLATES 14.1–3

Indian Creek, view southwest to Dome Mountain

LOCATION: 514.4 E, 4,967.1 N; elev. 2,350 m/7,707 ft)

DATES AND PHOTOGRAPHERS: 14.1, ca. 1885—J. P. Iddings (USGS); 14.2, 17 August 1972—D. B. Houston; 14.3, 14 August 1990—D. B. Houston

INTERVAL: Approximately 87 and 105 years. Camera points similar, note rock at arrow.

VEGETATION CHANGES: *Foreground* in 1972 was dominated by Idaho fescue, hairgrass, slender wheatgrass, and alpine timothy, with yampah, yarrow, and elk thistle as important forbs. Vegetation in the original appears to be dominated by mule's ears, but the forb was not present at the retakes, suggesting that the meadow was much wetter in the original scene. There was an increase in elk thistle and western coneflower by 1990. The foreground did not burn. *Middleground* shows a decrease in willow density; an increase in lodgepole pine, subalpine fir, and Engelmann spruce; and greater tree height in general. Western coneflower occurs in a dense stand at the base of the trees in both retakes. Idding's camp is visible at right in the original. *Background* forest of lodgepole pine and subalpine fir increased on the slopes of Dome Mountain. The original opening was created by a fire that burned the south side of Indian Creek around 1856.

This comparison shows a subtle change in the vegetation of a forest park over the past century, reflecting a possible reduction in soil moisture. Reduced soil moisture could be related to climatic change or to increased forest cover. This area is elk summer range, and moderate grazing occurred at the time of both retakes.

Upper Indian Creek is a natural travel route crossing the Gallatin Range, well used by wildlife and early peoples. As human use has increased in recent years, travel off maintained trails in the Gallatin Range has been restricted to reduce human disturbance of important grizzly bear habitat.

14.2

14.3

15.1

Plates 15.1–3

Indian Creek in Gardner's Hole, view west to Antler Peak and Quadrant Mountain

Location: 520.4 E, 4970.6 N; elev. 2,226 m/7,301 ft

Dates and Photographers: 15.1, 1905—F. J. Haynes (MHS); 15.2, July 1974—D. B. Houston; 15.3, 30 August 1990—M. Meagher

Interval: 69 and 85 years. Camera points similar.

Vegetation Changes: *Foreground* shows a decrease in willow density in the swale (arrow, 1905) and on the Gardner River bottom. Sagebrush appears to have increased in the swale between 1974 and 1990. *Middleground* sagebrush on the hill decreased in density and increased in size relative to its appearance during the Van Dyke and Deever cattle operation pictured in 1905. However, there has been an increase in density by 1990 to the left of the debris pile seen in the 1974 photograph. This appears to be an invasion into a drier site, comparable to the increase in the foreground. Scattered conifers have invaded the bottoms. *Background* forest at left and rear increased in density and tree height between 1905 and 1974, and began to invade the valley floor. These changes continued, as shown in the 1990

photo, but are less apparent on some sites because trees that burned in 1988 do not show as well against the background of sagebrush. In 1988, fire burned mostly on the ground in this area. Tree boles are more apparent in 1990 compared to 1974 and scattered dead trees are visible. In 1990 red-colored tree crowns (red tops) were visible at center rear to the photographer, indicating that trees were still dying from the effects of the 1988 fires. Most of the forest here is lodgepole pine.

The digging of an open water ditch upslope to the right, out of photo view, may have had localized effects on vegetation patterns.

The 1905 view shows the Van Dyke and Deever cattle herd and slaughter house. This was a summer season operation, established in 1895 as part of a Gardiner, Montana, business (L. Whittlesey, pers. comm.). Meat was transported to various park hotels in metal-sheathed wagons to protect the contents from bears. Travel was at night when necessary to keep the meat cool. Cattle skulls from this area have been brought in by hikers for identification.

15.2

15.3

16.1

PLATES 16.1–3

Upper Winter Creek, view northwest to Mount Holmes at left

LOCATION: 512.8 E, 4960.8 N; elev. 2,590 m/8,495 ft

DATES AND PHOTOGRAPHERS: 16.1, ca. 1885—J. P. Iddings (USGS); 16.2, 16 September 1971—D. B. Houston; 16.3, 15 August 1990—D. B. Houston

INTERVAL: Approximately 86 and 105 years. Camera point moved 15 m (49 ft) northwest because of an increase in conifers; note the conspicuous white rock.

VEGETATION CHANGES: *Foreground* and *middleground* represent subalpine herblands dominated by slender wheatgrass, mountain brome, stickseed, aster, and mountain dandelion. Big sagebrush, Rocky Mountain sagebrush, western coneflower, larkspur, and lupine were also present. Little change was evident in 1971, except for a decrease in big sagebrush. The showy flowers around the horse in the original were probably lupine, which was present but not in bloom in 1971. The sparsely vegetated area in right middleground is a snowbank site dominated by mountain dandelion and shows no change. Virtually the entire vegetated area burned during 1988,

except for scattered conifers and the meadow ridgetops, where big sagebrush persisted. Despite the fire, the 1990 species composition of the meadow was seemingly unchanged from 1971, except for less sagebrush. Standing crop of vegetation in 1990 seemed less than in earlier photos. *Background* shows that subalpine fir and whitebark pine had increased in density and area by 1971. The stands burned extensively in 1988. The tree that forced the change in camera points between 1885 and the retakes was cored in 1990 and found to be about 70 years old, so it became established two to three decades after Iddings photographed the scene. The original scene shows tree mortality typical of forest insect attacks.

Note that this meadow appears in the background of plates 18 and 19. The area is elk summer range. Considerable digging by grizzly bears occurred at this site in 1990. (Indeed, we waited for a sow and three yearlings to leave before rephotographing the scene.)

A marked trail now goes to the lookout atop Mount Holmes at 3,150 m (10,336 ft) elevation. Construction of a trail system in the park began in 1908. Prior to that, people used wildlife trails, some of which are better thoroughfares than anything we construct today. The 1890 vintage, army-built Christmas Tree park patrol cabin was located on the east flank of Mount Holmes near one of these wildlife trails. The cabin remnants burned in 1988.

16.2

16.3

17

Plates 17, 18, and 19

Winter Creek, view north to Mount Holmes

NOTE: *These plates are panoramic views. Together they constitute one comparative set. Each of the three views consists of three photos connected to form the whole. To do justice to the breadth of the views, we have spread the plates across six pages.*

LOCATION: 511.5 E, 4960.0 N; elev. 2,680 m/8,790 ft.

DATES AND PHOTOGRAPHERS: 17, ca. 1885—J. P. Iddings (USGS); 18, 25 August 1972—D. B. Houston; 19, 15 August 1990—D. B. Houston

INTERVAL: Approximately 87 and 105 years. Camera points similar.

VEGETATION CHANGES: *Foreground* at right in 1972 shows little change in a subalpine grassland dominated by slender wheatgrass, Idaho fescue, mountain brome, mountain dandelion, and wild buckwheat. The small shrub is mountain gooseberry. This site is an exposed ridgetop and receives

heavy summer elk use. Elk apparently aggregate on this windy knob to seek relief from biting insects. Extensive pocket gopher burrowing was also evident at the retakes. Virtually the entire scene burned in 1988, except for small stands of conifers near treeline and parts of the background meadow at right. The foreground grassland showed little change in composition following the burn, and the mountain gooseberry shrub was resprouting. *Middleground* in the original mosaic shows a subalpine fir–whitebark pine forest with what may be extensive forest insect effects. Forest increased in size, density, and distribution by 1972, most of it to be consumed in 1988 in what must have been a very hot fire. Understory vegetation was still sparse in 1990, consisting of scattered pinegrass and arnica. Meadow areas represent subalpine herbland that developed on limestone. These showed extensive burrowing by pocket gophers in 1972 (which probably also occurred in 1885 at the time of the first photos). Vegetation was dominated by slender

wheatgrass, Idaho fescue, mountain dandelion, yarrow, wild flax, aster, paintbrush, and harebell at the retakes. *Background* of subalpine herbland changed little, except that stands of big sagebrush burned in the 1988 fire. Subalpine fir and whitebark pine increased in density until 1972, but they also burned in 1988.

The entire area is important elk summer range. Grizzly bears also frequent the meadows. Mount Holmes was named in 1878 for W. H. Holmes, geologist and artist of the Hayden Surveys. The fire lookout was built in 1930. It is still used each summer to record fire starts (although these fires may now be allowed to burn) and to facilitate park radio communication.

18

19

20.1

Plates 20.1–3

Gallatin Range, view west to Crowfoot Ridge

Location: 506.2 E, 4968.8 N; elev. 2,650 m/8,691 ft

Dates and Photographers: 20.1, ca. 1885—J. P. Iddings (USGS); 20.2, 14 August 1972—D. B. Houston; 20.3, 11 August 1991—D. B. Houston

Interval: Approximately 87 and 106 years. Camera points moved about 6 m (20 ft) and 11 m (36 ft) north of original in 1972 and 1991, respectively, because of an increase in subalpine fir density and height.

Vegetation Changes: *Foreground* shows increased invasion of subalpine fir and whitebark pine into a wet meadow. Herbaceous vegetation at time of the retakes was dominated by rushes, sedges, hairgrass, bluegrasses, alpine timothy, cinquefoil, mountain dandelion, and bistort. Substantial pocket gopher activity occurred in the original and was conspicuous at both retakes. The foreground meadow and forest did not burn in 1988. Both retakes were photographed later in the growing season than was the original (note the snowbanks in the 1885 view). *Middleground* shows an increase in subalpine fir and whitebark pine at right. The fir and pine forest along the lakeshore burned in spot fires in 1988. *Background* shows little change in subalpine fir on Crowfoot Ridge in 1972. In 1988, forest beyond the lake burned in a very hot fire. Small stands of conifers on the ridgetops escaped burning.

The area is elk summer range, and the wet meadow showed substantial elk use at the time of both retakes. Crowfoot Ridge is composed mainly of Paleozoic limestone, sandstone, and shale deposited in shallow seas that covered the region several hundred million years ago.

The small alpine lake is unnamed. High elevation lakes such as this occupy biologically fragile habitat, with short growing seasons for vegetation. Because of this, overnight camping is not now permitted in these locations.

20.2

20.3

21.1

PLATES 21.1–3

Indian Creek, view southwest to Antler Peak

LOCATION: 518.9 E, 4970.1 N; elev. 2,260 m/7,412 ft

DATES AND PHOTOGRAPHERS: 21.1, ca. 1885—J. P. Iddings (USGS); 21.2, 25 July 1971—D. B. Houston; 21.3, 14 August 1991—D. B. Houston

INTERVAL: Approximately 86 and 106 years. Camera points similar.

VEGETATION CHANGES: *Foreground* and *middleground* show no apparent change in distribution or density of the willow community in 1971. At that time the lodgepole pine forest had recolonized the glacial moraine at the rear of the meadow, apparently following an earlier fire. The meadow and adjacent lodgepole pine stand at right burned during 1988 (except for left foreground, where sagebrush and shrubby cinquefoil shrubs persist). Wolf's willow and other shrubs were burned to the soil surface. Although some were apparently killed by the fires, profuse resprouting occurred during 1991. Big sagebrush was eliminated temporarily from the terrace edge below the burned lodgepole pine stand at right. A dense stand of native grasses and forbs dominated during 1991. Snags visible in the 1885 view had disappeared by 1971. However, in both retakes, the same tree shows at left. In 1971 it appeared to be dying at the top, but the lower branches had needles. By 1991 it was dead. Decomposition in this cool climate is slow, but eventually the roots will rot and the snag will topple and disappear. Causes of tree mortality were variable but probably included old age, insect attack, fire, and perhaps changes in the water table (temporary flooding). *Background* shows an increase in subalpine fir and whitebark pine on the slopes of Antler Peak. These slopes did not burn in 1988.

The area receives light to moderate year-round grazing by elk and moose but is primarily a spring, summer, and autumn range. Indian Creek was named in 1878 by the third Hayden Survey party after members noted the Bannock Indian Trail along the north bank.

21.2

21.3

22.1

Plates 22.1–2

Willow Park along Obsidian Creek, view south

Location: 520.9 E, 4967.0 N; elev. 2,240 m/7,347 ft

Dates and Photographers: 22.1, 1913—F. J. Haynes (MHS); 22.2, 16 August 1990—D. B. Houston

Interval: 77 years. Camera point moved about 15 m (49 ft) west of original and 5 m (16 ft) up a lodgepole pine tree because of increased forest.

Vegetation Changes: *Foreground* and *middleground* willows (several species) were 2–3 m (6.5–10 ft) tall in 1990. There is still considerable beaver activity at this site, with willow cuttings but no ponds. Willows in the right foreground and left middleground burned during 1988, and resprouting was sparse. *Background* lodgepole pine trees invaded the far edge of the meadow. Most of the lodgepole pine forest on the slopes at center and right burned during 1988.

This is one of the more predictable locations for watching moose. In the fall, the willows are often colorful with reds and yellows. Willows are complex taxonomically, and some species in Yellowstone Park are very sim-

ilar. This stretch of Obsidian Creek has had persistent beaver activity, compared to the ephemeral nature of beaver presence in many park locales.

22.2

23.1

Plates 23.1–2

Willow Park, view north to Bunsen and Electric peaks

Location: 521.0 E, 4965.0 N; elev. 2,240 m/7,347 ft

Dates and Photographers: 23.1, 1886—F. J. Haynes (MHS); 23.2, 16 August 1990—D. B. Houston

Interval: 104 years. Camera points similar.

Vegetation Changes: *Foreground* and *middleground* meadow in 1990 was dominated by nonnative timothy and smooth brome. Portions of the meadow burned during 1988. The site appears to have been grazed intensively in the original; horses and mules used by the travelers of the time may have been responsible for much of this. A decline in willows occurred along the small stream (closed arrow), and lodgepole pine invaded. The stream may have been mostly intermittent in recent years, as the bottom was grass-covered although a low flow occurred during 1990. Stream changes probably were related to the previous decade of mostly below-average winter snowpacks, and perhaps intensified by the summer drought of 1988. *Background* slope forests burned extensively during 1988, except for sites adjacent to the meadow at left and around Apollinaris Springs at right. Note the gray area at left in the original view (open arrow) suggestive of earlier fire (see pls. 25.1–3).

The meadow is grazed by elk in summer. Willow Park is located about halfway between Mammoth and Norris and must have been a campsite well used by people traveling with teams and wagons or buggies before automobiles were allowed.

Nonnative timothy is widespread in the park. In part, it was introduced and spread by early-day travelers' livestock. The grass is quite aggressive and able to outcompete native grasses such as alpine timothy. Smooth brome also is an exotic species.

23.2

24.1

Plates 24.1–3

Beaver Lake and Obsidian Cliff, view north down Obsidian Creek

Location: 521.5 E, 4,962.6 N; elev. 2,251 m/7,383 ft

Dates and Photographers: 24.1, ca. 1885–86—Haynes photo (NPS-YNP); 24.2, 16 July 1971—D. B. Houston; 24.3, 18 August 1990—M. Meagher

Interval: 85 and 105 years. Camera points approximate. The original view is closer to Obsidian Cliff.

Vegetation Changes: *Foreground* and *middleground* show succession from an open water/pond-lily stage to a beaked sedge meadow. Lodgepole pine invasion has begun, perhaps accelerated by the decade of mostly below-average winter precipitation during the 1980s and the summer drought of 1988. The tall inflorescence above the sedge at the center of the 1990 image is elephant's head (arrow). *Background* lodgepole forest at left rear in the first view showed dead trees, evidence perhaps of forest insect activity and earlier ground fire, as shown by fire-scarred trees. Trees at right center may have been killed by flooding as the beaver pond formed. Since

the original view, the density of the lodgepole forest has increased. In 1988 there was some ground fire at left. Canopy burn is apparent at rear behind Obsidian Cliff. Meadow burn was minor in this view.

The early view shows a line of early utility poles along the road. The second superintendent, P. W. Norris, built the first crude road in 1878, in part by building fires on the volcanic glass—obsidian—and then throwing cold water on the heated rock to fracture it (Haines 1977). The road in the 1885–86 view had been improved upon compared to Norris's original road, but it was still a narrow dirt track.

24.2

24.3

25.1

PLATES 25.1–3

Obsidian Cliff

LOCATION: 521.4 E, 4963.0 N; elev. 2,251 m/7,383 ft

DATES AND PHOTOGRAPHERS: 25.1, 1884—J. P. Iddings (USGS); 25.2, 28 June 1973—M. Meagher; 25.3, 17 July 1990—M. Meagher

INTERVAL: 89 and 106 years. Camera point approximate.

VEGETATION CHANGES: *Foreground* and *middleground* are similar. Lodgepole pine forest has increased in density and invaded the meadow edge. *Background* with entire cliff area burned prior to 1884 (the original view) and revegetated naturally with lodgepole pine forest. This earlier burn probably was part of the extensive forest fires of the 1850s or 1860s that burned much of the area between Swan Lake Flats, Norris, and the park's west entrance (Romme and Despain, computer data, Yellowstone GIS fire history). The Obsidian Cliff area burned again in 1988, but not quite as extensively. Trees at the cliff edge escaped fire, as did some on the slope at right adjacent to the cliff (open arrow, 1990 view). It is apparent that a good-sized lodgepole forest will grow again on some sites within 100 years after a fire. The conspicuous dark patches on the slopes below the cliffs in all three scenes are common junipers. In the 1990 view the ground cover may be showing impact from the numbers of people who walk up these lower slopes.

Obsidian Cliff presumably is the "mountain of glass" reputedly so clear that it supposedly proved to be in the line of sight when a fur trapper tried to shoot an elk! Swapping tall tales provided a major form of entertainment for these trappers of the mountain men era, roughly the 1820s and 1830s. Archeological evidence indicates considerable quarrying activity at the cliff by prehistoric people for perhaps 10,000 years (Cannon 1993). No collecting is permitted now, a necessary regulation because of the volume of park visitors.

The fires of the 1850s–1860s were probably the largest in the area that would become the park from the time of the extensive fires of the early 1700s to those in 1988.

26.1

Plates 26.1–3

Beaver Lake, view southwest from south edge of Obsidian Cliff

Location: 521.7 E, 4963.0 N; elev. 2,317 m/7,599 ft

Dates and Photographers: 26.1, ca. 1893—Photographer unknown (NPS-YNP); 26.2, 16 July 1971—D. B. Houston; 26.3, 31 August 1990—M. Meagher

Interval: Approximately 78 and 97 years. Camera points similar.

Vegetation Changes: *Foreground* and *middleground* illustrate pond succession in which a former beaver pond becomes dominated by sedges. The process was probably accelerated during the 1980s by below-average precipitation and by the drought of 1988. The pond may have been nearly abandoned by beaver by 1893. The forage source for beaver was probably willow. Even in the 1893 view willows appear to have been sparse, although a few willows were still present in 1990. Lodgepole pine trees continued to colonize the old dam, which was overgrown with sedge. The meadows did not burn in 1988, but some individual trees did, as did the forest at the right edge (closed arrow, 1990). Note that as the pond filled in, Obsidian Creek,

flowing diagonally toward the observer from the pond remnants, has formed a network of channels (reticulation). Even between 1971 and 1990, it shows much localized change. This indicates an old stream that cuts new channels as sediments are deposited on the relatively flat valley bottom. *Background* forest burned with varying degrees of intensity in 1988. The grayish areas to the rear in the 1990 view (open arrow) represent canopy burn. The barren-appearing area at left-center rear is the 1988 reburn of the 1976 Arrow fire. This hillside burned intensively because of large, already dead fuels from the fire 12 years before. Scarred trees throughout the area provide evidence of fires before 1988. The snags scattered in the forest in the 1893 view may have been caused by the extensive fires of the 1860s and 1870s (see pls. 25.1–3).

When Superintendent Norris built the first crude road here in 1878, his crew found a cache of iron beaver traps similar to those used by Hudson's Bay fur trappers (Haines 1977). Norris named Beaver Lake; at that time the beavers presumably were more active than now.

26.2

26.3

27.1

PLATES 27.1–3

Madison Junction, looking southwest at National Park Mountain

LOCATION: 511.0 E, 4943.0 N; elev. 2,073 m/6,799 ft

DATES AND PHOTOGRAPHERS: 27.1, ca. 1900–5—F. J. Haynes (MHS); 27.2, 26 August 1971—M. Meagher; 27.3, 14 August 1990—M. Meagher

INTERVAL: 65–70 and 85–90 years. Camera point moved to the west and slightly lower in 1971, and more so in 1990, because the site was altered when the road was relocated.

VEGETATION CHANGES: *Foreground* has been changed by road work and impacted by human foot travel. Area use intensified after a large campground was constructed nearby in 1962. *Middleground* sedge meadow is similar but tall willows at left (far edge of the river) and right (bend of the river) were gone by 1971. Sedge bottoms did not burn here in 1988. *Background* forest increased in density during the first interval. The area burned during 1988, and parts of National Park Mountain show the effects of crown fire, especially on top. The sparseness of trees in the original suggests that then, too, fire had occurred not many years before.

Note the suggestion of highlined trees—showing the distinctive browse line left by ungulate feeding—on the valley bottom in all the photographs (arrow, original). Elk habitually winter here, as increasing numbers of bison have been doing since 1980.

When private automobiles were admitted officially on 1 August 1915, the cost for a five-passenger car to enter was $7.50. Allowable speeds varied from 8 MPH when approaching sharp curves, to a maximum of 20 MPH at any time (Haines 1977).

27.2

27.3

28.1

Plates 28.1–3

Madison River, Seven Mile Bridge area, view west

Location: 502.9 E, 4945.3 N; elev. 2,070 m/6,789 ft

Dates and Photographers: 28.1, September 1912—U.S. Army Engineers (NPS-YNP); 28.2, 2 July 1973—M. Meagher; 28.3, 15 August 1990—M. Meagher

Interval: 61 and 78 years. Camera points approximate.

Vegetation Changes: *Foreground* relocation of the road has allowed revegetation, but remnants of the roadbed are still visible. Some meadow burn occurred in 1988, which probably caused the disappearance of the sagebrush visible at center right in the 1973 view. *Middleground* willows had disappeared by the 1990 view; note the skeletal remnants at right center. These willows apparently were killed gradually by too much water, too much of the time after the earthquake in 1959. Water levels were higher in 1973 because of the earlier photo date. Although not visible in the 1990 photo, Canada thistle and reed canarygrass have invaded the native vegetation (J. Whipple, pers. comm.). *Background* shows dying cottonwoods on

the river bottom in 1973 (arrow). Any remnants burned in 1988 when the area was swept by crown fire.

This area usually provides early winter range for elk. Since about the mid-1980s, groups of bison also have foraged seasonally on the bottoms. Increasing depths of snow often preclude ungulate use as winter progresses.

The location was affected by the 1959 Hebgen earthquake, which apparently caused a relative, but minor, drop in the river bed here and drowning of vegetation. Even in the fall, relative water levels are higher than they were before 1959. The epicenter of that earthquake was located just outside the west boundary of the park, north of West Yellowstone.

A pair of trumpeter swans nests here annually, but in years of high water the nest fails. The birds are successful often enough to replace themselves and ensure a nesting presence over the longer span of time.

29.1

PLATES 29.1–2

Cougar Meadows, view west at the Monida–Yellowstone Stage Company horse pasture site

LOCATION: 503.3 E, 4946.9 N; elev. 2,104 m/6,900 ft

DATES AND PHOTOGRAPHERS: 29.1, ca. 1905–10—E. W. Hunter (MHS); 29.2, 6 August 1990—M. Meagher

INTERVAL: Approximately 80–85 years. Camera points similar. Date of the original is presumed from the appearance of the establishment, which seems to have been here for at least several years prior to the original photo date.

VEGETATION CHANGES: *Foreground* in the original view probably was a native bunchgrass community, but there appears to be considerable impact from pasturing horses. In 1990, nonnative timothy was a major component of the grassland. These meadows burned in 1988. *Middleground* willows were gone by 1990. At the time of the original photo the creek must have contained water throughout the year, but it appears quite shallow and probably disappeared underground further downstream at that time, as it does now. The creek bed was dry in August 1990, with grasses growing on the dry creekbed when the site was rephotographed, but water flowed temporarily during the spring. The invading lodgepole pine and scattered sagebrush in the meadow burned in 1988. Skeletons of the sagebrush do not show in the 1990 photograph, being hidden by the tall grass, but could be found readily. *Background* of lodgepole forest burned extensively in 1988, with canopy fire. Also, note the difference in the skyline of the Madison Range to rear. In the original, the skyline may have been so indistinct that it was retouched in the photographic studio.

This area receives little summer ungulate use. There is moderate elk use in winter, and increasing numbers of bison have used these meadows seasonally since the mid-1980s. As winter progresses, deepening snows preclude most ungulate use, but beginning about 1990, bison have returned here in spring.

The Monida and Yellowstone Stage Company (owned by F. J. Haynes, the early-day photographer) operated from 1898 to 1913. This was the company summer horse pasture, complete with buildings. The two remaining abandoned buildings burned in 1988. The horse-pasturing activity probably did much to foster the introduction of nonnative timothy to these meadows.

29.2

30.1

Plates 30.1–3

Madison River just east of the Barns, view east

Location: 495.0 E, 4944.3 N; elev. 2,025 m/6,642 ft

Dates and Photographers: 30.1, 1917—J. E. Haynes (NPS-YNP); 30.2, 20 July 1974—M. Meagher; 30.3, 26 August 1990—M. Meagher

Interval: 57 and 73 years. Camera points moved slightly to the left for both retakes.

Vegetation Changes: *Foreground* of silver sagebrush-bunchgrass looks essentially unaltered. The abandoned road is discernable but has revegetated well. *Middleground* river banks show a decrease in scattered low willows, which had nearly disappeared by 1990. The banks indicated lower water levels in the river for the 1917 and 1990 photos; both were taken later in the season compared to 1974. The flats in the 1990 view had a washed-over appearance caused by a freshly deposited layer of fine silt. The high water of the rapid spring snowmelt in 1989 was probably responsible for scouring the surface and perhaps removing some trees, then leaving behind a silt layer as the water dropped. The light-colored patches in the 1990 view are long-stemmed dried grasses. These are visible perhaps because of the later photographic date and because the flats seem drier overall, with less sagebrush. The lodgepole pine forest generally increased in density and invaded open areas prior to the fires of 1988, but trees disappeared from the flats across the river between 1974 and 1990. During the 1970s and 1980s there was considerable pine bark beetle tree mortality in this locale. Some of these dead trees burned in 1988, and some were killed directly by the fire. Note that some lodgepole pines in the 1917 view also appear to have died from forest insect attack, these show as scattered gray tree trunks. *Background* plateau burned extensively in 1988; note trees silhouetted along the skyline at right center (arrow).

This original was captioned in an album belonging to Bessie Haynes Arnold, J. E. Haynes's sister, as "The Packard—his first car on Madison River 1917."

After 1988, early spring bison use increased steadily along the north river bank and adjacent burned forest. The bison appeared to be attracted by the early greening of plants such as Ross's sedge and the shoots of death camas. Fires had opened up the forest canopy, and the recent increases in bison numbers also forced them to seek these new foraging areas, a process facilitated by the snow-packed winter road system.

31.1

Plates 31.1–3

Sentinel Meadows from Flat Cone Spring, looking south

Location: 510.9 E, 4934.8 N; elev. 2,195 m/7,199 ft

Dates and Photographers: 31.1, 1871—W. H. Jackson (NPS-YNP); 31.2, 15 July 1972—M. Meagher; 31.3, 6 July 1991—M. Meagher

Interval: 101 and 120 years. Camera points similar.

Vegetation Changes: *Foreground* hot spring looks similar but the rim appears higher, with rougher detail, in the original. The spring may have changed activity enough to alter deposition patterns and permit normal erosion. Herbaceous vegetation has encroached on the far edges of the sinter deposits of this spring; the change is most apparent between 1972 and 1991. *Middleground* of wet sedge meadow looks unchanged. Lodgepole pines and a ground cover of forbs, grasses, and sedges have invaded siliceous sinter substrate at left. In contrast, the sinter area at right rear seems smaller but more defined, and the lower areas may be wetter. These changes illustrate that geothermal areas are dynamic, and varying ground temperatures and water levels influence vegetation shifts. *Background*

lodgepole forest shows snags that predate 1871. These trees may have been killed by pine bark beetles, as most of this forest was over 250 years of age by 1988 (W. Romme, pers. comm.). The forest increased in density and invaded some open areas until 1988. In 1988 the crown fires were extensive in this locale; note the skylined trees at right rear (arrow). Even so, the fires skipped patches of trees, such as those at the right base of the conical hill. The conical hill is most obvious in 1991 after the 1988 fire exposed its shape. It was formed of glacial till, probably because of localized hot water that melted ice during the Pinedale glaciation, as with similar hills nearby (Fournier et al. 1994).

These meadows receive elk and bison use during the fall, winter, and spring. Elk are more likely to utilize the drier sites, while bison use sedge meadows.

Steep Cone at middleground center (sometimes called Sentinel Cone) is one of three prominent hot spring mounds in this meadow "guarding the upper valley"—the sentinels of Sentinel Creek (Whittlesey 1988:137).

32.1

Plates 32.1–3

Fountain Flats, Lower Geyser Basin, looking south from the Porcupine Hills

Location: 514.9 E, 4935.0 N; elev. 2,256 m/7,399 ft

Dates and Photographers: 32.1, September 1912—U.S. Army Engineers (NPS-YNP); 32.2, 26 August 1971—M. Meagher; 32.3, 6 July 1991—M. Meagher

Interval: 59 and 79 years. Camera points adjusted slightly because of conifer tree growth, emphasized by the limber and lodgepole pine branches that intrude into the scenes of the retakes.

Vegetation Changes: *Foreground* of the original already had been disturbed by early roads and trails, cavalry summer encampments, and tourist activities. Ditching in the sedge meadow and other scars have healed naturally in this mesic, geothermally influenced area. Because the 1991 scene was taken in early July, the vegetation appears darker, with comparatively moister conditions. However, the 1991 view also shows extensive bare whitish patches of dry siliceous soils. The interspersion of wet and dry at this early date probably reflects more than a decade of win-

ter drought. *Middle* and *background* show a gradual increase in the density and distribution of lodgepole forest, with gradual invasion of meadow edges and openings on suitable sites. The fires of 1988 burned forest in the middle distance, especially at left (arrow). The white expanses at the rear edges of the flats are deposits of siliceous sinter from the geothermal activity of the Lower Geyser Basin. Note a few steam columns rising.

The Fountain Hotel, visible at rear in 1912, opened in 1891 and ceased operation in 1903 but was not razed until 1927. The telegraph line paralleled the early road. In the 1912 view the dark animals grazing on the flats are cattle. Cattle were few in number and grazed here during the summer for only a few years.

Bison and elk use the flats during fall-winter-spring. Summer use is more limited. The meadow vegetation here is short because of the thermally influenced growing conditions (Despain 1990). In the drought of 1988 these meadows had a reddish cast in summer as spike-rush was prominent among the sedges.

32.2

32.3

33.1

PLATES 33.1–2

Near Clepsydra Geyser, Lower Geyser Basin, looking southwest

LOCATION: 514.9 E, 4932.9 N; elev. 2,220 m/7,281 ft

DATES AND PHOTOGRAPHERS: 33.1, ca. 1885—J. P. Iddings (USGS); 33.2, 20 June 1973—M. Meagher

INTERVAL: 88 years. Camera points approximate.

VEGETATION CHANGES: *Foreground* appearance of siliceous sinter deposits and water patterns has changed, probably with shifts in geothermal activity. *Middleground* at the edge of the siliceous sinter flat shows invasion of ground cover, mainly grasses and sedges. *Background* hill had burned over just prior to the original photo, then reforested with lodgepole pine. The area had considerable fire in 1988, but no burned sites are visible in this scene.

This part of the Lower Geyser Basin has been a major tourist attraction since the early days of the park. The old Fountain Hotel about 1 km (0.5 mi) eastward offered comparatively luxurious accommodations for 350 guests when it opened in 1891 (Haines 1977). Bison and elk spend fall, winter, and spring in the adjacent meadows.

33.2

34.1

PLATES 34.1–3

Midway Geyser Basin, view northwest from the south end

LOCATION: 513.8 E, 4929.1 N; elev. 2,211 m/7,252 ft

DATES AND PHOTOGRAPHERS: 34.1, 1871—W. H. Jackson (NPS-YNP); 34.2, 13 September 1971—M. Meagher; 34.3, 13 September 1990—M. Meagher

INTERVAL: 100 and 119 years. Camera points similar.

VEGETATION CHANGES: *Foreground* below shows increased ground cover except for the disappearance of the common juniper at left, and shows small, site-specific, geothermally influenced changes. Most of the dense vegetation close to the river is sedge, with rushes and seasonal forbs such as yellow monkeyflower and fringed gentian. Note that the geothermal rivulet in the center foreground has cut down more deeply with concurrent narrowing of its channel since 1871. Details have changed in the river (arrow) as the small island was submerged and worn away between 1871 and 1990. No remnants of the stump at right remained by 1971, although decomposition is slow here. Tourists may have removed the stump for firewood. *Middleground* during the first interval shows a loss of common juniper from the slope at right. Lodgepole pine forest increased in density and invaded suitable sites. Note the highlining of scattered trees in both retakes. The trail visible at the base of the slope at right in the original was reestablished by 1990. This area is heavily used by bison and some elk. In summer, anglers and sightseers also use the trail. *Background* shows the effects of the extensive fires of 1988.

One of the Twin Buttes is the prominent landmark at rear. This scene served as the setting for a Defenders of Wildlife art print created in 1989 by Monte Dolack to advocate the return of the wolf to Yellowstone. In early 1995, an experimental population of 14 wolves was brought to the northern part of the park to begin the reestablishment process.

34.2

34.3

35.1

Plates 35.1–3

Midway Geyser Basin, view west northwest from atop cliffs on east side

Location: 513.5 E, 4930.0 N; elev. 2,287 m/7,501 ft

Dates and Photographers: 35.1, 1871—W. H. Jackson (USGS); 35.2, 13 September 1971—M. Meagher; 35.3, 13 September 1990—M. Meagher

Interval: 100 and 119 years. Camera points similar but cliff edge omitted.

Vegetation Changes: *Foreground* and *middleground* generally show the invasion and increased density of lodgepole on the sinter substrate of the basin. From back to front, one strip of trees has increased, one reinvaded, one decreased, and one is a new invasion, illustrating the variety of changes that may occur in thermal basins where hot water flow patterns and temperatures change over time. The strip of dead trees in the original may also reflect fire (note background). Scattered foreground trees burned in 1988. *Background* forest was roughly 150 years old in 1871 (W. Romme, pers. comm.), so a pine bark beetle outbreak probably caused the tree mortality visible as gray standing dead trees. Thereafter, the lodgepole forest appears to have increased in uniformity and density. The fires of 1988 left grayish-appearing areas in the standing forest. Note the skylined tree snags on top of the Twin Buttes in the 1990 view; these indicate a crown fire in 1988.

This area is used seasonally by elk and especially by bison. They travel along the meadow edge at the far side of the siliceous sinter flat and along the near side of the river bank. Steam near the center of the scenes rises from Excelsior Geyser. The immense eruptions of the 1880s for which the geyser was named apparently were sufficient to break the internal "plumbing" and enlarge the crater. It was dormant until small eruptions of 2–2.5 m (6–7 ft) were seen in 1985 (Whittlesey 1988).

35.2

35.3

36.1

PLATES 36.1–3

Midway Geyser Basin, looking southeast along the Firehole River from the north and east side

LOCATION: 513.2 E, 4930.3 N; elev. 2,211 m/7,252 ft

DATES AND PHOTOGRAPHERS: 36.1, 1872—W. H. Jackson (USGS); 36.2, 4 September 1972—M. Meagher; 36.3, 13 September 1990—M. Meagher

INTERVAL: 100 and 118 years. Camera points similar.

VEGETATION CHANGES: *Foreground* appears to have changed from scattered bunchgrasses with some forbs to more general grass cover. The bank sedges appear less dense than in the original view. *Middleground* lodgepole forest increased in area and density. Between 1872 and 1972 a small new island formed in the river; by 1990 it appears to be slightly larger. At left the river has deepened the curve of the sedge-covered bank. *Background* in 1990 shows grayish areas of forest that burned in 1988. Note the similarity of the skylined trees at right rear in 1872 and 1990, suggesting that a forest fire occurred here not long before 1872.

Midway Geyser Basin was commonly called Hell's Half Acre in the early years of the park. Bison forage along the Firehole River banks in winter and new calves may be seen here in spring as groups forage the river bottom on newly green sedges and grasses.

In the 1872 view, the effect of the slower shutter speed available for early cameras resulted in a blurring of steam clouds and riffles in the river. However, vegetation and ground surface detail often was remarkably sharp.

36.2

36.3

37.1

PLATES 37.1–3

Firehole River below Castle Geyser, looking northwest

LOCATION: 513.0 E, 4923.3 N; elev. 2,241 m/7,350 ft

DATES AND PHOTOGRAPHERS: 37.1, 1871—W. H. Jackson (NPS-YNP); 37.2, 4 September 1972—M. Meagher; 37.3, 10 September 1990—M. Meagher

INTERVAL: 101 and 119 years. Camera points similar.

VEGETATION CHANGES: *Foreground* and *middleground* show increased extent and density of the sedge and grass ground cover. The hot water flow from the cone on the far river edge has changed; the near cone shows erosion and/or vandalism. Note that after 1871 a geothermal rivulet appeared at the base of the near cone at left. *Middle* and *background* lodgepole pines increased in size and density until the fires of 1988. The hill at left rear burned in 1988, as did the plateaus. The grayish areas in the lodgepole pine forest reflect crown fire.

The temperature of the Firehole River warms more than it would otherwise because of the inflow of thermally heated water from the geyser basins. In summer, temperatures become high enough to cause the fish population to move to the cooler waters of tributary streams. Ungulates, mainly bison, may concentrate here in winter.

As in plate 36.1, the riffles in the 1871 view are smoothed by the slower shutter speed of the camera used. But even so, over the 119 years represented by the photos, the riffle patterns are amazingly similar.

37.2

37.3

38.1

Plates 38.1–3

Punchbowl Spring, Upper Geyser Basin

Location: 511.7 E, 4923.4 N; elev. 2,232 m/7,320 ft.

Dates and Photographers: 38.1, ca. 1885—J. K. Hillers (USGS); 38.2, 7 July 1972—M. Meagher; 38.3, 11 September 1990—M. Meagher

Interval: Approximately 87 and 105 years. Camera points similar.

Vegetation Changes: *Foreground* has changed greatly. Some of this may have been caused by human activity such as trampling, with effects probably compounded by natural geothermal change. Water overflow now occurs at the opposite side of the spring, out of view here. *Background* probably burned during the early 1870s, since most of the trees had fallen by 1885. This apparently was a small fire because most of the area had not burned since the early 1700s (W. Romme, pers. comm.). A respectable forest grew in the next 100 years before the area burned again in 1988.

Between about 1909 and 1913, the Wylie Camping Company had a permit to pipe hot water from this spring to a nearby tent-camp tourist facility (L. Whittlesey, pers. comm.). The tent-camp system originated by

William Wylie provided low-cost accommodations in contrast to the hotels. Mr. Wylie of the "Wylie Way" first called this spring the Fairies Well (Whittlesey 1988). Some seasonal use by elk and bison occurs in this area.

38.2

38.3

39.1

PLATES 39.1–3

Pyramid Cone, an extinct geyser cone east of Punch-bowl Spring, Upper Geyser Basin, looking northwest

LOCATION: 512.0 E, 4923.8 N; elev. 2,232 m/7,320 ft

DATES AND PHOTOGRAPHERS: 39.1, ca. 1885—J. P. Iddings (USGS); 39.2, 18 July 1972—M. Meagher; 39.3, 9 September 1990—M. Meagher

INTERVAL: Approximately 87 and 105 years. Camera points similar.

VEGETATION CHANGES: *Foreground* and *middleground* in both retakes are drier; ground cover changed from a sedge-rush to a forb-sedge-arrowgrass community by 1972. Overall, the wetlands appear to have decreased. Walk construction and relocation disturbed the flat (visible in 1972), but natural revegetation during the last 20 years has mostly concealed the human-caused disturbances. We cannot identify the four distinctive dark blobs at right center on the flats of the original. *Background* lodgepole forest increased in density and size and invaded the sinter substrate of the mound by 1972. A crown fire burned through in 1988, charring even young trees.

The annual plant Ross's bentgrass is endemic to Yellowstone Park and is unique to the Firehole geyser basins. It grows where steam rises to the soil surface and condenses (Despain 1990). Dispersal of its annual seed production, and thus its perpetuation, may be dependent upon transport on the muddy hooves of bison and elk that use the Firehole geyser basins, especially for winter range (J. Whipple, pers. comm.).

39.2

39.3

40.1

PLATES 40.1–3

Upper Geyser Basin Hotel, replaced by the Old Faithful Inn, from Beehive Geyser

LOCATION: 513.7 E, 4923.1 N; elev. 2,241 m/7,350 ft

DATES AND PHOTOGRAPHERS: 40.1, ca. 1885—F. J. Haynes (NPS-YNP); 40.2, 12 September 1972—M. Meagher; 40.3, 9 September 1990—M. Meagher

INTERVAL: Approximately 87 and 105 years. Camera points similar.

VEGETATION CHANGES: *Foreground* in both retakes appears to show more sinter detail; this is probably related to a geothermal change, with overflow from Plume Geyser at the observer's feet. This geyser did not exist in 1885. *Middleground* is amazingly similar, given the amount of disturbance caused by both human and wildlife presence. Note the shape of individual conifers across the river in 1885. Thick branches at ground level probably reflected protection by the winter snows of that time, but highlining occurs in all views. *Background* of the 1990 photograph shows the effects of the 1988 fires. A fire storm burned behind the Old Faithful Inn. Much of the gray cast represents trees killed by the crown fire but still standing in 1990.

The early hotel of the 1885 view was called the Shack and was classified as dangerous by Assistant Superintendent Weimer when it was built in 1885 (Haines 1977). Fire accidentally, and perhaps fortunately, destroyed it in 1894. The Old Faithful Inn, built in 1904, survived the 1988 fire storm because of fire protection efforts and because the inn is surrounded by parking lots and otherwise barren open space.

40.2

40.3

41.1

Plates 41.1–3

Old Faithful Geyser from the top of the Old Faithful Inn

LOCATION: 513.5 E, 4922.6 N; elev. 2,256 m/7,399 ft

DATES AND PHOTOGRAPHERS: 41.1, 1 October 1917—J. E. Haynes (NPS-YNP); 41.2, 13 September 1972—M. Meagher; 41.3, 11 September 1990—M. Meagher

INTERVAL: 55 and 73 years. Camera points similar.

VEGETATION CHANGES: *Foreground* and *middleground* show the effects of high levels of human use. Note that utility poles crossing the edge of the Old Faithful sinter deposits in 1917 have long since been removed. Likewise, the original photo shows footpaths close to the geyser cone that are mostly gone by 1972, with people confined to the observation boardwalk. Lodgepole pine tree reproduction probably has been precluded by human trampling on many sites. *Background* appearance of the lodgepole forest in 1917 may be due to pine bark beetles' causing defoliated and dead trees. In contrast, the fires of 1988 produced some of the same grayish cast in the 1990 scene, but it appears much more patchy, probably because of the mosaic of burn

intensity. The slope at the left edge in the 1990 view is more open. Most of this view burned in the early 1700s, making the forest about 250 years of age in 1988.

The railed platform atop the inn (visible in pls. 40.2–3) from which these photographs were taken is accessed by a stairway within the inn that opens onto the roof below the top. Public access to this platform is no longer possible for safety reasons, nor would the space accommodate present-day crowds.

We do not know the date of the first construction of a boardwalk around Old Faithful Geyser, but one has been there for many years. Boardwalks serve two purposes; they are intended to protect people as well as the geothermal features.

41.2

41.3

42.1

PLATES 42.1–2

Shoshone Geyser Basin, view north up Shoshone Creek

LOCATION: 516.3 E, 4911.3 N; elev. 2,380 m/7,806 ft

DATES AND PHOTOGRAPHERS: 42.1, 1871—W. H. Jackson (USGS); 42.2, 25 July 1973—D. B. Houston

INTERVAL: 102 years. Camera angles similar in views but retake is from further back.

VEGETATION CHANGES: *Foreground* and *middleground* demonstrate the effects of changes in geothermal activity on vegetation. A large geyser occurs just beyond the photo edge in the right foreground. Lodgepole pine has invaded a former thermal site in left middleground. Trees in right middleground are lodgepole pine and subalpine fir. *Background* in the original shows a large number of dead trees in a lodgepole pine forest. Both subalpine fir and Engelmann spruce now occur in the forest understory. Note that the older forest appears more even against the skyline. This area did not burn in 1988; the aging of the forest makes it increasingly vulnerable to fire in the future.

Osborne Russell visited the basin in 1839 and described in some detail the geyser known to the fur trappers as Hour Spring (Haines 1955). Shoshone Lake and the geyser basin derive their name from the Shoshone Indians, who lived mainly to the west and south of the park, but entered the park area at times. The Sheepeaters, related to the Shoshone-Bannock peoples, were the only residents at the time of park establishment.

43.1

PLATES 43.1–2

Three Rivers Junction, southwest or Bechler corner, view north

LOCATION: 508.7 E, 4903.6 N; elev. 2,220 m/7,281 ft

DATES AND PHOTOGRAPHERS: 43.1, 1921—J. E. Haynes (MHS); 43.2, 23 July 1990—M. Meagher

INTERVAL: 69 years. Camera point slightly higher and to the west.

VEGETATION CHANGES: *Foreground* of grasses, sedges, and young conifers is not appreciably different. *Middle* and *background* appear to have similar ground cover. Subalpine fir has invaded and increased in the middle areas. In the background there appears to have been a forest fire prior to the original photo. Subalpine fir has come in on many sites, with lodgepole pine on top of the plateaus. Dead but standing subalpine fir trees in the retake background probably were killed in another forest fire that burned here in 1940.

Three Rivers Junction was named in 1920 by W. C. Gregg "because neither we nor others would call it anything else" (Whittlesey 1988:155).

The three streams that join here form the Bechler River, encountered by the southern division of the Hayden Survey in 1872 (Haines 1977). At the time of the original photograph there were proposals to dam the Bechler River to provide irrigation for agricultural lands in Idaho. There was also a road proposed through this lovely canyon, another idea that fortunately was not pursued.

43.2

44.1

PLATES 44.1–3

South slopes of Mount Everts

LOCATION: 528.6 E; 4976.5 N; elev. 2,010 m/6,592 ft

DATES AND PHOTOGRAPHERS: 44.1, ca. 1885—J. P. Iddings (USGS); 44.2, 18 September 1970—D. B. Houston; 44.3, 12 August 1990—D. B. Houston

INTERVAL: Approximately 85 and 105 years. Camera point for retakes moved 30–60 m (108–197 ft) east because of increased forest cover.

VEGETATION CHANGES: *Foreground* of dense coniferous forest has changed little on the steep north-facing slope above Lava Creek. The scene did not burn in 1988. *Background* shows a substantial increase of conifers, mostly Douglas-fir, on the lower and upper slopes, and the summit of Mount Everts. Comparatively little change in patterns occurred in the sparse herbaceous vegetation on the steep, harsh south-facing slopes, and some groups of shrubby Rocky Mountain juniper retained the same configuration throughout. Erosion has continued. Dead trees suggest an earlier forest insect attack, disease, or fire on the edge of a grove of Douglas-fir in the original (below the rimrock at left center). In the 1990 image, scattered mortality of Douglas-fir is visible along Lava Creek and on Mount Everts as a result of spruce budworm activity.

This area is winter range for elk, mule deer, bighorn sheep, and an occasional moose.

Truman C. Everts, a member of the Washburn-Langford-Doane exploring expedition of 1870, wandered lost for 37 days after becoming separated from the others. The naming of the mountain confers upon him a sort of immortality that he otherwise might not have achieved. Everts was found on the Blacktail Plateau to the southeast: reportedly, he was most ungrateful for his rescue, believing that he would have made his way out of the wilderness unaided (Haines 1977).

44.2

44.3

45.1

PLATES 45.1–3

Approximately 0.4 km (0.25 mi) north of Wraith Falls on the Mammoth-Tower Road

LOCATION: 530.0 E, 4976.2 N; elev. 2,048 m/6,720 ft

DATES AND PHOTOGRAPHERS: 45.1, 1924—W. J. Cribbs (NPS-YNP); 45.2, 28 August 1972—D. B. Houston; 45.3, 29 July 1990—M. Meagher

INTERVAL: 48 and 66 years. Camera point for retakes moved about 10 m (33 ft) north because of increased forest cover.

VEGETATION CHANGES: *Foreground* and *middleground* show change from an extensive beaver pond to a willow-sedge-grass meadow (although a beaver was in the process of reconstructing a small lodge on a stream in the meadow at the time of the 1972 retake). Lodgepole pine, Engelmann spruce, and subalpine fir had invaded the edges of the meadow by 1972. The meadow and adjacent small conifers burned during 1988. Robust stands of grasses and sedges, with scattered willows, occurred by 1990. *Background* shows a minor reduction in aspen along the forest-grassland boundary. There was little change in distribution of the lodgepole pine and Douglas-fir forest until crown and understory fires burned extensively in

1988. A number of Douglas-fir trees that appear to be alive in the 1990 retake had severely scorched trunks and will likely succumb to the burn. Many of the young Douglas-fir and big sagebrush plants on the toe of the slope at right were killed by the fire.

The change from active beaver pond to sedge-grass meadow seems to have been common in the park after the 1920s, but the ecological forces driving the vegetation shifts are complex. Beaver populations appear to have irrupted during the early 20th century, perhaps in response to increased abundance of aspen for food. Subsequently, beaver numbers dropped sharply, but the animals maintain a constant, if less conspicuous, presence within the park.

In much of Yellowstone, beaver activity sites appear to be quite ephemeral. Some sites sustain activity for only a few years, enough time for one or two sets of kits. Then the beaver move on. The park does not seem to be prime beaver habitat. We have seen dams made of sagebrush in some of these ephemeral sites.

45.2

45.3

46.1

Plates 46.1–3

Lower Blacktail Deer Creek, view east across the Blacktail Plateau

Location: 532.5 E, 4979.6 N; elev. 1,950 m/6,396 ft

Dates and Photographers: 46.1, 1929—C. P. Russell (NPS-YNP); 46.2, 9 August 1972—D. B. Houston; 46.3, 8 August 1990—D. B. Houston

Interval: 43 and 61 years. Camera points approximate.

Vegetation Changes: *Foreground* between 1929 and 1972 shows little change except for minor increases in the shrubs—common rabbitbrush and horse-brush. Dominant herbaceous vegetation was Idaho fescue, bluebunch wheatgrass, and needlegrasses, with hairgrass and aster in wetter sites. Sagebrush burned throughout the scene in 1988. By 1990, a grassland again dominated by robust Idaho fescue, needlegrasses, and other bunchgrasses grew vigorously in the burn. *Middleground* shows a decline in aspen and suggests an increase in big sagebrush in 1972. In the 1988 fires the aspen and lodgepole pine stands along the stream burned; profuse aspen sprouting was occurring at the burned sites by 1990. Dominant grasses in the wetter sites were Idaho fescue and hairgrass; in the dry sites, bluebunch wheatgrass and junegrass. *Background* bare-appearing slopes have vegetation dominated by bluebunch wheatgrass and junegrass. These were essentially unchanged in 1972. (Sites appear less harsh in the 1972 retake, but this is due to differences in lighting.) The open arrow (1972) marks an erosion site that is part of a complex of mineral licks used by ungulates. A minor decline in shrubs, possibly shrubby cinquefoil or willow, occurred in the swale to the left of the arrow in the 1972 image. Fire in 1988 burned the big sagebrush from the swales, and cinquefoil appears to have been eliminated from the site above the mineral lick. The bunchgrass steppe across the creek burned except for the ridgetops. Dark-colored patches on the slopes in 1990 (arrow) were charcoal from burned big sagebrush plants that were surrounded by dark green, vigorously growing native grasses.

The area is elk winter range. Elk, mule deer, and pronghorn summer here. The valley of Blacktail Deer Creek is surfaced by glacial deposits from the Pinedale glaciation, the last remnants of which vanished about 10,000 years ago—but a blink in geologic time. About 20,000–30,000 years ago the Pinedale ice covered most of what is Yellowstone National Park today (Pierce 1979, Good and Pierce 1996).

46.2

46.3

47.1

PLATES 47.1–3

Northern range, view northwest toward Electric Peak from the east edge of the Blacktail Plateau

LOCATION: 534.8 E, 4978.2 N; elev. 2,107 m/6,910 ft

DATES AND PHOTOGRAPHERS: 47.1, 1900—U.S. Army Engineers (NPS-YNP); 47.2, 18 May 1972—D. B. Houston; 47.3, 5 May 1992—M. Meagher

INTERVAL: 72 and 92 years. Camera points similar.

VEGETATION CHANGES: *Foreground* and *middleground* areas support an Idaho fescue-big sagebrush grassland. An increase in big sagebrush occurred during the first interval, but the fires of 1988 removed much of it. Some of the lodgepole pines invading the grasslands also burned. The pond shows emergent vegetation above the water surface in 1992, indicating that it is shallower. Note highlining of conifers in the open meadow at left in the 1992 image. Isolated trees and many of those along meadow edges showed more browsing and the mechanical effects of the breakage of lower branches and rubbing by elk and bison in recent years. Limber pines grow near the photo point; these are the branches that protrude into the 1972 view. Some of these trees burned in 1988, leaving the skeletal branches in the 1992 view. *Background* had some increase in conifers on the flank of Mount Everts during the first 72 years. There was a mosaic of burned and unburned forest after the 1988 fires, but little is apparent in this view. Electric Peak did not burn.

This area is elk range from winter to spring; bison travel through. After a moratorium in 1968 on management of the population by removals within the park, elk numbers roughly tripled by the early 1980s. The consecutive winters of 1976–1977 and 1977–1978 were exceptionally mild, with mostly mild winters prevailing in the northern part of the park since early 1981 (winter drought). An interaction of climatic influences with the biology and behavior of elk appeared to be responsible for the population changes (Houston 1982).

The spring of 1992 was early; April was warm and dry. As a consequence, snowmelt, runoff, and plant growth were all several weeks early. Note the near absence of snowbanks in 1992, even though the photo was taken in early May, especially when compared to the earlier photographs. Note also that the pond level reflects this and the cumulative overall winter drought from the early 1980s to the early 1990s.

47.2

47.3

48.1

Plates 48.1–3

Upper Geode Creek, view north to Hellroaring Mountain

Location: 539.7 E, 4976.7 N; elev. 2,320 m/7,609 ft

Dates and Photographers: 48.1, August 1918—U.S. Forest Service (NPS-YNP); 48.2, 2 August 1971—D. B. Houston; 48.3, 7 August 1990—D. B. Houston

Interval: 53 and 72 years. Camera points similar.

Vegetation Changes: *Foreground* supported a vigorous stand of native grasses in all three scenes—needlegrasses, Idaho fescue, and bluegrasses. The area did not burn in 1988. *Middleground* shows little change in the bunchgrass steppe of Idaho fescue and bluebunch wheatgrass. The Douglas-fir stands continued to increase in abundance and stature. Note that the area of sparse herbaceous vegetation in the retakes (arrow, 1971) was present in the original. The powerline there in 1971 (pole visible near arrow) was removed in 1972. *Background* Douglas-fir and grassland likewise show little change except for minor increases in forest density. The

background area at extreme right burned in 1988 and conifers were killed, but this cannot be seen in the photograph.

This area is in the heart of the park's northern winter range. It has received consistent use by elk and yet has shown little change in 72 years. The northern Yellowstone elk numbered just over 19,000 for the winter count of 1993–94 (J. Mack, pers. comm.). At times, hundreds of elk are scattered across these hills, making the snow an expanse of feeding craters. Apparently, the elk "know" the proper areas to forage (Wallace et al. 1995).

48.2

48.3

49.1

PLATES 49.1–3

Elk Creek, view west

LOCATION: 545.0 E, 4975.2 N; elev. 1,950 m/6,396 ft

DATES AND PHOTOGRAPHERS: 49.1, 23 July 1921—E.R. Warren (SUNY ESF, Archives); 49.2, 14 August 1971—D. B. Houston; 49.3, 6 August 1990—D. B. Houston

INTERVAL: 50 and 69 years. Camera points similar.

VEGETATION CHANGES: *Foreground* has an active beaver pond in 1921, ringed by aspen and containing scattered willow. Warren (1926) described the willows as "mostly dead with a few living." The beaver dam was in the upper right corner of the pond, here partially obscured by aspen. The pond was deserted by 1923. Retakes show a sedge meadow with hairgrass on drier sites. Remnants of the beaver lodge were present but are difficult to see in the 1971 retake. Engelmann spruce had invaded the far edge of the sedge meadow. The sedge-hairgrass meadow burned partially during 1988, but it is little changed from 1971 in the 1990 retake. *Middleground* of the original view shows a big sagebrush grassland with some invasion of Douglas-fir. A substantial increase in Douglas-fir occurred in both retakes.

Douglas-fir invaded the grassland and nearly replaced the aspen grove at left (arrow, original). In 1988 the steppe burned, killing small conifers and scattered big sagebrush plants. In 1990 the site was dominated by robust stands of native grasses. *Background* shows an increase in conifers (mostly Douglas-fir, with lodgepole pine and subalpine fir) on the east-facing slopes and ridgetops. The appearance of the vegetation in the original suggests that this change represents recolonization of a former burn. In 1988 the forest and sagebrush steppe burned in patches, killing Douglas-fir and big sagebrush.

Many of the changes shown in the initial comparison reflect a reduced frequency of fires. A fire-scarred tree cut in this vicinity in the 1970s showed a mean interval between fires of 51 years for the previous 303 years. Although the various construction and foraging activities of beaver clearly contributed to the changes observed, a complex interaction of ecological factors appeared to be involved. Mountainous terrain such as this does not seem to foster large, long-lasting beaver colonies (Hill 1982). The heavy snowpack sometimes melts abruptly, turning small streams into torrents that wash out beaver dams and fill the ponds with silt. Extensive willow flats cannot form along these headwater streams, so the food source is limited and the beaver disperse when it is gone for the time being.

49.2

49.3

50.1

PLATES 50.1–3

View west southwest down the Yellowstone River, 2.5 km (1.5 mi) below the confluence with Elk Creek

LOCATION: 542.8 E, 4978.7 N; elev. 1,800 m/5,904 ft

DATES AND PHOTOGRAPHERS: 50.1, ca. 1885—J. P. Iddings (USGS); 50.2, 11 August 1971—D. B. Houston; 50.3, 11 August 1990—D. B. Houston

INTERVAL: Approximately 86 and 105 years. Camera points similar; note pattern of stones on cliff edge.

VEGETATION CHANGES: *Foreground* ridgecrest above the cliff is sparsely vegetated and shows little change except for a minor increase in size and number of Rocky Mountain juniper; the snag present in 1971 had fallen by 1990. Bluebunch wheatgrass was the dominant grass on the site. The foreground did not burn during 1988. A small clump of nonnative cheatgrass was in the right foreground in 1990. Remarkably few changes have occurred in the rocks and shrubs on the cliff face. *Middleground* shows an increase in big sagebrush in the grassland at left across the river. This scene did not burn in 1988. *Background* of Douglas-fir forest increased except for individuals killed by western spruce budworm (a native insect) during the

1980s. Douglas-fir has almost completely replaced the aspen stand (arrow) visible in the original photo.

The ridgecrest site with sparse vegetation is part of an intensively grazed bighorn sheep and elk winter range. The increased forest cover probably reflects a reduction in frequency of natural fires.

The rock exposures to the right are nonvolcanic conglomerates of Eocene age (Prostka et al. 1975). The area is part of the Black Canyon of the Yellowstone, formed largely of dark, metamorphosed, Precambrian rock. The canyon is generally rugged to impassable. The route followed by the Bannock Trail and by early explorers lay to the south of this section of the Yellowstone River.

50.2

50.3

51.1

Plates 51.1–3

Lower Hellroaring slopes, view northeast

Location: 544.2 E, 4979.2 N; elev. 1,830 m/6,002 ft

Dates and Photographers: 51.1, 27 August 1943—McDougall and Grimm (NPS-YNP); 51.2, 26 August 1974—D. B. Houston; 51.3, 11 August 1990—D. B. Houston

Interval: 31 and 47 years. Camera points similar.

Vegetation Changes: Vegetation in the original was described as green rabbitbrush, Idaho fescue, and needle-and-thread grass. It was the same in the retakes and the site did not burn during 1988.

This exposed upper slope on the northern winter range is intensively grazed each winter by elk (and some bison) and shows no appreciable change in vegetation over 47 years. We have seen several thousand elk scattered at one time across the Hellroaring slopes.

The large glacial erratic boulder probably was deposited as the Pinedale glaciers receded. Note the Rocky Mountain juniper growing behind the erratic, barely visible in 1943. It is common on the northern range to see trees growing like this because of a moist microzone created by a boulder. In the winter, a layer of snow makes such scenes deceptive, turning the erratics into "buffalo rocks" to the casual eye.

51.2

51.3

52.1

Plates 52.1–3

Tower Junction, view north to Little Buffalo Creek

Location: 546.7 E, 4973.8 N; elev. 1,920 m/6,297 ft

Dates and Photographers: 52.1, ca. 1885—J. P. Iddings (USGS); 52.2, 25 August 1970—D. B. Houston; 52.3, 6 August 1990—D. B. Houston

Interval: Approximately 85 and 105 years. Camera points similar.

Vegetation Changes: *Foreground* of bunchgrass steppe in the original appeared to contain scattered rabbitbrush plants. At the time of the retakes, the native grasses under the big sagebrush canopy were dominated by Idaho fescue and needlegrasses. Fore and middleground did not burn in 1988 and show little change in the 1990 retake, except for mortality of some big sagebrush plants and increased height of Douglas-fir. *Middleground* benches across the Yellowstone River support a sagebrush grassland in all views. As in the foreground, the benches may have lacked an extensive sagebrush component in the original (see the extreme left of the view), but this is difficult to determine. Conifers have increased. *Background* slopes show forest invasion into grassland. The dark gray vegetation in the original (as above the boulder at right) was aspen, growing as dense, small stems. The aspen stands remaining in the retakes were characterized by scattered large trees, and the understories of the stands were dominated by young Douglas-fir. Background slope burned spottily during 1988; a decline in big sagebrush occurred on the burned sites, but this is difficult to detect in the retake.

This area is important elk winter range. Iddings took a series of photos of the impressive boulders deposited in this vicinity during the retreat of the Pinedale glaciers. The vegetation changes shown here are representative of changes that have occurred over large areas of the northern winter range. We attribute much of the change to a reduction in the frequency of fire.

52.2

52.3

53.1

PLATES 53.1–3

Tower Junction, view south through a field of glacial erratic boulders

LOCATION: 546.8 E, 4973.6 N; elev. 1,920 m/6,297 ft

DATES AND PHOTOGRAPHERS: 53.1, ca. 1885—J. P. Iddings (USGS); 53.2, 25 August 1970—D. B. Houston; 53.3, 6 August 1990—D. B. Houston

INTERVAL: Approximately 85 and 105 years. Camera points similar.

VEGETATION CHANGES: *Foreground* shows the addition of big sagebrush to the former bunchgrass-rabbitbrush community between 1885 and 1970, and a marked increase in the sagebrush after 1970. Perennial grasses under the big sagebrush canopy were dominated by Idaho fescue and several species of needlegrass at the time of the retakes. The scene did not burn in 1988 and shows little change except for scattered mortality of big sagebrush plants. *Background* slopes show grassland with two low, dense aspen stands in the original scene (the boulder adjacent to the stand at right is about 2.5 m/8.3 ft high). Scattered Douglas-fir trees of different sizes were present, snags indicating the occurrence of earlier fires. The retakes show invasion of big sagebrush into the grassland; replacement of aspen by Dou-

glas-fir and big sagebrush; highlining of some of the trees by ungulates (the small Douglas-fir at the extreme left in the original appears to have been browsed, arrow); and the invasion of Douglas-fir into the sagebrush-grassland.

Increases in big sagebrush and Douglas-fir, coupled with the decline in aspen, reflect in part the changes expected from the absence of fires. Until the beginning of the 20th century, fires may have burned in this locale at intervals of 20-25 years (Houston 1973).

Big sagebrush is a volatile fuel and is probably important as a carrier of fire in the big sagebrush grassland of the northern range. In the absence of fire, wet summers may kill old big sagebrush locally but foster large numbers of seedlings.

53.2

53.3

54.1

ground burned during 1988 killing both big sagebrush and Douglas-fir. By 1990, the grassland was dominated by robust blue-bunch wheatgrass, needlegrasses, wildrye, and lupines. Big sagebrush seedlings, up to 30 cm (12 in) tall, were recolonizing the area. The sedge meadow at lower left burned intensely; the accumulated organic layers burned down to mineral soil. *Background* shows an increase in Douglas-fir and proba-bly big sagebrush, with a decline in aspen. Aspen in the original had the appearance of the foreground stand—that is, dense repro-duction with no large overstory trees. Stands in the original showed the effects of ungu-late browsing on the margins. Remnant aspen stands in the retakes showed no reproduction. Junction Butte did not burn in 1988 and shows little change in the 1990 retake.

This area near the confluence of the Yel-lowstone and Lamar rivers is an impor-tant elk and bison winter range. Fire-scarred trees cut in this vicinity in the early 1970s suggested a mean fire frequency of 20–25 years until the 20th century. Reduction in fire frequency undoubt-edly had a role in vegetation change.

The butte was named in 1878 by the third Hayden Survey because of its prominence at the confluence of the Yellowstone and Lamar rivers (Whit-tlesey 1988).

Plates 54.1–3

Tower Junction area, view east across Yellowstone River to Junction Butte

Location: 546.7 E, 4974.8 N; elev. 1,980 m/6,494 ft

Dates and Photographers: 54.1, 1900—U.S. Army Engineers (NPS-YNP); 54.2, 15 July 1972—D. B. Houston; 54.3, 13 August 1990—D. B. Houston

Interval: 72 and 90 years. Camera point moved 15 m (49 ft) west and uphill because of the aspen's increased height.

Vegetation Changes: *Foreground* of the original was occupied by a low, dense stand of aspen (probably 3–5 m/10–16 ft tall, based on size of rock at left). Evidence of browsing occurs on the outer stems. The stand in the 1972 retake had matured and showed no recruitment of stems into the overstory. Big sagebrush dominated the understory. In 1988, these large aspen stems were killed by fire. Profuse sprouts up to 1 m/3 ft tall (inset photo) occurred by 1990, but numbers subsequently decreased. *Middle-ground* in 1972 shows an increase in Douglas-fir and possibly in big sage-brush on the Idaho fescue–bluebunch wheatgrass grassland. The middle-

54.2

54.3

55.1

PLATES 55.1–3

Lamar River, view southwest to Prospect Peak

LOCATION: 552.5 E, 4973.5 N; elev. 1,890 m/6,199 ft

DATES AND PHOTOGRAPHERS: 55.1, 1905—U.S. Army Engineers (NPS-YNP) (the "1818" is an identification number); 55.2, 17 July 1973—D. B. Houston; 55.3, 7 August 1990—D. B. Houston

INTERVAL: 68 and 85 years. Camera points approximate.

VEGETATION CHANGES: *Foreground* of sagebrush steppe has changed little except for local increases in the density of big sagebrush. Dominant grasses at the time of both retakes were Idaho fescue and needle-and-thread. The valley bottom did not burn here in 1988. *Middleground* across the Lamar River likewise shows little change, except for a decrease in willow or alder around a spring. Dominant grasses again were Idaho fescue and needle-and-thread; shrubs, common and green rabbitbrush and big sagebrush. *Background* of the 1973 retake shows an increase in Douglas-fir and a decline in aspen on Specimen Ridge, at left, and at lower elevations on Prospect Peak. Additional changes between 1973 and 1990 are not appar-

ent in the views: spot fires burned on Specimen Ridge in 1988, and Prospect Peak had extensive fire on the upper and middle slopes.

The road, which apparently was newly constructed in the original view, has since been abandoned and the road bed has revegetated naturally. A sharp eye will note traces of it, but in many places these pre–motor vehicle roads "sat rather lightly on the land." Earth-moving work was done with horse-drawn equipment and by hand. Some effort may have been made to recontour the road cut when the alignment was changed, but for many sites little attempt at restoration occurred. Sites of human activity were simply abandoned.

The Lamar River was originally known as the East Fork of the Yellowstone. In 1835, fur trapper Osborne Russell wrote: "I almost wished I could spend the remainder of my days in a place like this" (Haines 1955:27).

55.2

55.3

56.1

Plates 56.1–3

Lamar Valley about 2.5 km (1.6 mi) east of Junction Butte, view east to Druid Peak

Location: 551.5 E, 4973.2 N; elev. 1,890 m/6,199 ft

Dates and Photographers: 56.1, August 1918—U.S. Forest Service (NPS-YNP); 56.2, 2 August 1971—D. B. Houston; 56.3, 7 August 1990—D. B. Houston

Interval: 53 and 72 years. Camera points similar.

Vegetation Changes: *Foreground* in the original appears to have supported rabbitbrush and bunchgrasses. Both retakes show grassland dominated by Idaho fescue, needlegrasses, and junegrass. Shrubs were big sagebrush and green rabbitbrush. The rabbitbrush may have been less abundant in the retakes or merely obscured by the grasses. The 1990 photograph also shows shrubby horse-brush. *Middleground* of Idaho fescue grassland shows little change in the 72 years. Conifers in all three photographs show the effects of highlining by ungulate browsing. Foreground and middleground did not burn in 1988. *Background* shows little change, except for a noticeable increase in Douglas-fir forest between 1918 and 1971. Even the aspen shows little change (arrow, 1990).

This is an important elk and bison winter range, and the site represents a heavily grazed steppe that shows little change over 72 years. Utility poles present in 1971 had been removed by 1990.

The Pinedale glaciation brought the many glacial erratics scattered in the lower Lamar Valley on top of finer rock debris. Although remnants of glaciers persisted locally until about 10,000 years ago, this valley has probably been ice-free for at least 11,000 to 12,000 years.

Paleontological evidence suggests that a mammalian community similar to that of the present has occupied this area for the past 1,700–2,000 years (Hadly 1990). This is consistent with pollen records (Whitlock and Bartlein 1993), which suggest that the vegetation and appearance of the Lamar Valley have been much the same for nearly 2,000 years.

56.2

56.3

57.1

PLATES 57.1–3

View north on lower Slough Creek

LOCATION: 554.0 E, 4975.0 N; elev. 1,890 m/6,199 ft

DATES AND PHOTOGRAPHERS: 57.1, 7 August 1923—E. R. Warren (SUNY ESF, Archives); 57.2, 17 July 1973—D. B. Houston; 57.3, 7 August 1990—D. B. Houston

INTERVAL: 50 and 67 years. Camera points similar.

VEGETATION CHANGES: *Foreground* changes are most apparent in the reduction of willow. The willows appear to be dying in the original, but the dead branches do not have the hedged appearance of shrubs that have received intensive browsing by ungulates. The foreground otherwise shows little change; note the chokecherry bush at right (open arrow), cropped from the 1973 view. Dominant herbaceous vegetation in the foreground included bluegrasses, hairgrass, and wildrye (apparently the same clumps of wildrye occur at left-center in all the photographs, closed arrow, 1973), with sedges dominating the marsh area along the oxbow (above the arrow). *Middleground* also shows a small decline in willow and aspen. Herbaceous vegetation was similar to that in the foreground, except that

the alien timothy grass dominated some sites. The oxbow channel has filled with vegetation in both retakes compared to the original. The foreground and middleground did not burn in 1988. *Background* shows little change in the sagebrush grassland; dominant grass was Idaho fescue, with bluebunch wheatgrass and junegrass on drier areas. A decline in the density of aspen occurred in the swales and along the streams as stands increased in height. By 1990 the large aspen stems had died and the understories of the stands were dominated by nonnative timothy. Douglas-fir increased in area and density on the slopes and continued to invade the grassland along the ridgetop. Only a few small clumps of sagebrush burned during 1988.

E. R. Warren's notes (1926) suggested that extensive beaver activity occurred here just before the 1920s. Remnants of beaver dams are found throughout the area; note the beaver cuttings in the 1923 photograph.

57.2

57.3

58.1

PLATES 58.1–3

Druid Peak, view north across Lamar River from the top of Specimen Ridge

LOCATION: 560.0 E, 4967.4 N; elev. 2,440 m/8,003 ft

DATES AND PHOTOGRAPHERS: 58.1, ca. 1885—J. P. Iddings (USGS); 58.2, 27 August 1970—D. B. Houston; 58.3, 8 August 1991—D. B. Houston

INTERVAL: Approximately 85 and 106 years. Camera point for retakes 50–60 m (164–197 ft) higher because of an increase in forest cover.

VEGETATION CHANGES: *Foreground* of burned forest underwent a regrowth of conifers not apparent in the retakes because of the change in photo point (itself imposed by the increase in conifers). There has been considerable erosion from the exposed ridge and one of the petrified logs present in the original was gone by 1970. *Middleground* shows changes in the channel of the Lamar River with consequent changes in the locations of the small cottonwood and willow communities. Even in 1885, cottonwood trees were sparse along the river, but a small grove became established after that date (open arrow, 1991). An Idaho fescue–big sagebrush steppe dominated the valley bottom. The valley floor south of the river burned during 1988, and big sagebrush was eliminated temporarily. *Background* of conifers increased on the south slopes of Druid Peak. Little change is detectable in

the Idaho fescue and bluebunch wheatgrass grassland. Several ridgetops and upper slopes in this area showed 60 percent or more bare ground in 1970. These same sites show similar low vegetation density in the original (arrow, 1970). The area of sparse trees at left center in the original also suggests considerable bare ground, as in 1970. Aspen stands (arrow, original) decreased in area after 1885. The small size of the conifer and aspen trees suggests that a fire occurred shortly before the original photo was taken. The background did not burn during 1988 and conifers continued to increase in size.

The Lamar Valley is an important elk and bison winter range. Bighorn sheep occur on Druid Peak and on the foreground slopes of Specimen Ridge. This photo represents our earliest view of the south central portion of the valley. Despite the poor quality of the view, it shows limited amounts of riparian vegetation present in the 19th century, the early ("natural") occurrence of eroded slopes, and the increase of forests on bighorn sheep range that is typical of much of the northern winter range.

Trapper Osborne Russell wrote about this "Secluded Valley" in 1836 (Haines 1955:46), commenting: "There is something in the wild romantic scenery of this valley which I cannot nor will I, attempt to describe but the impressions made upon my mind while gazing from a high eminence on the surrounding landscape one evening as the sun was gently gliding behind the western mountain casting its gigantic shadows across [sic] the vale were such as time can never efface from my memory."

58.2

58.3

59.1

Plates 59.1–3

Lamar Valley, view south to Specimen Ridge

Location: 561.6 E, 4970.2 N; elev. 1,980 m/6,494 ft

Dates and Photographers: 59.1, 1898—A. Nelson (UW); 59.2, 10 July 1970—D. B. Houston; 59.3, 7 August 1990—D. B. Houston

Interval: 72 and 92 years. Camera points approximate.

Vegetation Changes: *Foreground* displays little change in the distribution of either big sagebrush or the grassland until fire in 1988 burned the big sagebrush in most of the valley bottom south of the river. *Middleground* of the 1970 retake shows relatively little change in the sagebrush steppe, with the exception of the replacement of a riparian shrub community (at left) by mesic grassland on an old channel of the Lamar River. Remnants of the shrub community (outside the scene) suggest that it was composed of species such as Geyer's willow and mountain alder. Big sagebrush was eliminated temporarily across much of the valley bottom south of the river when the area burned in 1988. The river bank is more apparent in the 1990 retake because of different lighting and the absence of sagebrush. *Background* shows that coniferous forests have increased throughout the 92 years on

the north-facing slopes. Big sagebrush and aspen (arrow) declined on the lower slopes, as did the bunchgrass steppe on the upper slopes. Aspen stands appear to have been composed of small, very dense stems in the original. In contrast, aspen in the retakes were large, occurred at lower densities, and showed no successful reproduction. Aspen understories had been invaded by Douglas-fir, spruce, and lodgepole pine; this is most apparent in 1990. One of the large Douglas-fir trees (now dead) in the aspen above the willow thicket in the original, showed multiple fire scars. Patches of the background forests burned during 1988. Dying trees were apparent in 1990, but these are difficult to detect in the photo.

This is important elk and bison winter range, and bighorn sheep occupy the upper slopes and cliffs year-round. Note the herd of elk in the 1898 view, below and to the right of the arrow. As shown here, forests have invaded grasslands on bighorn ranges in many sites in the park.

Specimen Ridge was named for the abundant 50-million-year-old petrified trees exposed throughout. Successive layers of forest were buried by gravel conglomerates, ash sandstones, airfall ash deposits, and a few lava flows. The ancient forests included sycamore, walnut, and magnolia, species that now grow far from Yellowstone Park (Fritz 1985).

59.2

59.3

60.1

Plates 60.1–3

Soda Butte, view northeast up Soda Butte Creek

LOCATION: 567.1 E, 4969.5 N; elev. 2,030 m/6,658 ft

DATES AND PHOTOGRAPHERS: 60.1, 1871—W. H. Jackson (NPS-YNP); 60.2, 20 July 1971—D. B. Houston; 60.3, 7 August 1990—D. B. Houston

INTERVAL: 100 and 119 years. Camera points similar.

VEGETATION CHANGES: *Foreground* and *middleground* of the original show a willow and alder community on the Soda Butte floodplain. Other early photos (pl. 61.1) taken at the same location suggest that the density of willow beyond Soda Butte is exaggerated because of the photo angle. Willow declined markedly by 1971. The meadow consisted of rushes, sedges, hairgrass, and reedgrass, and seemed unchanged throughout. Although willows do not appear in the retakes, in 1990 willows were colonizing a gravel bar along Soda Butte Creek about 150 m (164 yd) southeast of the camera point. Beaver had constructed an extensive series of ponds on the floodplain by 1900 (pls. 61.1–3). What Jackson had called "Soda Spring" in the foreground of the 1871 view appears to have been excavated quite recently. The area at left shows a sagebrush steppe with considerable disturbance along a trail. Other Jackson photos clearly show abundant big sagebrush on the upper terrace around Soda Butte at this time. The formerly bare, harsh-looking floodplain terrace was completely vegetated in the retakes. *Background* shows an increase in forest distribution from 1871 to 1990, especially at right where trees have recolonized an earlier burn.

Fire suppression efforts prevented the 1988 fires from burning into the Soda Butte Creek drainage from the Lamar River.

This area is near the upper, eastern end of the northern range, and represents important bison and elk winter range. Cast antlers (arrow) indicated that elk wintered here more than a century ago. The hot spring that formed the cone has been inactive during historic time.

61.1

Plates 61.1–3

Soda Butte Creek, additional views northeast up Soda Butte Creek

LOCATION: 567.1 E, 4969.5 N; elev. 2,030 m/6,658 ft

DATES AND PHOTOGRAPHERS: 61.1, 1884—F. J. Haynes (MHS); 61.2, 18 July 1972—D. B. Houston; 61.3, 1900—U.S. Army Engineers (NPS-YNP)

INTERVAL: 87 years. These three views are intended to show the dynamic changes at this site. The 1900 army photograph most resembles views in plates 60.1–3.

VEGETATION CHANGES: *Fore* and *middleground* of the 1884 view and 1972 retake are quite similar to the 1871 view (pl. 60.1). They are included here to show that the density of willow in the earliest view may be exaggerated by angle of the photograph. Willows as seen in the early photographs at this particular site have generated much interest since the park's early days. Causes for the striking decrease since the turn of the century have provoked debate; hence our inclusion of these additional early views. Beaver had constructed an extensive series of ponds on the floodplain of Soda Butte Creek by the time of the 1900 view (open arrow); the ponds apparently remained

until the early 1920s. In the 1900 view the bare upper edge of the bank at left probably has been trampled by human activity, judging by the small dock in the pond, constructed perhaps by the soldiers who lived at the nearby Soda Butte Soldier Station. Note the floating barrel—whiskey? *Background* conditions are comparable to those seen in plate 60.1. Bighorn sheep winter on the slopes of Barronette Peak (arrow, 1972 retake) where they occupy several caves during periods of adverse weather.

Soda Butte was named in 1870 by prospectors. To the casual eye, no evidence remains of a nearby patrol station used by the army and then the park service until about 1937. Nor are there remnants of the buildings and activities of early-day squatters or of the assistant superintendents of the early 1880s, known derisively as rabbit catchers because of their ineffectiveness as a police force (see Haines 1977).

61.2

61.3

62.1

PLATES 62.1–3

Soda Butte Creek, view west to Barronette Peak

LOCATION: 574.8 E, 4982.5 N; elev. 2,260 m/7,412 ft

DATES AND PHOTOGRAPHERS: 62.1, ca. 1885—J. P. Iddings (USGS); 62.2, 25 August 1970—D. B. Houston; 62.3, 7 August 1991—D. B. Houston

INTERVAL: Approximately 85 and 106 years. Camera point for retakes moved 15–30 m (49–98 ft) north due to forest development.

VEGETATION CHANGES: *Foreground* of an extensive willow thicket on the floodplain of Soda Butte Creek in 1885 had been replaced by various conifers and by mesic grassland by 1970. A charred snag in the original (just right of center) provides evidence of past fires. By 1991, small willow shrubs and herbaceous vegetation had increased on the floodplain at left (sedges, nonnative timothy, clovers, rushes). Lodgepole pine had also increased. No portion of the scene burned in 1988. *Middleground* conifers (mostly subalpine fir and lodgepole pine, and some Engelmann spruce) expanded into forest parks. The original photo shows evidence of fire, insects, or disease in the conifers. The road in the original was abandoned, probably about the mid-1930s when it was rebuilt on the south side of this part of the creek (Culpin 1994), and has been reclaimed naturally by vegetation. One of the stumps visible above the road (1885, arrow) was found at the time of the 1971 retake. By 1991 the floodplain beyond the creek supported increased herbaceous vegetation, with alders and willows around the stump (open arrow). *Background* shows little overall change in the distribution of forest on Barronette Peak, although one stand present at the forest border in the original was absent at the 1971 retake, and there was colonization of a site directly below the peak by 1991.

The replacement of willow communities by grassland and forest is graphically demonstrated in these photos. A few moose use the area year-round, but this is a deep-snow locale, well outside the usual winter range for elk. Some browsing by elk and mule deer probably occurs at other seasons, yet it seems unlikely that ungulate browsing was the only force driving the decrease in willow. A possible reduction in lateral movement of the stream on the flood plain is suggested by less exposed gravel in the retakes.

Barronette Peak is composed of massively layered Absaroka volcanic rocks of Eocene age that rest directly upon Paleozoic sedimentary rocks (Fritz 1985). The contact occurs at about the level of the forest line. The peak was named in 1878 for "Yellowstone Jack" Barronett, soldier of fortune and early guide and army scout in the park (Haines 1977; spellings of early names sometimes vary).

62.2

62.3

63.1

Plates 63.1–3

Pebble Creek, view northeast across the upper meadows to Meridian Peak

Location: 573.4 E, 4985.4 N; elev. 2,418 m/7,930 ft

Dates and Photographers: 63.1, 1921—F. L. Carter (NPS-YNP); 63.2, 24 August 1974—D. B. Houston; 63.3, 8 August 1992—M. Meagher

Interval: 53 and 71 years. Camera points similar but slightly forward in the 1992 view.

Vegetation Changes: *Foreground* appears different in the 1992 view because of the shift in the photo point. The original shows a dense, tall (1–2 m/3–6.5 ft) willow community on the floodplain. Taller willows persisted adjacent to the creek but appear to have declined during the first interval, with a further decrease between 1974 and 1992. Meadow vegetation, most apparent in the retakes, was sedge and reedgrass. The retakes show scattered low Wolf's willow and less frequent Booth's willow; these were probably the same species as the more abundant willows of the original. *Middleground* forest burned in 1988, after some increase during the first photo interval. The forests were lodgepole pine with some Engelmann spruce and

subalpine fir. The tops of the two adjacent ridges remained unburned. *Background* forests did not burn. Meridian Peak supports mainly subalpine fir and whitebark pine forests, with some Engelmann spruce.

This area is elk and moose summer range. Moose may winter here in low density but snows are deep. Mountain goats introduced north of the park are sometimes seen on the peaks of this northeast quarter of the park, but they are not native to any locale near Yellowstone.

Meridian Peak was snow covered in the original. Detail was lost in the process of copying the original snapshot. The park's east boundary traverses the crest of the peak.

64.1

Plates 64.1–3

Republic Creek, Shoshone National Forest, view north to the Beartooth Plateau area

Location: 583.6 E, 4981.9 N; elev. 2,530 m/8,298 ft

Dates and Photographers: 64.1, ca. 1885—J. P. Iddings (USGS); 64.2, 29 August 1972—D. B. Houston; 64.3, 12 August 1991—D. B. Houston

Interval: Approximately 87 and 106 years. Camera points similar.

Vegetation Changes: *Foreground* and *middleground* willow decreased throughout the 106 years spanned by the photos. Scattered willows persisted on the lowest floodplain (below forked tree at right, arrow in 1972), and at the left edge of the meadow, but lodgepole pine was invading the remaining willows at both sites. Small patches of willows above and right of the m-stick identified as Eastwood's and Farr's willows were unchanged between 1972 and 1991. Dominant grasses in the foreground meadow in both retakes were hairgrass, mountain brome, alpine timothy, and sedges; dominant forbs were broad-leaved bluebells, cinquefoil, fleabane, groundsel, and cow-parsnip. The forest has increased in area and density since 1885, and was dominated by lodgepole pine, subalpine fir, and Engelmann spruce. Note increased height of individual trees in 1991. No portion of the scene burned during 1988. Considerable pocket gopher activity occurred in the meadow, and moose sign was common in 1991. More gravel was exposed in the streambed in the original than in retakes, suggesting that more lateral stream activity occurred in 1885. *Background* shows little change beyond increased height of individual trees. The retake of another Iddings photograph in the collection (USGS no. 343, not used here), taken from Republic Pass about 1885, shows increased density of forests along the length of Republic Creek.

This area receives light summer foraging by moose and elk. Note that the vegetation changes shown at this site outside Yellowstone are similar to those that have occurred in the park. The Beartooth Plateau beyond, at more than 3,100 m (10,167 ft) in elevation, lies well above tree line and is accessible by automobiles for only about four months of the year. The growing season is brief in the harsh climate, so the landscape is biologically fragile. In these conditions, biological change is so slow that it may occur in geological time.

64.2

64.3

65.1

PLATES 65.1–3

Republic Pass, view northwest across the headwaters of Cache Creek to Amphitheater Mountain

LOCATION: 582.6 E, 4978.0 N; elev. 3,050 m/10,003 ft

DATES AND PHOTOGRAPHERS: 65.1, ca. 1885—J. P. Iddings (USGS); 65.2, 16 August 1970—D. B. Houston; 65.3, 12 August 1991—D. B. Houston

INTERVAL: Approximately 85 and 106 years. Camera points similar, note rock in center foreground, 1885 and 1970.

VEGETATION CHANGES: *Foreground* shows little change in vegetation. In 1970 this subalpine meadow had sedges and bluegrass as dominant cover; small lupines and mountain dandelion were also present. The area showed moderate to abundant elk use in 1970, as indicated by beds, droppings, and feeding areas. Bighorn sheep sign and pocket gopher mounds were also present. In 1991 the composition was similar to that of 1970, with hairgrass, bluegrasses, Idaho fescue, slender cinquefoil, silvery lupine, and Jacob's ladder. Summer elk grazing occurred throughout the 106 years spanned by the photographs. The meadow did not burn in 1988. *Middleground* is a steep southeast-facing slope composed of Absaroka volcanics, where stands

of conifers show little change. Elk and bighorn sheep trails occurred on the slope in 1970 (arrow, 1991). *Background* shows some increase in coniferous forests on Amphitheater Mountain in 1970, but forests of whitebark pine, subalpine fir, and scattered Engelmann spruce burned in the headwaters of Cache Creek during 1988.

Little or no change is apparent in herbaceous vegetation on this elk summer range in the 106-year interval. The patterns of erosion on the harsh volcanic slopes show little change. The Absaroka volcanic sequences of Amphitheater Mountain form some of the most rugged terrain in Yellowstone National Park. Early Eocene volcanoes supplied the material that formed these volcanic rocks 50–55 million years ago.

In 1869, Adam Miller, J. H. Moore, Bart Henderson, and James Gurley lost their horses and supplies cached on Cache Creek to Indians. They escaped across this pass into Republic Creek, panning for gold and discovering the manganese-stained outcrop that led to the development of the Republic Mine. The town below, part of the New World mining district, became Cooke City (Lovering 1930).

66.1

Plates 66.1–3

Cache Creek, view northeast to the Thunderer

LOCATION: 575.0 E, 4969.0 N; elev. 2,230 m/7,314 ft

DATES AND PHOTOGRAPHERS: 66.1, ca. 1880—H. B. Calfee (NPS-YNP); 66.2, 13 September 1972—D. B. Houston; 66.3, 12 August 1991—D. B. Houston

INTERVAL: Approximately 92 and 111 years. Camera points adjusted because of increased forest; this placed the retake point farther back.

VEGETATION CHANGES: *Foreground* with dense big sagebrush in 1880 shows a decline by 1972 that accelerated dramatically when the 1988 fires burned across this meadow. Dominant herbaceous species in 1972 were slender wheatgrass, mountain brome, needlegrasses, nonnative timothy, alpine timothy, hairgrass, yampah, and sedges. After the foreground meadow burned in 1988, the species composition was not greatly different than that recorded during 1972. Robust nonnative timothy, yampah, graceful cinquefoil, yarrow, wheatgrasses, and Idaho fescue dominated. *Middleground* shows meadow invasion by lodgepole pine and subalpine fir. The scattered aspen in the original had been mostly replaced by conifers by

1972, although a few large trees persisted in the adjacent forest. The original is the only early image in the collection that shows an aspen stand composed of large, sparse-appearing trees. The forest burned completely from the meadow edge to the Thunderer in 1988. Trees that burned in 1988 (1991 view) can be matched with living trees present in 1972. *Background* of whitebark pine and subalpine fir shows a minor increase by 1972 (largely obscured because of increased height and density of the middleground forest). Even isolated patches of forest on the peak burned during 1988.

Most of the drainage of Cache Creek burned intensely in 1988 and strong prevailing winds from the southwest drove the fire front as though through a chute. The term the fire crews used for this creek was "cooked."

The area is elk and bison summer range. The Thunderer was named in 1885 by the Hague U.S. Geological Survey as "seemingly a great focus for thunderstorms" (Whittlesey 1988:155). These summer storms can be dramatic, locally eroding quantities of Absaroka volcanics into adjacent streams.

66.2

66.3

67.1

PLATES 67.1–3

Lamar River trail between Cache and Soda Butte creeks; looking southwest

LOCATION: 567.2 E, 4965.0 N; elev. 2,122 m/6,960 ft

DATES AND PHOTOGRAPHERS: 67.1, September 1931—J. Joffe (NPS-YNP); 67.2, 15 August 1972—M. Meagher; 67.3, 8 August 1991—M. Meagher

INTERVAL: 41 and 60 years. Camera points similar.

VEGETATION CHANGES: *Foreground* shows an initial increase in big sagebrush. Volatile sagebrush was eliminated temporarily by fire in 1988. *Background* of lodgepole pine forest across the Lamar River shows some increase between 1931 and 1972. The slopes burned in the 1988 fires, with patches of crown fire as well as stands that went untouched, resulting in a mosaic of fire effects.

These flats are summer bison range, and some elk use the area, especially in spring, summer, and early winter. The slopes receive moderate elk use in summer.

In 1921, during the heyday of the Buffalo Ranch (now Lamar Ranger Station), an immense log fence was constructed across the Lamar River just north of the photo point to prevent the bison from coming down into the hay fields on the valley bottom during the summmer. By 1952, only a few bison were artificially fed in winter, but hay was cut in the Lamar Valley as late as 1956 to provide some of the feed for National Park Service horses used in the park in summer. Forty years after construction, fence remnants still could be seen on the flats north of the Lamar River. The last vestiges were burned by the fires of 1988.

67.2

67.3

68.1

Plates 68.1–3

Parker Peak trail, a knob 4 km (2.5 mi) northwest of Parker Peak, looking northwest at the ridges above Miller Creek

Location: 585.6 E, 4953.8 N; elev. 2,920 m/9,577 ft

Dates and Photographers: 68.1, 8 September 1931—J. Joffe (NPS-YNP); 68.2, 14 August 1972—M. Meagher; 68.3, 20 August 1991—M. Meagher

Interval: 41 and 60 years. Camera points similar.

Vegetation Changes: *Foregrounds* are similar. Minor differences in the appearance of meadow vegetation probably reflect the variations that occur between growing seasons. *Middleground* whitebark tree trunk has paleness emphasized by sunlight on the bark. Note the fire scar at the base. The one-sided shape was caused by the prevailing wind direction of fierce winter storms that are particularly harsh at these higher elevations. *Background* shows an increase in forest density and area. Fire in this area in 1988 was of moderate intensity, leaving behind a mosaic of fire effects in the forest. In the 1991 view, burned areas have a grayish cast, most apparent to the left. The subalpine meadows of the area often did not burn well, if at all.

The Parker Peak locale is summer elk range. This area was outside the original straight east boundary of Yellowstone Park. The boundary was revised in 1929 to conform more to the drainage divides of the Absaroka Mountains. Elk hunting likely took place in fall near the photo location prior to the change (and occasional poaching continues to the present).

The individual in the center of the 1931 photo is Floyd Gibbons, identified as a war correspondent, and a guest of the park. His brother Don is probably the individual at left (similar hats!).

68.2

68.3

69.1

PLATES 69.1–3

Parker Peak trail, a knob 4 km (2.5 mi) northwest of Parker Peak, looking south toward Castor and Pollux peaks

LOCATION: 585.7 E, 4953.5 N; elev. 2,924 m/9,590 ft

DATES AND PHOTOGRAPHERS: 69.1, 8 September 1931—J. Joffe (NPS-YNP); 69.2, 14 August 1972—M. Meagher; 69.3, 20 August 1991—M. Meagher

INTERVAL: 41 and 60 years. Camera points approximate.

VEGETATION CHANGES: *Foreground* covered with subalpine/alpine vegetation appears similar in all three photographs. Annual variation in the very short growing seasons may have caused slight differences. Forbs such as stonecrops and lupines, and some of the bluegrasses and alpine fescue, grow here. *Background* burned moderately in 1988, but this does not show particularly in the 1991 photo. The effects may be more apparent with time.

This area is elk summer range. This pack trip along the east boundary may have been organized in part as a general reconnaissance of the lands transferred from the U.S. Forest Service to Yellowstone National Park in 1929. Castor and Pollux peaks were named by the Hague U.S. Geological Survey in 1893 (Whittlesey 1988). The Gibbons brothers (as in pl. 68.1) are the men silhouetted (Don left, Floyd right).

70.1

PLATES 70.1–3

Parker Peak, east-west escarpment north of main peak, looking toward the slopes above Miller Creek

LOCATION: 587.5 E, 4953.6 N; elev. 2,950 m/9,675 ft

DATES AND PHOTOGRAPHERS: 70.1, ca. 1885—J. P. Iddings (USGS); 70.2, 14 August 1972—M. Meagher; 70.3, 29 July 1992—M. Meagher

INTERVAL: 87 and 107 years. Camera points similar.

VEGETATION CHANGES: *Foregrounds* remain very similar despite the high erodibility of the Absaroka volcanics; careful comparison between 1885 and 1992 shows nearly identical details of shape and placement of surface rocks (arrow, 1992). *Middleground* trees increased in number and size prior to the fires of 1988. The surviving large tree at left is a whitebark pine. *Background* shows appreciable forest increase from 1885 to 1972. The mosaic burn of 1988 left a patchwork of effects that will probably be more apparent in the future. In the 1885 view the mature dead trees in the forest at right in the creek bottom (below the arrow, toward the lower right corner) suggest remnant effects of an earlier fire. This seems more probable than forest insect attack in this location.

The Parker Peak area of the east boundary is important summer elk range. At the time of the 1992 retake, a large grizzly bear had been seen frequenting the meadow just out of the view to the left. Years with a good production of whitebark pine seeds attract bears to higher elevations in late July and into fall.

70.2

70.3

71.1

PLATES 71.1–3

Pyramid Peak summit, looking northeast

LOCATION: 574.5 E, 4939.5 N; elev. 3182 m/10,437 ft

DATES AND PHOTOGRAPHERS: 71.1, October 1931—G. Baggley (NPS-YNP); 71.2, 1 August 1973—M. Meagher; 71.3, 3 September 1993—M. Meagher

INTERVAL: 42 and 62 years. Camera points approximate.

VEGETATION CHANGES: *Foreground* vegetation of alpine tundra is similar in all three photographs. Plant density appears comparable. Forb composition (stonecrop, a low-growing lupine, asters) is probably comparable also, but appearance varies with time of year. The cairn visible at the edge of the summit in the 1973 and 1993 views marks the east park boundary. This cairn was built after the 1931 view, probably by the Bandy survey party in the late 1930s. *Background* scene toward Frost Lake burned moderately in 1988; but the effects are difficult to discern in the 1993 view.

The summit of Pyramid Peak receives limited summer elk use. Growing season here is always very short; in 1993 the summer weather was so cold late into the season that the green vegetation was sparse to nonexistent even before the killing frosts occurred. Elk were not seen at the highest elevations during aerial surveys that summer.

The original east boundary of Yellowstone ran north-south along 110° longitude. In 1929 the east boundary was changed along much of its length to conform to the hydrologic divide of the Absaroka Mountains, placing much of this scene within the park.

71.2

71.3

72.1

PLATES 72.1–3

View south across Rainy Lake

LOCATION: 547.3 E, 4972.9 N; elev. 1,950 m/6,396 ft

DATES AND PHOTOGRAPHERS: 72.1, ca. 1885—J. P. Iddings (USGS); 72.2, 29 August 1973—D. B. Houston; 72.3, 6 August 1990—D. B. Houston

INTERVAL: Approximately 88 and 105 years. Camera points similar.

VEGETATION CHANGES: *Foreground* and *middleground* suggest a decline in the water surface area and an increase in emergent vegetation (cattails and bulrushes), likely influenced by road construction along the west shore and across the northwest portion of the lake. Increased growth of emergents was apparent in the 1990 retake. Middleground forests did not burn during 1988 and showed little change. *Background* shows evidence of earlier fires in the original. The forest (above the autos) burned in patches during 1988, but dead trees are difficult to detect in the retake. A fire-scarred tree cut within 40 m (130 ft) of the camera point indicated fires around 1810, 1840, and 1876, as well as at several earlier dates. The aspen clones in the original were small dense stems that apparently resprouted following the fires. Only a few scattered, large aspen remained at the time of the retakes. Douglas-fir and lodgepole pine have increased dramatically. A few Rocky Mountain junipers occurred on the slope. Note that several trees in the photographs appear highlined from ungulate browsing. Big sagebrush was the dominant shrub on the slope; bluebunch wheatgrass was the dominant grass.

The change in forest density and composition likely reflects a reduced frequency of natural fires. The area is elk winter range and also home to low densities of moose year-round. According to Whittlesey (1988), the lake was named by Superintendent Roger Toll (1929–35) because small springs made the surface appear as if rain were striking the water.

72.2

72.3

73.1

PLATES 73.1–3

View southeast up the Yellowstone River near Bumpus Butte

LOCATION: 547.8 E, 4972.3 N; elev. 1,980 m/6,494 ft

DATES AND PHOTOGRAPHERS: 73.1, 1871—W. H. Jackson (NPS-YNP); 73.2, 19 July 1971—D. B. Houston; 73.3, 6 August 1990—D. B. Houston

INTERVAL: 100 and 119 years. Camera points approximate.

VEGETATION CHANGES: *Middleground* shows relatively little change in distribution of vegetation on steep slopes above the river, except that Douglas-fir increased in density. There was scattered mortality of Douglas-fir trees from spruce budworm attacks during the 1980s. The grasses were mainly Indian ricegrass and bluebunch wheatgrass. Ephemeral erosion rills occur on this steep slope following intense rains. The ridgecrest in the retakes showed 60 percent bare ground and was probably in similar condition in the early photo. The middleground did not burn. *Background* also shows an increase in the density of Douglas-fir forest. The area of sparse vegetation at left (arrow) was present in all three photographs. Specimen Ridge burned spottily during 1988 and Douglas-fir were killed.

The area is bighorn sheep and elk winter range, and the ridgetops and slopes receive heavy winter grazing. A layer of columnar basalt is prominent below the ridgetop. Below the basalt the next layer represents stream gravels deposited 1.5 million years ago by an earlier Yellowstone River. The ridgetop is lake sediment, deposited when the Yellowstone River was blocked farther downstream by a glacial dam (Keefer 1972).

73.2

73.3

74.1

PLATES 74.1–3

Tower Fall area, view east across the canyon of the Yellowstone River

LOCATION: 548.7 E, 4971.0 N; elev. 2,010 m/6,592 ft

DATES AND PHOTOGRAPHERS: 74.1, ca. 1885—J. P. Iddings (USGS); 74.2, 19 July 1971—D. B. Houston; 74.3, 8 August 1990—D. B. Houston

INTERVAL: Approximately 86 and 105 years. Camera points similar.

VEGETATION CHANGES: *Middle* and *background* show essentially no change in the pattern of herbaceous vegetation on the west-facing ridge. Grasses present in both retakes were bluebunch wheatgrass, Indian rice-grass, junegrass, and Sandberg's bluegrass. A minor increase in the density of conifers, mostly Douglas-fir, has occurred since 1885 on the ridgetop at right and between the layers of columnar basalt. The colonization on the steeper sites suggested that the slopes may be more stable with time. Note particularly that some of the dead trees present in the original remain in place in 1990. The appearance of several trees in all the photos suggests highlining from ungulate browsing. The ridgecrest featured in the photos did not burn in 1988. Most of the Douglas-fir forest at right background on Specimen Ridge burned and the trees were killed.

The area receives heavy winter grazing by bighorn sheep and elk, and by spring the ridgecrest is carpeted with ungulate droppings. The pattern of sparse vegetation is unchanged over time, and is considered to represent a naturally occurring zootic climax because of the influence of ungulates. Two other early photos taken along this same ridge by Iddings and W. H. Jackson show similar conditions (both also U.S. Geological Survey photos).

The two layers of columnar basalt are a striking feature of the east wall of the canyon. The rocks between the basalt flows are formed from ancient stream gravels deposited about 1.5 million years ago.

Basaltic flows in Yellowstone are much less common than the rhyolitic flows that cover much of the plateau. The youngest rhyolite flows in the park are about 70,000 years old (Christiansen 1984). There is no reason to believe Yellowstone's volcanic history is at an end.

74.2

74.3

75.1

PLATES 75.1–2

Antelope Creek drainage, looking at Mount Washburn

LOCATION: 546.5 E, 4966.7 N; elev. 2,234 m/7,327 ft

DATES AND PHOTOGRAPHERS: 75.1, ca. 1910—E. W. Hunter (MHS); 75.2, 16 July 1991—M. Meagher

INTERVAL: Approximately 81 years. Camera points close but the timing of the original makes the appearance of the foreground view deceptive. The original was photographed in the evening, and probably in August. The year in which the original was taken was estimated from the appearance of the aspen stands, likely 20–30 years old at least, and from the fact that the road to the top was constructed in 1905. The existence of the road would have made it much easier for the photographer to reach this site.

VEGETATION CHANGES: *Foreground* in 1991 shows less big sagebrush. Before 1988, the area was a sagebrush grassland grading to subalpine meadow on some sites. Sagebrush burned extensively here in 1988, but by 1991, young big sagebrush was apparent. The clumped appearance in the retake of 1991 represents a mix of wild rose, arrowleaf balsamroot, and cinquefoil. The aspen stand of 1910 was reduced to two dead trees by 1991 (by 1995 these were gone). *Middleground* shows a considerable decrease in aspen; stands appear less vigorous, and conifers have been invading. In the original photo, the aspen down the slope from the viewer already lacked lower branches, and no reproduction can be seen (open arrow, original). *Background* of conifer forest shows increased density and height between 1910 and 1991, and conifer trees had invaded meadow edges. The fires of 1988 burned extensively in this drainage, with crown fire in the grayed areas below and to either side of Mount Washburn. Forest composition was a mix of lodgepole pine and extensive Engelmann spruce, with some subalpine fir and whitebark pine at higher elevations.

The meadows of Antelope Creek are elk and grizzly bear summer habitat. Female grizzlies raise their young here; this is a good location for them to prey on elk calves and forage on lush meadow vegetation. The area is restricted for human access now to allow bears to live undisturbed by recreational use. Bears (and other wildlife) are commonly observed from the road, which is behind and above the photo site.

Note the tiny square shape of the lookout at the highest point on Mount Washburn (arrow, retake). The lower level of the building is open to the public, affording shelter from the nearly constant wind while visitors enjoy the expansive view to the south.

75.2

76.1

Plates 76.1–3

Mount Washburn, south side looking toward Dunraven Pass

Location: 543.8 E, 958.7 N; elev. 2,760 m/9,052 ft

Dates and Photographers: 76.1, September 1912—U.S. Army Engineers (NPS-YNP); 76.2, 3 September 1972—M. Meagher; 76.3, 15 July 1992—M. Meagher

Interval: 60 and 80 years. Camera points approximate, moved somewhat forward.

Vegetation Changes: *Foreground* ground cover of subalpine vegetation appears little changed, regardless of any differences in timing of the photographs. Herbaceous vegetation was colonizing the road edges by 1972. *Middle* and *background* forest, which is predominantly subalpine fir–Engelmann spruce with some whitebark pine, shows an increase in size, density, and area covered. The 1988 fires burned scattered stands in this view.

This old road is a part of the Chittenden Road, named for H. M. Chittenden, the army engineer officer who built it in 1903–4. It is now used as a hiking trail to the summit of Mount Washburn. Note another section of abandoned road at left rear (arrow, 1992), across Dunraven Pass. The pass was named for the eleventh Earl of Dunraven, who visited the park in 1874 and recounted his travels in *The Great Divide*.

At this elevation, the growing season is short and cool to cold. Trees grow slowly, and herbaceous vegetation requires much time to invade barren sites, particularly where soils are poorly developed. Vegetation patterns persist for a long time. Scars from human activity, including trampling by feet, are long lasting.

76.2

76.3

77.1

PLATES 77.1–3

Chittenden Road near Dunraven Pass, view northeast to Mount Washburn

LOCATION: 542.5 E, 4958.2 N; elev. 2,770 m/9,085 ft

DATES AND PHOTOGRAPHERS: 77.1, ca. 1905–10—Haynes photo (NPS-YNP); 77.2, 16 August 1971—D. B. Houston; 77.3, 10 August 1991—D. B. Houston

INTERVAL: Approximately 64 and 84 years. Camera points similar.

VEGETATION CHANGES: *Foreground* and *middleground* are typical sub-alpine herbland with scattered stands of subalpine fir and whitebark pine. Herbaceous vegetation at retakes was dominated by larkspur, stickseed, mountain dandelion, mountain brome, and other characteristic subalpine grasses. Note that the subalpine vegetation has reclaimed the abandoned road bed (open arrows, far edge of the road, both retakes). Trees have increased appreciably in height. *Background* shows little change in poorly vegetated snowbank sites adjacent to the road on Mount Washburn. Small increases in area and density of conifer stands have occurred, but overall changes are minor. A small stand of trees on the ridge at left burned during 1988 (arrow, 1991).

The area serves as summer range for elk, moose, and mule deer. The present fire lookout at 3,123 m (10,243 ft) atop Mount Washburn, visible in the retakes, was constructed in 1940, although use of the mountain top as a fire lookout probably was common after the road was opened for travel in 1905. The top of the mountain was lowered slightly by leveling to provide a small parking surface—an example of humans as agents of geomorphic change.

77.2

77.3

78.1

PLATES 78.1–2

Chittenden Bridge area, east side south of road, view north toward Mount Washburn

LOCATION: 540.4 E, 5950.9 N; elev. 2,365 m/7,757 ft

DATES AND PHOTOGRAPHERS: 78.1, ca. 1890s, probably early September— W. H. Jackson (CSHS); 78.2, 19 September 1975—M. Meagher

INTERVAL: 80-85 years. Camera points similar.

VEGETATION CHANGES: *Foreground* of silver sagebrush has decreased in density. More of the shrubs were visible in midsummer, before the grasses reached maximum height. Seasonal differences in forbs and grasses account for some differences in appearance, but changes in species composition have occurred, with nonnative timothy prevalent now. Annual variation in precipitation probably accounts for differences in grass height (1975 was a wet year). *Middleground* forest at the canyon rim appears to have decreased, probably because of development (road, trails). Note the double-crowned lodgepole at right in both photos. This stand increased considerably in size and density during the photo interval.

This area probably was subjected to limited summer horse grazing during the period of the old Canyon Lodge operation nearby (1923–56). A deeply entrenched trail runs from left to right across the meadow, not visible here in the tall grass. The fires of 1988 were close but did not burn this site.

78.2

79.1

PLATES 79.1–3

Alum Creek, Hayden Valley, view northwest from southeast side

LOCATION: 541.0 E, 4946.8 N; elev. 2,342 m/7,681 ft

DATES AND PHOTOGRAPHERS: 79.1, 9 July 1909—U.S. Army Engineers (NPS-YNP); 79.2, 27 July 1971—M. Meagher; 79.3, 12 July 1991—M. Meagher

INTERVAL: 62 and 82 years. Camera points approximate.

VEGETATION CHANGES: *Foreground* has been disturbed by road construction and human activity. The modern road, built in the 1930s, acted as a levee in preventing the seasonal high water level apparent in the 1909 view, caused by the increased flow of the Yellowstone River at right. The retakes show that the modern road also has a damming effect to the left, with the creek channeled into one culvert (closed arrow, 1991) before it joins the Yellowstone River. This has created a semi-marsh on the creek bottom, and likely caused the increase in sedges visible on the right side. *Middleground* sagebrush grassland looks essentially the same. Both big and silver sagebrush appear somewhat denser and more extensive over the 82-year span

of the photos, but individual sites vary somewhat. Lodgepole pine invaded a few sites. The meadows did not burn in 1988. *Background* in 1909 shows a fairly recent burn, 20–25 years old, judging by reproduction. The hillside at left and lower right had reforested by 1971. Scattered gray tree trunks in the 1971 view indicate bark beetle activity. The lower edge of the forest changed little between 1909 and 1971, except for the establishment of trees on the terrace at left center (above the three bison, 1991). The lack of change is probably maintained by soil differences. For the same reason, patches of meadow at upper left in both retakes (below open arrow, original) appear as nonforested sites in the 1909 photograph. The 1988 fires burned a more extensive area of the background compared to 1909.

Bison were absent from the valley between the late 1890s and 1936. Their numbers increased slowly after roughly three dozen were reintroduced in that year. These bison were trucked from the Buffalo Ranch in the Lamar Valley, along with others for release on the Firehole River, to reestablish a Mary Mountain subpopulation (release totaled 71). Bison use this locale throughout the year, but numbers are greatest during summer and fall.

The horseman in the first view appears to be an army trooper.

79.2

79.3

80.1

Plates 80.1–2

Crater Hills, Hayden Valley, looking north

LOCATION: 541.3 E, 4944.5 N; elev. 2,370 m/7,773 ft

DATES AND PHOTOGRAPHERS: 80.1, 1881—F. J. Haynes (NPS-YNP); 80.2, 15 July 1971—M. Meagher

INTERVAL: 90 years. Camera points similar.

VEGETATION CHANGES: *Foreground* shows increased density of big sagebrush. *Middleground* shows decreased sagebrush at left, while at right the ground cover has changed from what may have been a sagebrush island to more extensive but less dense bunchgrass-forb vegetation. Ground cover on the thermal sites at right has increased and has changed slightly in distribution, suggesting a change in ground temperature. *Background* shows increased size and density of lodgepole pine at the base of the hills. Trees have invaded the geothermally influenced substrate, suggesting that the heat has lessened or shifted at this site. Shifts are not uncommon in thermal areas. In 1881 those trees present appear to have had denser basal branches; the decreased density in 1971 may reflect rubbing and other mechanical impact from increased ungulate presence, primarily bison for this site. Some lodgepole pine may have had repetitive top injury with a resulting low mat-forming shape at left center.

Most of Hayden Valley, including this area, did not burn in 1988. Bison use the meadow sites in the rest-rotation fashion typical of this nomadic species. In winter they sometimes occupy areas of warm ground. These sites are too warm to support forage (or snow) but may ameliorate the energy costs of winter, because the animals can move easily and can bed down on relatively warmer ground. In harsh conditions, even without forage, it is easier to survive here. Some elk use this area in summer. Grizzly bears forage for rodents and meadow vegetation and use carcasses of bison that have died naturally.

80.2

81.1

Plates 81.1–2

Crater Hills, Hayden Valley

LOCATION: 541.0 E, 4945.0 N; elev. 2,390 m/7,839 ft

DATES AND PHOTOGRAPHERS: 81.1, 1871—W. H. Jackson (NPS-YNP); 81.2, 3 July 1972—M. Meagher

INTERVAL: 101 years. Camera points similar.

VEGETATION CHANGES: *Foreground* mud spring has become more viscous in character, suggesting a change in available water and the water table. The original photo probably was taken as much as a month later, and available water can vary during the season as well as annually. *Middleground* suggests that the entire area may be drier. The drainage rills from the edge of the bank at left are less distinct, and the rivulet of water that earlier flowed across the geothermal substrate toward the mud spring has disappeared. Herbaceous ground cover has decreased to the right underneath the sparse lodgepole pine trees. Those same trees in the earlier photo show clustered branches at ground level and then a bare section of trunk. In the 1972 retake, those trees still present are dead. *Background* sagebrush at left now appears mostly limited to the tops of the hills. The stand of lodgepole is taller and denser. The sparse appearance in 1871 may reflect earlier ground fire, but this area did not burn in 1988, nor does it show evidence of fire recently.

The shape of the trees in the 1871 view suggests ungulate impact. Elk are an unlikely source, because they mostly summer in Hayden Valley and their use of this particular site is limited. (An occasional bull elk may stay the winter, as may also have occurred a century ago.) Bison utilize the valley throughout the year, and a few bulls consistently winter in this thermal area. They would not browse, but might have done enough rubbing to remove low branches, without affecting the very lowest limbs. Snow probably covered the lowest limbs during earlier winters, as winters were consistently harsher a century ago.

81.2

82.1

PLATES 82.1–3

Upper Alum Creek thermal area, southwest corner of Hayden Valley

LOCATION: 533.2 E, 4940.4 N; elev. 2,378 m/7,799 ft

DATES AND PHOTOGRAPHERS: 82.1, ca. 1900—U.S. Army Engineers (NPS-YNP); 82.2, 10 July 1972—M. Meagher; 82.3, 19 July 1991—M. Meagher

INTERVAL: 72 and 91 years. Camera points similar.

VEGETATION CHANGES: *Foreground* appears to have become moister since the original photo, and somewhat tussocky. There also appears to be some local change in the geothermal substrate; the two are probably related. By 1972 the vegetation seemed coarser, with sedges the most likely dominant. However, the 1991 view also suggests that the vegetation is being cropped by grazing to a greater extent than in 1972. This boggy, poorly drained bottomland is grazed intensively by bison during much of the year. *Middle* and *background* show increased density and extent of big sagebrush. Grasslands appear similar, although visually dominated by sagebrush. The exposure (arrows, 1900 and 1972) of silt-clay deposits in old lake bed sediments appears comparable. Lodgepole pine is similar in extent, with disappear-

ance and replacement of trees on the same general sites. Note the shapes in the first view; there are limbs to ground level. However, the far left tree of the right group with its shorter bottom branches suggests that elk may have browsed here earlier, or bison may have rubbed on and broken the limbs, with a subsequent release of growth. In the two later views the trees are without bottom limbs, and a few individuals have died. This site did not burn in 1988.

Bison use this area throughout the year. The appearance of the trees probably correlates with changes in bison numbers. Exterminated from this locale by about the mid-1890s, bison were reintroduced in 1936. They rub on trees, especially while shedding and during breeding season, eventually killing some. Most impact is on individual trees, isolated stands, and along meadow edges. Charred wood on isolated dead trees and their remnants suggested that grass fires may have swept the valley at times.

Note the herd of elk in the first photograph. Elk from Yellowstone's northern winter range spent the summer here, as they do now.

83.1

PLATES 83.1–3

Trout Creek, Hayden Valley, at the west edge of the road

LOCATION: 543.0 E, 943.2 N; elev. 2,345 m/7,691 ft

DATES AND PHOTOGRAPHERS: 83.1, 1898—C. D. Walcott (USGS); 83.2, 1 September 1972—M. Meagher; 83.3, 12 July 1991—M. Meagher

INTERVAL: 74 and 93 years. Camera points similar but a little closer.

VEGETATION CHANGES: *Foreground* slope has been disturbed by construction and maintenance of the present road. It has functioned as a partial dam on Trout Creek since the 1930s. *Middleground* shows a change in the amount of water flowing through the meander as seen in 1898, because the creek cut across the neck (below closed arrow, 1972), creating another face on the cutbank where Pleistocene lake bed sediments are exposed. By 1972, willows appear to have replaced a few clumps of what may be low-growing willow or perhaps silver sagebrush in the original. Changes in water table probably account for the increase in willows visible in the 1972 image and for the decrease by 1991. A line of sagebrush marks the old road at upper right, more apparent in 1972 than in 1991 (open arrow). Sagebrush general-

ly increased in density and spread to some new sites by 1991. These meadows did not burn in 1988. Note also that the 1898 and 1991 views suggest ungrazed sedge. Bison were not present in 1898 because they had been extirpated from this locale. By 1972, the localized increase in water table because of the road's damming effect, combined with use of the valley by only a few hundred bison, may have resulted in a lusher appearance. By 1991, an increasing bison population used this area more than in 1972, but even so, a July photograph in 1991 would not show the cumulative summer grazing by bison that a September 1972 photograph would record for this particular site. *Background* vegetation has increased on the creek bluffs except the face at left, which is being actively cut by the changed creek. Note the bison foraging here.

The early road apparently was abandoned shortly after the original photograph was taken. This must have been a difficult track to keep intact, as evidenced by log cribbing at the bottom of the eroded cutbank in the original. An army-period road camp was located beyond the right edge of the original view; likely the present road alignment was in use by 1898.

83.2

83.3

84.1

PLATES 84.1–2

Yellowstone River south of Hayden Valley, by the Sulphur Cauldron, view north

LOCATION: 545.0 E, 4941.5 N; elev. 2,350 m/7,707 ft

DATES AND PHOTOGRAPHERS: 84.1, 1871—W. H. Jackson (NPS-YNP); 84.2, 1 September 1971—M. Meagher

INTERVAL: 100 years. Camera point moved somewhat to right.

VEGETATION CHANGES: *Foreground* has been altered by road construction. *Middle* and *background* show a general increase in size, density, and extent of forest, mostly lodgepole pine. Increase may not be as great as it appears because of the masking effect of taller trees on some meadows. A careful look at the far bank of the Yellowstone River indicates that herbaceous vegetation increased considerably during the 100-year time interval. This area did not burn in 1988. However, the shadings of gray in the 1871 view at right rear and the interspersion of dead trees within the forest at left rear suggest fire prior to the first scene, recent enough to be visible in 1871.

We do not know the identity of the kilt-wearing man shown at left foreground in the 1871 photo (Thomas Moran perhaps, the artist of the expedition), but we may presume that the weather at the time was relatively warm and likely free of biting insects.

84.2

85.1

PLATES 85.1–2

Yellowstone Lake, just south of Lake Ranger Station, looking southeast

LOCATION: 548.5 E, 4933.4 N; elev. 2,260 m/7,740 ft

DATES AND PHOTOGRAPHERS: 85.1, ca. 1885—J. P. Iddings (USGS); 85.2, 22 August 1971—M. Meagher

INTERVAL: 86 years. Camera points similar.

VEGETATION CHANGES: *Foreground* appears to have changed from a wet sedge meadow to a slightly drier moist meadow of sedges, grasses, and forbs. Some natural drainage channels appear to have changed or filled in. This area did not burn in 1988. *Middleground* shows silting in and shrinking of the lagoon, with invasion of sedge and decrease of willow. This is a natural aging process for lakes. Lodgepole pine at right is gone. *Background*, however, shows an increase in forest along the lakeshore.

Meadow receives summer-fall use by occasional bison, elk, and moose. Human impact appears to be minimal on this scene in spite of nearby developments for tourists. Indeed, people have lived in this locale for 10,000 years (Cannon et al. 1995). Blood residue analyses of stone tools indicated that these people used a variety of animal foods, including rabbit, deer, elk, and bison.

85.2

86.1

Plates 86.1–3

Pelican Creek, looking northeast toward the Sulphur Hills

Location: 550.9 E, 4934.1 N; elev. 2,366 m/7,760 ft

Dates and Photographers: 86.1, 1939—Photographer unknown (NPS-YNP); 86.2, 17 July 1972—M. Meagher; 86.3, 12 July 1991—M. Meagher

Interval: 33 and 52 years. Camera points similar.

Vegetation Changes: *Foreground* and *middleground* show the disappearance of willows, a change probably related to an interaction of two factors. The East Entrance road crosses the delta of Pelican Creek downstream from the view. In spite of a bridge, the road partially dams the creek. The effect of this is increased by the episodic uplift of the Sour Creek resurgent dome north of the Pelican area. Between 1922 and 1985, uplift of about 1 m (3.3 ft) occurred, relative to Sylvan Pass as zero. This activity appears to be related to the 600,000-year-old Yellowstone Caldera (see part 2, "Assembling the Yellowstone Landscape"). A period of uplift in the dome would increase the stream gradient slightly, adding to the damming effect of the road. Also, when the dome inflates, back-flooding from the Yellowstone

River raises the level of Yellowstone Lake in this area (Cannon et al. 1995), which would raise the water level at the mouth of Pelican Creek *below* the road bridging. An impression of the higher water table is shown in the immediate foreground. Higher water levels are evident in 1991 despite recent winters with average or below average snowpack. This scene did not burn in 1988. *Background* forest in 1991 shows evidence of a 1981 lightning-caused forest fire (arrow).

Moose use this area in late summer, although less so in recent years, probably because of the decrease in willows. Winter use by bison increased greatly beginning in the early 1980s. However, access to forage here may be precluded as winter progresses, bringing deeper and more consolidated snow.

The road was reconstructed for automobiles in 1934, with a much more solid base than the earlier wagon road. Stream flow was constricted into a few culverts. The activity of the resurgent dome since the end of the Pleistocene has resulted in complex interactions that affect the level of this northeast section of the Yellowstone Lake shoreline (Cannon et al. 1995). Archeological evidence indicates that people have used these shorelines for at least 10,000 years.

86.2

86.3

87.1

PLATES 87.1–2

East Entrance road, meadows northeast of Squaw Lake (Indian Pond), looking northwest

LOCATION: 554.8 E, 4934.4 N; elev. 2,377 m/7,800 ft

DATES AND PHOTOGRAPHERS: 87.1, 1930—Photographer unknown (NPS-YNP); 87.2, 4 July 1972—M. Meagher

INTERVAL: 42 years. Camera points similar.

VEGETATION CHANGES: *Foreground* and *middleground* show no discernible changes in the meadow although native grasses were cut for hay at the time of the original photograph. *Middle* and *background* show encroachment of lodgepole pine forest into the meadow. The forest appears taller and denser. This location did not burn in 1988.

Cutting of wild hay here reflected a time when park resources were utilized to manage the park. Hay cutting at this location was infrequent, however, and may have occurred only this one summer. The meadows receive limited summer grazing by elk and deer. Bison use was limited to a few bulls until the last decade, when groups of cows and young began to use the area in fall and early winter, before the snow is too deep.

Indian Pond was the original name of the small lake nearby and is again in use, although maps still show Squaw Lake. This is good grizzly bear habitat. A particularly large grizzly bear that frequented this area in 1916 injured guide Ned Frost and killed teamster Frank Welch. The bear was blown up in a dynamite trap while raiding a road camp some miles to the east (a method of removal that would not be used now).

87.2

88.1

Plates 88.1–3

The Mudkettles on upper Pelican Creek, view north

Location: 561.1 E, 4242.4 N; elev. 2,442 m/8,009 ft

Dates and Photographers: 88.1, 14 June 1931—G. M. Wright (NPS-WASO); 88.2, 27 June 1973—M. Meagher; 88.3, 3 September 1991—M. Meagher

Interval: 42 and 60 years. Camera points similar.

Vegetation Changes: *Foreground* substrate consists of Pleistocene lake bed sediments (from an earlier version of Yellowstone Lake). On the small hill that is the immediate foreground, the available soil moisture is limited and supports mainly forb growth in all views. Just below are grasses and sedges that appear unchanged. The site is part of a major north-south travel route for the northern Yellowstone elk and the Pelican Valley bison. Visible wildlife trails at left decreased between 1931 and 1973, then increased by 1991. This may reflect the major elk reductions of the 1960s as well as local shifts in travel patterns. *Middleground* is geothermally influenced. Grasses and sedges appear to have increased, but this may be partly due to the lateness of the 1991 image. Lodgepole pine colonized suitable sites.

Note the shape in 1973 of the double-trunked lodgepole in the center, with basal limbs below a limbless section. This may also reflect much lower ungulate numbers. However, new trees became established and grew regardless of increased ungulate presence. Overall patterns appear quite similar. *Background* shows forest increase and colonization of older burns, as at left rear. The 1988 fires reburned this site to some extent but were moderate here, allowing young lodgepole pines to survive. The pattern of the 1988 fires shows in the rear as a grayish cast across the forest (arrow, 1991 view).

This narrow north-south valley is a major travel route for wildlife, including grizzly bears, which utilize winterkilled bison carcasses and prey on elk calves. It is elk summer range and bison fall-winter range.

88.2

88.3

89.1

Plates 89.1–3

Pelican Cone, looking north

Location: 564.0 E, 4944.0 N; elev. 2,940 m/9,643 ft

Dates and Photographers: 89.1, October 1931—G. Baggley (NPS-YNP); 89.2, 7 July 1973—M. Meagher; 89.3, 10 September 1990—M. Meagher

Interval: 42 and 59 years. Camera points similar.

Vegetation Changes: *Foreground* has been subjected to considerable human impact since 1931, especially after the lookout was constructed in 1937. Until the last few years, the lookout was supplied regularly by horse and mule pack strings. Whitebark pine trees grow in the immediate foreground. *Middle* and *background* show extensive reforestation after an earlier fire (estimated from the appearance in the 1931 view to have occurred perhaps 20–25 years previously). The 1988 fires burned much of this view. Signs of fire are most obvious on the hill at right middle, but the mottled grayish pattern of the forest at right rear is also due to these fires. The forest was composed mainly of lodgepole pine, with Engelmann spruce on the more moist and north-facing sites. Subalpine fir and whitebark pine could be found at higher elevations. The spire-like trees on the slope below the viewer are subalpine fir. Hellroaring Mountain (arrow, 1990), on the north side of the Yellowstone River, can be seen against the skyline.

Fire burned across the top of Pelican Cone in 1994, but the lookout survived. Considered a historic building, it is still used at times for monitoring fire activity and for park radio communication, as circumstances require. From this high vantage point, a research project documented that grizzly bear use is negatively affected by high levels of human recreational use (Gunther 1990). The bears used the valley much less during daylight hours, or went elsewhere in the park, as numbers of hikers in the valley increased.

89.2

89.3

90.1

PLATES 90.1–3

Mirror Plateau, head of the north fork of the Mirror Fork of Timothy Creek, looking southeast

LOCATION: 566.8 E, 4954.7 N; elev. 2,756 m/9,039 ft

DATES AND PHOTOGRAPHERS: 90.1, 1916—J. E. Haynes (MHS); 90.2, 6 September 1973—M. Meagher; 90.3, 13 September 1991—M. Meagher

INTERVAL: 57 and 75 years. Camera points similar.

VEGETATION CHANGES: *Foreground* in the 1916 photo probably was taken earlier in the season, perhaps in late July or early August (the lupine is in bloom). Ground cover otherwise appears similar, with a dense subalpine meadow of grasses and sedges. Note that the meadow appears to have received more extensive grazing in 1991 than in 1973. These meadows did not burn in 1988. The dark patch near the center of the meadow is a small seep. In 1916 there was water in the depression, but it was dry in 1973. By 1991 it was much larger, with a little water. The enlargement was probably caused by increased numbers of elk and especially bison using this meadow in summer. *Middle* and *background* show an increase in forest density and height between 1916 and 1973, with some tree colonization along meadow edges. The appearance of the forest in 1916 suggests the effects of an earlier forest fire. The forest burned in 1988.

This is summer range for northern Yellowstone elk and bison. For years, the bison that ranged here in summer-fall came from Pelican Valley and the Lamar. In recent years bison also have moved from Hayden Valley to the Mirror Plateau. In 1992, an estimated 2,000 bison were seen at one time in the open meadows of the Mirror Plateau, some of them in this one.

The Absaroka Mountains, which form most of the park's east boundary, are skylined in the distance. Saddle Mountain is at left and Notch Mountain at right (arrows, 1991).

90.2

90.3

91.1

PLATES 91.1–3

Turbid Springs on Bear Creek, looking west

LOCATION: 599.2 E, 4932.4 N; elev. 2,409 m/7,901 ft

DATES AND PHOTOGRAPHERS: 91.1, ca. 1905—Photographer unknown (UW); 91.2, 4 July 1972—M. Meagher; 91.3, 7 September 1990—M. Meagher

INTERVAL: 67 and 85 years. Camera points similar.

VEGETATION CHANGES: *Foreground* is a sinter-geothermal substrate that is essentially unchanged since 1905. Creek flow and gravel bars have altered slightly. *Middle* and *background* show increased forest density. The original photo probably was taken sometime during August, because it is unlikely that tourists (as the group of people appear to be) would have been able to travel this route much earlier. The meadow in the original appears to show some impact from grazing and trampling by camping parties. Because the 1972 photo was taken in early July, the ground cover is shorter, but it appears to have become gradually denser and drier between 1905 and 1990, with a change from a higher proportion of sedges to more grasses. The thermal area may be less active now. The semiopen area behind the hot springs became a meadow dense with nonnative timothy sometime between 1905 and 1972. Curly dock, also an exotic plant, was present by 1990. In 1988, ground fire burned through the stand of lodgepole pine (behind the campers in the 1905 photo); some snags can be seen in the background in the 1990 view.

Some bison and elk use occurs seasonally. In winter, bison traveling between Pelican Valley and the shore of Yellowstone Lake may pass through.

This site is adjacent to the first road built between the East Entrance and Fishing Bridge, which opened to public use on 10 July 1903 (Culpin 1994). The nonnative timothy now widespread in the park probably was brought first to this locale along with the horses and mules used for transportation. This meadow was likely often used as a campsite, because people camped wherever they wished and this was a convenient location. Road access no longer exists to the site; the old alignment serves as a trail.

91.2

91.3

92.1

PLATES 92.1–2

Upper Witch Creek thermal area, looking southwest at Factory Hill

LOCATION: 537.6 E, 4906.0 N; elev. 2,439 m/7,999 ft

DATES AND PHOTOGRAPHERS: 92.1, 26 September 1940—J. E. Haynes (MHS); 92.2, 4 August 1992—M. Meagher

INTERVAL: 52 years. Camera points similar. View retaken earlier in the day to improve the angle of the light on the background.

VEGETATION CHANGES: *Foreground* similar, with minor changes in the patterns of the mosses and forbs such as stonecrop. These minor shifts in ground cover are probably related to changes in soil temperature, which is known to vary over time in geothermal areas. *Middleground* shows some increase in ground cover and colonization by lodgepole pine. Ground cover appears to have changed from moss and stonecrop to more grasses. A field check in September 1991 showed a similar appearance, so the early August date of the 1992 retake did not account for the differences in vegetation. *Background* shows the effect of crown fire across much of Factory Hill in 1988. Young trees growing in an avalanche chute burned that year. The arrow in the retake indicates a patch of young trees that did not burn, but were flattened to the downhill side probably by an avalanche after 1988. The appearance of these trees can be deceptive as to the cause of their demise, but there was no indication of historic fire on the slopes of Factory Hill before 1988 (W. Romme, pers. comm.). Avalanches function as localized agents of change, contributing to the vegetation patterns caused by natural disturbances.

The fires of 1988 were sufficiently intense here to require a brief evacuation of the fire lookout atop Mount Sheridan (beyond the mountaintop in this view). This historic lookout is manned most summers for a variety of administrative communication needs, aside from the reporting of fire starts. Natural fires (lightning-caused) are allowed to burn on a case-by-case basis. Hikers may notice traces of the old fire road that accessed Witch Creek and Heart Lake, in use at the time of the original photo.

Factory Hill was named about 1885 by the Hague U.S. Geological Survey, because of N. P. Langford's description of nearby steam vents giving "the appearance of a New England factory village" (Whittlesey 1988:54).

92.2

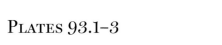

Plates 93.1–3

Overlook Mountain, looking northeast at the South Arm of Yellowstone Lake

Location: 549.5 E, 4899.7 N; elev. 2,842 m/9,321 ft

Dates and Photographers: 93.1, 1889—J. P. Iddings (USGS); 93.2, 18 July 1972—M. Meagher; 93.3, 10 September 1990—M. Meagher

Interval: 83 and 101 years. Camera point for the 1972 view moved slightly forward because of forest encroachment from the rear; point for 1990 retake virtually identical to the 1972 location.

Vegetation Changes: *Foreground* appears lusher in both retakes. This may reflect the slight shift of location from the first view or milder winters with slightly longer growing seasons. Differences also may reflect annual variation in precipitation. The first view probably was taken later in the growing season than the second. Note the whitebark pine trees that bracket the 1889 view. Unburned whitebark pines formed the forest behind the photographer in 1972; they burned in 1988. The small dead tree at the left in the original is probably a whitebark pine. *Middleground* in 1990 shows the extensive burn of 1988. The spire-topped trees in all three views are

subalpine fir, many of which burned in 1988. The round-topped whitebark pine downslope from the photographer in 1972, which also burned in 1988, shows the shape typical of this high elevation species. The delta of Grouse Creek in the center appears drier, with fewer willows than in 1889. Conifers increased on the delta between 1972 and 1990. *Background* is similar, to the extent discernible. The Promontory, between South and Southeast arms, and the east side of Southeast Arm did not burn in 1988.

These high elevation meadows are important summer range for the southern Yellowstone elk herd. These elk winter on the National Elk Refuge in Jackson Hole, along with other elk from summer ranges south of Yellowstone Park.

Arnold Hague (1887:27) referred to Grouse Creek as "a broad bottom filled with willows." The Hague surveys (U.S. Geological Survey) made in Yellowstone National Park during the 1880s and 1890s covered an amazing amount of rugged country by horseback, supplied by pack train.

93.2

93.3

94.1

Plates 94.1–3

Big Game Ridge, looking north at Mount Hancock

Location: 547.5 E, 4886.9 N; elev. 2,927 m/9,600 ft

Dates and Photographers: 94.1, ca. 1900—S. Leek (UW); 94.2, 16 July 1973—M. Meagher; 94.3, 9 August 1990—M. Meagher

Interval: 73 and 90 years. Camera points similar.

Vegetation Changes: *Foreground* vegetation is within a snowbank site. Variation in plant density is apparent among the photo comparisons, as at right center (arrow). The site shows a decrease in herbaceous vegetation between 1900 and 1973, but by 1990 there appears to be an overall increase, much of it forbs such as mountain dandelion. Some of this variation probably occurred because of differences in the seasonal dates of the photographs; the August 1990 date would allow a longer period of growth. Also, the appearance of the foreground vegetation probably varies annually in response to the time and rate of snowmelt, temperature variation, summer precipitation, stage of growing season for that particular year, pocket gopher activity, and intensity of elk grazing. *Middle* and *background* show a slight increase in forest cover and density between 1900 and 1973. A crown fire burned this forest in 1988.

This is summer range for the southern Yellowstone elk herd that winters in Jackson Hole. The ridgecrest forms an east-west travel route for wildlife as well as people and approximates the park's south boundary. Theodore Roosevelt hunted big game near here about 1890, outside the park (Whittlesey 1988).

94.2

94.3

95.1

PLATES 95.1–3

Big Game Ridge, view north toward Heart Lake and Chicken Ridge

LOCATION: 549.7 E, 4886.9 N; elev. 3,049 m/10,000 ft

DATES AND PHOTOGRAPHERS: 95.1, 19 August 1915—V. Bailey (NA); 95.2, 13 August 1969—G. Gruell (USFS); 95.3, 31 July 1991—M. Meagher

INTERVAL: 54 and 76 years. Camera points similar. The 1991 retake showed more background to include fire-caused changes.

VEGETATION CHANGES: *Foreground* and *middleground* show limited change in the subalpine herbland since 1915. Some increase in herbaceous vegetation may have occurred on deeper soils, but other sites show an apparent decrease between 1969 and 1991. These high elevation sites vary annually, sometimes greatly, in response to weather conditions and animal activity. *Middle* and *background* show an increase in subalpine fir and whitebark pine trees in the basin; the 1988 fires burned some of these. Crown fire burned across much of the forest beyond the basin.

This important elk summer range was first named Elk Ridge by the Hayden Survey in 1872 (Whittlesey 1988). The views are expansive in all directions from the top of this ridge, making it seem like the top of the world.

5.2

5.3

96.1

Plates 96.1–3

Upper Yellowstone River just south of Hawk's Rest in the Bridger-Teton National Forest, view southwest up the Atlantic Creek drainage

LOCATION: 574.0 E, 4882.2 N; elev. 2,409 m/7,901 ft

DATES AND PHOTOGRAPHERS: 96.1, fall 1930—G. F. Baggley (NPS-YNP); 96.2, 27 August 1974—M. Meagher; 96.3, 22 August 1991—M. Meagher

INTERVAL: 44 and 61 years. Camera points approximate.

VEGETATION CHANGES: *Foreground* indicates a drier meadow than formerly. The taller willows in the original appear to have given way to a lower form, perhaps Wolf's willow, by 1974. More tall willows appear again during the second interval (allowing for a slight change in perspective). Patches of willows burned in 1988, such as to the left of the left rock and at right-center. *Background* forest increased in density and height, and trees invaded meadow edges between 1930 and 1974. In 1988 the forests burned fairly extensively except at higher elevations and in the bottoms. Snags barely visible at higher elevations (arrow, 1930) may indicate earlier fire.

Atlantic Creek and the Upper Yellowstone have been a travel route for people for centuries. This is part of the Thorofare, known to and much traveled by the fur trappers of the 1820s to 1840s (Whittlesey 1988) as the only easy southern route to the Yellowstone Plateau. For the same reason, Native Americans undoubtedly used the route prior to the trappers' arrival.

Hague wrote: "The broad valley is occupied wholly by meadows and hills and was at no distant day occupied by a very large number of beaver" (1887:95). Although the sites in use by beaver undoubtedly have changed, the animals are present in the area now. Note the two moose in the center of the 1930 view.

96.2

96.3

97.1

PLATES 97.1–3

Eagle Peak from Mountain Creek

LOCATION: 578.2 E, 4903.0 N; elev. 2,561 m/8,399 ft

DATES AND PHOTOGRAPHERS: 97.1, ca. 1889—J. P. Iddings (USGS); 97.2, 8 August 1973—M. Meagher; 97.3, 30 August 1991—M. Meagher

INTERVAL: 84 and 102 years. Camera points similar.

VEGETATION CHANGES: *Foreground* shows a gradually drier meadow. Between 1889 and 1973, willows disappeared. During the next two decades the vegetation seems to have shifted from a wetter meadow of sedges and rushes to a slightly drier one; in 1991 it was comparatively drier underfoot, offering easier walking. Species are likely the same, but some shifts in the relative composition of the community may have occurred, such as an increase in tufted hairgrass. *Background* forest burned in 1988, but Eagle Peak shows little change except that the unburned trees are taller.

This area receives some summer-fall elk use. Eagle Peak was named in 1885 by the Hague survey of the U.S. Geological Survey (Whittlesey 1988). Eagle Pass on the right (east) flank is a major crossing of the Absaroka Mountains; a maintained trail makes travel easier.

Photographic dates and hence growth of vegetation are probably comparable in the three views. Early expeditions such as the Hague geological surveys did most of their traveling in this locale in August and early September, because of snow. Mountain passes could be impassable before mid-July at the earliest. Hague wrote: "The snows cover these mountains the greater part of the year. It is everywhere evident that these snows do not disappear much before the first of September; indeed there are many snow drifts 100 ft. long and 20 or 40 ft. thick which last the year around. Many of the amphitheatres in the mountains carry these snow-fields. In consequence the range is very well watered" (1988:76–78).

97.2

97.3

98.1

PLATES 98.1–3

Table Mountain, view west from a tributary of Mountain Creek

LOCATION: 577.2 E, 4904.8 N; elev. 2,730 m/8,954 ft

DATES AND PHOTOGRAPHERS: 98.1, ca. 1889—J. P. Iddings (USGS); 98.2, 8 August 1973—M. Meagher; 98.3, 15 September 1992—M. Meagher

INTERVAL: 84 and 103 years. Camera points similar; 1992 view somewhat closer.

VEGETATION CHANGES: *Foreground* seems progressively drier throughout the 103 years. The shrubs at the bottom edge of the 1889 view may be low-growing willow. The meadow appears to have changed from predominantly sedge growth to more of a sedge-grass community. The dead standing trees in the 1889 view appear to have been killed by a fire, perhaps several to 10 years before the photo was taken. *Middleground* appears to be drier than in the 1889 view. Willows visible along the creek in the original had mostly disappeared by 1973 and trees masked the creek. Willows appeared to be gone from the 1992 view. In spite of the extensive fire in 1988, trees at the front of the stand survived, perhaps because conditions there were more

open and moist. The vagaries of wind also may have been a factor in their survival. Fire commonly creates a mosaic of burned and unburned forest. Trees gradually invaded the meadow over the entire time spanned by the photos; note the new young trees coming in at right (arrow) in 1992. *Background* shows increased forest height and density prior to the crown fire that burned here in 1988. Trees on the slopes of Table Mountain did not burn in 1988. In those higher locations the combination of sparse fuels and localized wind patterns may have prevented much fire.

This area receives some summer-fall elk use, and mule deer probably are present at low densities.

Finding the deceptively hard-to-locate photo point for the retakes generated great admiration for Iddings's original photograph. Considerable effort must have been required to take the original with one of the beautiful but large and cumbersome varnished wood cameras used at the time. Cameras and glass plate negatives had to travel on horseback or on mules, making the results nothing short of phenomenal.

98.2

98.3

99.1

PLATES 99.1–3

Langford Cairn on the Southeast Arm of Yellowstone Lake, view southeast from the top

LOCATION: 563.5 E, 4909.7 N; elev. 2,696 m/8,842 ft

DATES AND PHOTOGRAPHERS: 99.1, 1871—W. H. Jackson (NPS-YNP); 99.2, 7 August 1973—M. Meagher; 99.3, 31 August 1991—M. Meagher

INTERVAL: 102 and 120 years. Camera points similar but adjusted slightly for the view in 1991.

VEGETATION CHANGES: *Foreground* changed little during the second interval; the top of Langford Cairn did not burn. Big sagebrush and bunchgrasses both increased during the first interval. *Middle* and *background* show generally increased size and density of forest, mainly lodgepole pine. Meadow invasion by trees is apparent on the flats at right rear, but note that the meadow pattern across the center remains quite similar in all three views. These long-lasting meadow patterns apparently are controlled by soil (edaphic) factors. Colter Peak is the highest mountain to the rear. The Turret shows as a round knob just beyond the right flank of Colter Peak. Some of the forest that burned in 1988 shows near the top of the long open ridge at right rear.

These meadows receive some summer and fall elk use. Mule deer are present at the same time, but appear to be fewer in number. The feature was named for N. P. Langford of the 1870 exploring expedition, apparently because of a misconception that Langford sketched Yellowstone Lake from its top (Whittlesey 1988).

9.2

9.3

100.1

Plates 100.1–3

Langford Cairn, view south across the delta of the Yellowstone River in the Southeast Arm

Location: 563.5 E, 4909.7 N; elev. 2,696 m/8,842 ft

Dates and Photographers: 100.1, 1871—W. H. Jackson (USGS); 100.2, 7 August 1973—M. Meagher; 100.3, 31 August 1991—M. Meagher

Interval: 102 and 120 years. Camera points similar but adjusted forward in the 1991 view for maximum expanse of delta.

Vegetation Changes: *Foreground* shows more grass and big sagebrush, the change most noticeable between 1871 and 1973. In 1991, because of the camera point change, the immediate foreground is different. In the *middleground,* as on the lower slopes of Langford Cairn, the forest cover is essentially the same with a small amount of invasion into the meadows. *Background* does not show well because of smoke haze in 1991. The fires of 1988 burned slopes across the delta on the west side of the river, but this is not apparent in the 1991 photograph. The delta appears to have been wetter in 1871 than in 1973. This may have some relationship to activity in the resurgent dome (Sour Creek) of the caldera and consequent episodic changes in

relative lake levels (Hamilton 1987, Locke and Meyer 1994; see also pls. 86.1–3). As channels collect silt and change, deltas build up and would be expected to change to somewhat drier conditions. Invasion of scattered conifers on higher sites suggests this, even though there may be slightly more water apparent in the lower sites. Willows are extensive (dark gray) and have invaded new substrates (closed arrow), but have disappeared from sites that became drier (light gray, open arrow). A careful comparison among the views shows a number of sites where these changes have occurred.

The delta is used by moose, mostly in summer and fall, and a few winter here. Elk use the area mainly in the fall, but recent mild winters have allowed some to remain into the winter. This is one of the few places in the park that supports long-term beaver activity.

The wilderness seen from the perspective of Langford Cairn shows little of human activity. Yet it encapsulates biological time as seen in the photo collection. Change is visible as conifers invade the meadows, willows appear and disappear, the channel of the river moves, sometimes influenced by beaver activity. Underscoring all of this is the influence of geology as the resurgent dome inflates and deflates, changing the water levels of the lake. But the broad patterns of the vegetation and the landforms are similar throughout. Biological time is superimposed on geological time; both are removed from the world of human affairs.

2

0.3

[213]

PART 2

The Physical and Biological Framework

Assembling the Yellowstone Landscape: Geology

We think that the Yellowstone hotspot is fundamental to the dynamics of both tectonics and glaciation; it produced . . . uplift of the greater Yellowstone region, and . . . a hotspot track (eastern Snake River Plain) through which storms carry snows to the greater Yellowstone area.

PIERCE & GOOD (1992)

The geological past sets the stage in various ways for the biological scene of Yellowstone National Park as we know it. The interplay of geological forces and events resulted in the landforms and geomorphology of the present landscape and also influenced the climate that prevailed over time, both locally and regionally. Geological events determined the parent bedrock as well as surface outcrops and deposits. In turn, these dictated the soils that formed to cover the land. And finally, the geological history is fundamental to perhaps the most popular and best known expression of geology in Yellowstone: Old Faithful Geyser, the signature feature of the myriad hot springs, geysers, and lesser expressions of geothermal influence throughout Yellowstone National Park. It seems both fitting and essential to treat the geological history of the area as the prologue for biological time.

Parts of the Yellowstone landscape we see today originated long before the Yellowstone hotspot, during the Precambrian era some 2.7 billion or more years ago. The dark outcrops of gneisses and schists of the Black Canyon of the Yellowstone and elsewhere near the north boundary are metamorphosed remnants rearranged by time and geological events. These basement rocks were brought to the surface late in the Precambrian during a long period of uplift and erosion in the region, of which few surface features remain in the Yellowstone area. Later, vast quantities of sediments accumulated in waters of the Paleozoic and Mesozoic eras. These became deposits such as the Cretaceous shales of Mount Everts (pls. 7.1–3). The long period of deposition was followed by large-scale mountain building, the Laramide orogeny, which uplifted the Rocky Mountains between 100 and 50 million years ago as the North American and Pacific crustal plates collided. Subsequently, Eocene volcanoes erupted some 50 to 40 million years ago to create the Absaroka volcanic deposits and bury ancient forests that are now the petrified forests of the area (pls. 58.1–3, 59.1–3). After the volcanic eruptions, millions of years of uplift and erosion followed, until volcanism commenced again. Thus, many of the details of the present landscape are the legacy of this lengthy earlier geologic history, superimposed and rearranged on the stage created by more recent forces.[1]

The forces that generated the present mountain-ringed and punctuated high plateau that is the Yellowstone National Park area began about 16 million years ago. These forces were first expressed some 600 km (375 mi) to the southwest of the present Yellowstone Plateau, roughly at the conjunction of the present states of Idaho, Oregon, and Nevada. A plume of magma from the earth's mantle apparently formed below the lithospheric crust and created a hotspot, similar to those that form oceanic islands such as Hawaii. As the North American plate moved to the southwest across the mantle plume, the top of the plume spread and mushroomed, while the neck served as a chimney through which molten rock continued to funnel to the base of the lithospheric plate. A complex transfer of energy from mantle to crust resulted in uplift, faulting, and volcanism in the region. Some 10 million years ago the hotspot was 200 km (125 mi) southwest of Yellowstone, near present-day American Falls, Idaho. From there, a series of progressively younger volcanic fields mark the trace of the hotspot toward the park as the plate moved across the magma plume. Today, the Snake River Plain marks the hotspot track toward Yellowstone. Faulting and subsidence created this trench approximately 90 km (56 mi) wide, bounded by mountains and floored with overlapping calderas and basaltic lava flows (fig. 8).[2]

About 2 million years ago the southwestward movement of the crustal plate resulted in the surface positioning of the hotspot here, to form the Yellowstone Plateau volcanic field. Three volcanic cycles each culminated in explosive pyroclastic eruptions from crustal magma chambers, forming three partially overlapping calderas dated at 2.1, 1.3, and 0.6 million years old. The youngest was first identified in the late 1950s but the older calderas had been obscured by later geological events and were recognized only in the last few decades.

For about 600,000 years prior to formation of the youngest Yellowstone caldera, rhyolitic lavas from slowly forming ring fractures oozed intermittently across the plateau surface. A triggering mechanism that is not yet well understood allowed a massive degassing of magma in the crustal chamber, resulting in an explosive eruption and collapse of the chamber roof. This formed a somewhat oval caldera of 2,590 km^2 (1,000 mi^2) located more or less centrally in the park (fig. 9). Probably in a matter of hours or a few days, approximately 1,000 km^3 (240 mi^3) of pyroclastic material was ejected.[3]

This is geology at work on a scale not easy to imagine. At 240 *cubic*

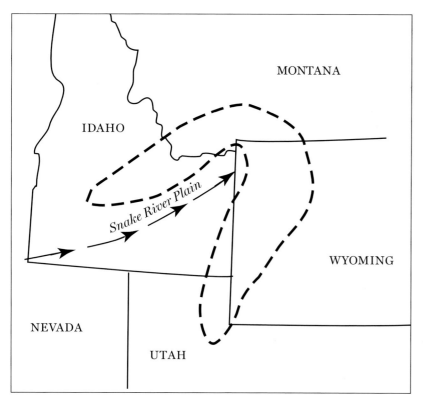

Fig. 8. *Track of the Yellowstone hotspot, spanning hundreds of miles and 15 million years. Adapted from Pierce and Morgan (1992).*

miles, the volume of material involved was immense. The caldera stretches from Old Faithful almost to Mount Washburn in the north and beyond Yellowstone Lake to the east. (By contrast, in its 1980 eruption, Mount St. Helens ejected less than half of a single cubic mile of material.) Afterward, the caldera was partially filled by rhyolitic surface lava flows and by sediments. Yellowstone Lake lies partly within the caldera; West Thumb basin was created by a comparatively small caldera that formed within the larger one about 150,000 years ago. Volcanic activity continued intermittently as surface flows until about 70,000 years ago—a mere moment ago in geological time.

Geophysical studies suggest that volcanism could recur. Remarkably, a series of releveling measurements across the 0.6 million-year-old caldera showed approximately 700 mm (2.6 ft) of uplift just in the mere 55-year period prior to 1985. This localized uplift was greatest toward the northeast edge of the caldera, adjacent to the Sour Creek resurgent dome. The uplift appeared to wax and wane, with subsidence in the late 1980s. Thus, part of the earth itself changed elevation within the time frame of the photo comparisons. (There are few places on earth where two biologists could not consider landscape levels to be constant during their studies.) Geophysical evidence derived from seismic experiments, earthquake data, and gravity measurements suggested a "partial melt body" (presumably magma) perhaps 5–6 km (3–4 mi) below the earth's surface. Volcanic

activity could either represent the waning stages of the third caldera-forming cycle or might indicate the start of a fourth. At present geophysicists cannot distinguish between the two scenarios, but there is no reason to believe that Yellowstone's volcanic history terminated with past events.[4]

Active faulting and broad regional uplift accompanying the presence of the hotspot in the Yellowstone locale will surely continue. The uplift created the present horseshoe-shaped bow of mountains, some 0.5 km (0.3 mi) higher than surrounding terrain and open to the southwest. Here the terrain is contiguous with the Snake River Plain, the direction of the prevailing regional winds as they sweep across the Yellowstone Plateau and encounter the higher mountains formed by the uplift at the crest of the bow to the east and north (fig. 8). As the winds lift over the mountains they lose much of the moisture they contain, which falls as rain and snow. Thus the hotspot would appear to be partly responsible for the most recent major phase of Yellowstone's geologic history—the ice.[5]

Pleistocene glaciations covered much of what is now Yellowstone, carving some stream courses, blocking and changing others, creating glacial lakes that are now interior valleys, and depositing surface material as moraines, glacial erratics, and other debris.[6] Although earlier glaciations occurred, evidence from only the last two periods has persisted to the present. Bull Lake was the earlier of the last two glacial periods; the maximum occurred about 150,000 years ago. Volcanism continued during and between some glacial periods, adding to a more complex geological history than the simplified version presented here. For instance, rhyolite lava flows occurred on the west side of the park between the last two glacial episodes. The presence of these flows blocked some ice movement westward, forcing more of the Pinedale ice mass—the last glaciation—north down the Yellowstone Valley.

The Pinedale glaciation covered nearly 90 percent of the park at its maximum about 30,000 years ago. Large masses of ice built up on the Yellowstone Plateau, focusing generally on the higher elevations and mountainous areas (fig. 10). From high divides, ice masses flowed outward. The northern Yellowstone outlet glacier covered most of the north half of the park area, and had five interconnected ice caps, extending from the Gallatin Range eastward across the plateau to the upper Lamar River and the Beartooth Plateau. Ice built up along the Absaroka Mountains further south to form the southern Yellowstone ice mass. At one time over Yellowstone Lake the ice cap was more than 1,000 to 1,200 m (3,200–4,000 ft) thick, although it did not function as one huge homogenous mass. Subunits of glaciers commonly built up and melted at somewhat different rates. The ice mass may have remained near maximum in extent until about 20,000 years ago. The complex record left as moraines, erratics (pls. 51.1–3, 53.1–3, 56.1–3), striations, and other glacial evidence indicated differing times and sometimes directions of ice flow. Much of the Pinedale ice was gone by 14,000 years ago, but remnants persisted locally to about 10,000 years ago. This transition marked the onset of the Holocene.

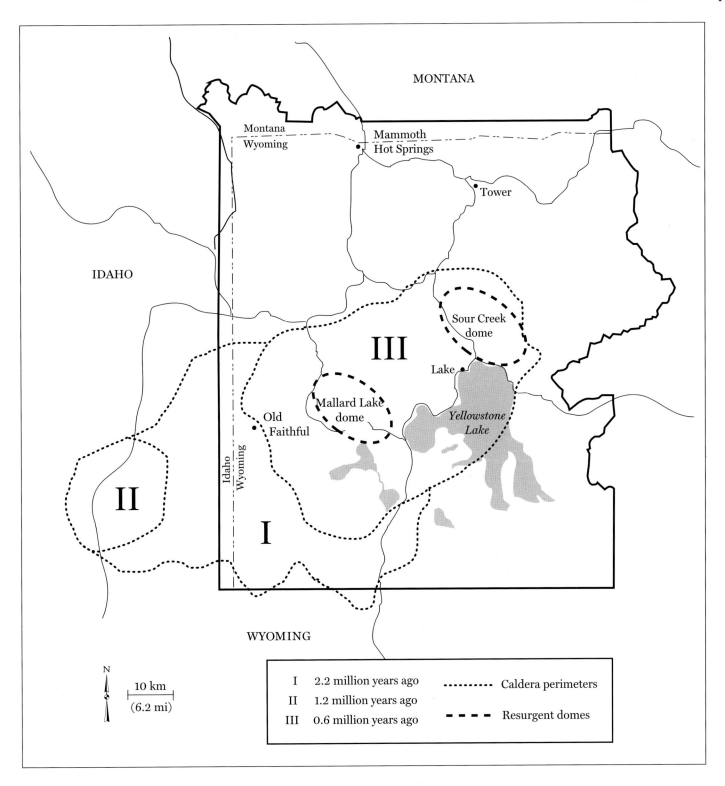

MONTANA

Montana
Wyoming

Mammoth
Hot Springs

• Tower

IDAHO

Sour Creek
dome

III

Lake

Mallard Lake
dome

Yellowstone
Lake

Old
Faithful

Idaho
Wyoming

II

I

WYOMING

N

10 km
(6.2 mi)

I	2.2 million years ago	·········· Caldera perimeters
II	1.2 million years ago	
III	0.6 million years ago	▬ ▬ ▬ Resurgent domes

Aside from geologic events such as earthquakes and volcanism, uplift and erosion serve as continual and opposing forces that have much to do with the present Yellowstone scene. Both usually are more gradual forces in their expression over time. But not always. The high east boundary of the Absaroka Mountains was formed by uplift of highly erodible Eocene

Fig. 9. *Calderas of the Yellowstone volcanic field. The most recent Yellowstone caldera (III) formed approximately 600,000 years ago. From Fournier et al. (1994).*

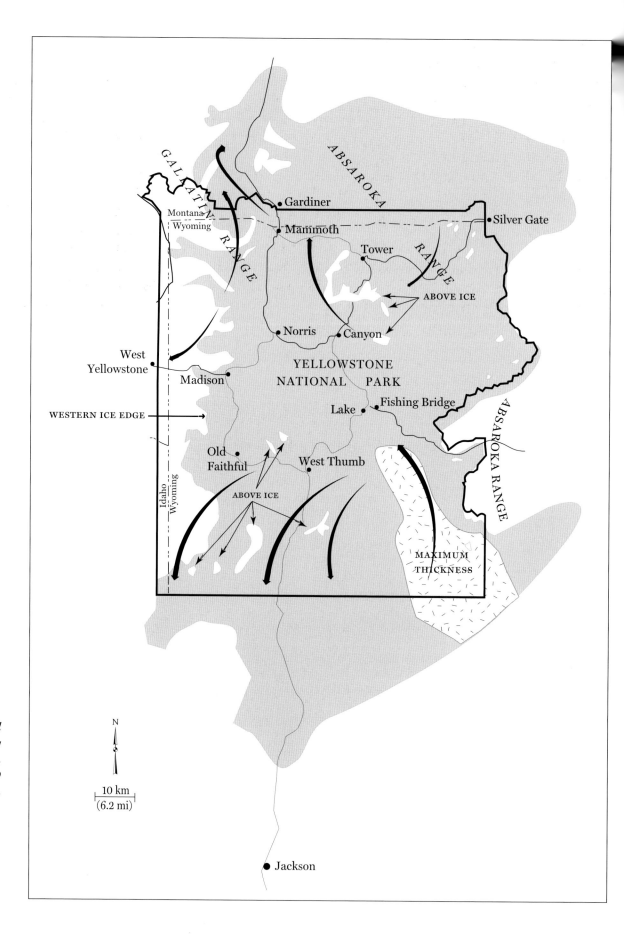

Fig. 10. *Maximum extent of Pinedale ice in and around Yellowstone National Park, indicated by shading. This was the most recent major glaciation, with much of the ice disappearing a mere 12,000 years ago. Adapted from Fritz (1985), Pierce (1979), and Pierce and Good (1992).*

volcanic rocks and rock fragments (pls. 70.1–3). These are the source of much of the turbidity and sediment load seen at times in tributaries of the Yellowstone River drainage in the park. Quite localized summer thunderstorms can be traced to the site of rainfall by following a silted stream course to its incised head near the boundary. Commonly, only one or two drainages may show temporary siltation from these thunderstorm events. Annually, spring snowmelt brings down silt and boulders to be deposited as alluvial fans. Quantities moved during snowmelt can be enormous; sediment discharge averaged over 251 metric tons (281 tons) daily for Soda Butte Creek in 1985 and 1986. Some years this runoff peaks as a fairly major event over a few warm days; these occurrences may shift stream channels and build point bars or leave widespread deposits of silt and rock where the gradient slows. The braided floodplain and shifts of gravel bars seen on lower Soda Butte Creek are a striking example of the deposition of a waterborne erosion load that occurs where the gradient

lessens (pls. 60.1–3, 61.1–3). From the air or a high vantage point, the valley bottom has a flattened, filled-in look. The typical U-shape of a glacial valley—scoured here by the Pinedale ice—has been filled by deposition from glacial outwash and waterborne erosion.[7]

Comparatively rapid erosion of the Absaroka Mountains with deep young canyons (pls. 66.1–3) suggested relatively recent uplift of perhaps 1 km (0.6 mi) with the forces generated by the hotspot. Peaks locally may be as much as 1.9 km (1.18 mi) above the valley floor.[8] Erosion here is an inevitable and ongoing force, particularly as uplift continues (pls. 70.1–3).

As the track of the Yellowstone hotspot demonstrates, geological change forms a continuum operating today and inseparable from the present biological scene. We often fail to recognize this, simply because of the shortness of human time. Even so, the comparative photographs show changes in the form of erosion, landslides, geothermal activity shifts, movements of stream channels, and shifts in surface elevation.

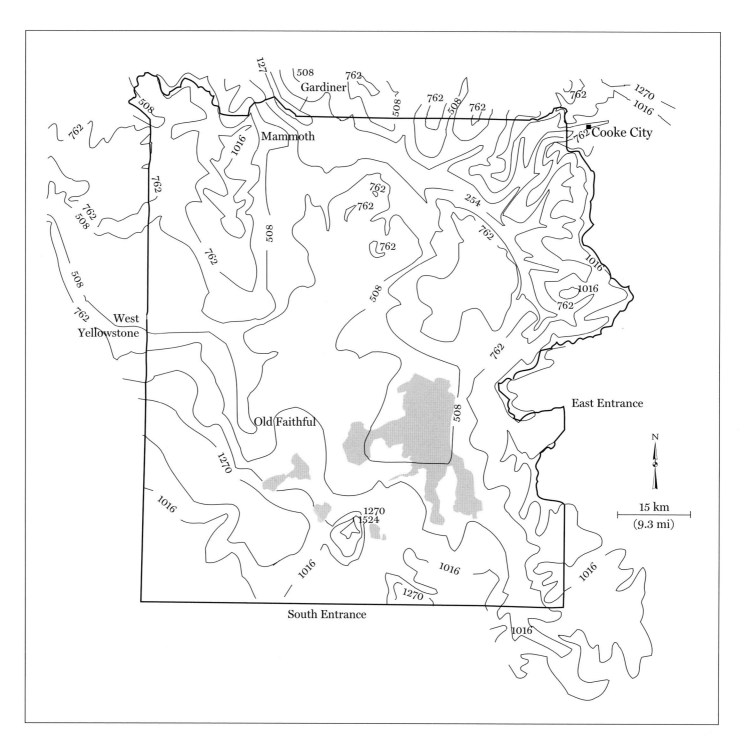

Fig. 11. *Mean annual snowfall (cm) 1958–72, Yellowstone National Park. Modified from Farnes's 1974 map, as presented in Dirks and Martner (1982). Yellowstone GIS.*

Setting the Stage: Climate and Soil

We attribute the heterogenous pattern of Holocene climatic change in Yellowstone to (1) the effects of the amplification of the seasonal cycle of solar radiation in the early Holocene and (2) the manifestation of these effects in a topographically complex landscape.

WHITLOCK AND BARTLEIN (1992)

The present climate of Yellowstone Park is relatively severe. Summers are short and cool; winters are long and cold, with snow covering the plateau for six to eight months. Within that generalized regime, the climate can be highly variable in time and space according to a hierarchy of influences. Significantly, the park has two contrasting climatic regimes: summer-dry/winter-wet climates prevail in southern and central areas; summer-wet/winter-dry in the north. These contrasting climates are controlled indirectly by large-scale atmospheric circulation patterns and directly and more locally by solar radiation and topography. These two differing weather regimes generate quite different patterns of vegetation. Moreover, mountainous sites receive more precipitation and are cooler than are valley sites, resulting in elevational climatic gradients.[1]

Long-term climatic patterns prevail at given locations, regardless of considerable variation in weather, daily and annually. For instance, Mammoth Hot Springs at elevation 1,900 m (6,239 ft) near the northern edge of the park has a mean annual temperature of 4.3°C (34.3°F); annual precipitation averages about 42 cm (16.8 in). Lake Station at 2,360 m (7,744 ft) on the shore of Yellowstone Lake is somewhat colder and wetter with a mean annual temperature of 0.2°C (32.1°F) and precipitation of 47 cm (18.8 in). Much of the precipitation falls as snow, creating a striking pattern of environmental differences across the park (fig. 11). Cooke City, for example, averages 762 cm (25 ft) of snowfall while Gardiner receives 127 cm (4 ft) or less. (Snow on the ground is always less than total snowfall.)

LONG-TERM CLIMATIC TRENDS

Broad climatic change drives regional vegetation change. Hence, a sense of the magnitude of climatic change is essential for understanding the dynamics of vegetation and landscapes, even at the temporal and spatial scales of our photo comparisons.

The Pinedale glaciation here spanned perhaps 50,000 years, from 60,000 to 10,000 years ago, and provided a convenient climatic baseline against which to compare subsequent trends. As described earlier, 20,000 years ago most of the area that became Yellowstone National Park was covered by an ice field that exceeded 1,000 m (3,280 ft) in thickness. Mean annual temperatures at the maximum extent of glaciation may have been as much as 10–15°C colder than at present, whereas the cold late-glacial climates of 14,000–11,500 years ago were about 4–5°C colder. By 10,000 years ago, summer temperatures were about as now.[2]

The rising temperatures that terminated the Pinedale glaciation and set the Holocene stage culminated in a generally warmer and drier period. The rise was rapid; by 9,500 years ago, pollen and fossil beetle evidence indicates that summers were even warmer than at present. During the warmest period, mean annual temperatures here were probably 1–2°C higher than now; precipitation might have been 40 cm (16 in) less. Some 5,000 years ago the thermal maximum ended with cooler and generally wetter climate.[3]

Within this broad post-Pleistocene pattern the changes in temperature and moisture varied both geographically and in time. In southern Yellowstone National Park the maximum post-glacial warming occurred from roughly 9,000 to 5,000 years ago; this part of the park has become progressively cooler and wetter since. In contrast, northern areas warmed after the Pleistocene but became progressively drier.[4]

After the thermal maximum of the early Holocene, cooler climates returned, which included several neoglaciations. A small but important neoglaciation marked the Little Ice Age in western North America. The coldest part of this occurred from roughly 1650 to 1890 A.D. in Yellowstone, although the moraines formed in the park during this period have not been dated. An analysis of tree rings from lower elevations of the park indicated that the later part of this neoglaciation was comparatively more severe; rings dating from 1751 suggested that winters of the 1860s and those from about 1885 to 1900 were unusually cold. Moreover, the greatest winter precipitation since the mid-18th century occurred from about 1877 to 1890.[5]

Weather records for Mammoth Hot Springs show considerable variation and suggest trends both annually and for winter (fig. 12).[6] Temperatures have risen more than 1°C since the beginning of the 20th century. This appreciable increase mirrors change reported throughout much of the northern hemisphere. The trend to warmer temperatures is the subject of considerable debate within the scientific community; many scientists believe the change has been driven by humans altering the composition of the atmosphere through increased burning of fossil fuels (the "greenhouse effect"). Others remain unconvinced, pointing to a strong

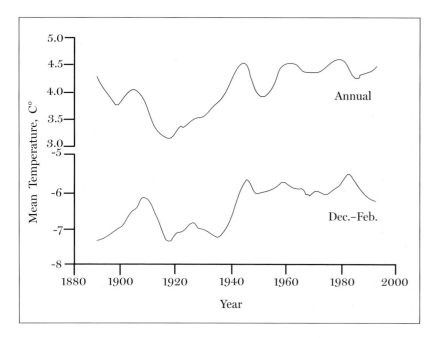

Fig. 12. *Annual and midwinter (December–February) temperature trends at Mammoth, Yellowstone National Park.*

correlation between temperature changes during the past 130 years and the variation in length of the solar cycle.

Measurements of annual and winter precipitation at Mammoth Hot Springs (fig. 13) show alternating periods of high and low precipitation, but the trends suggest a general decline since the late 19th century (pls. 81.1–2). Precipitation declined sharply during the drought of the 1930s and has done so more gradually since the late 1960s. The 1970s brought comparatively severe winters, in marked contrast to the 1980s, a decade of winter drought. However, note that the annual precipitation dropped less sharply; this happened because of a number of very wet summers.[7]

Winter temperatures and snow cover combine to limit the access of large herbivores to winter forage; consequently, winter conditions set upper limits to their population sizes in the park. An index of relative winter severity was produced by combining monthly precipitation and temperature records.[8] The severity index for 1888–1990 on Yellowstone's northern range not only demonstrated striking annual variability but suggested a trend to comparatively milder winters (fig. 14). We will return to the issue of ungulates, climate, and vegetation (see part 3, "Grazing Dynamics").

We draw a number of lessons from this examination of climatic trends in relation to the interpretation of the photographs. First, the climate of Yellowstone has changed continually on the scale of millennia, centuries, and decades; these changes have affected vegetation. Our earliest photos show vegetation at the end of the Little Ice Age. The climate of that cold period affected natural vegetation and the resulting landscapes as well as

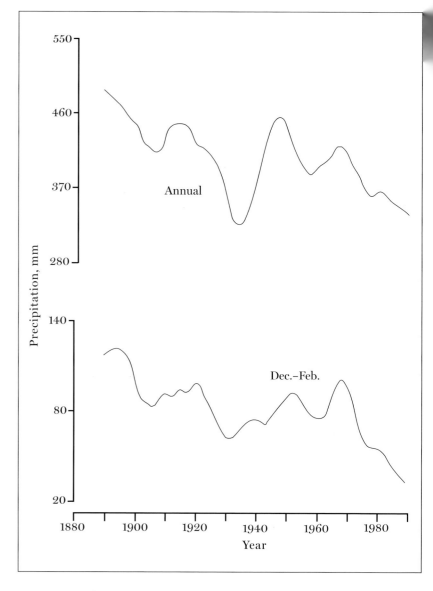

Fig. 13. *Annual and midwinter (December–February) precipitation trends at Mammoth, Yellowstone National Park.*

human populations and agriculture.[9] Many of the large trees visible in the early forest scenes (and in retakes) became established during this neoglaciation. Because of the ensuing climatic change, there is no particular reason to think that when these older forests die (because of fire, insects, blowdown, and age), the sites will be colonized by forests that are the same. Second, some of the photo comparisons hint tantalizingly at climate as the direct influence on the subtle vegetation shifts observed—granting the difficulties of separating climatic effects from localized influences such as ungulate grazing and rubbing, episodic seed production, or the interaction of several factors. For example, several of the comparative sets of photographs show changes in plant composition from a wet meadow type to drier grasslands. We do not expect the photographs

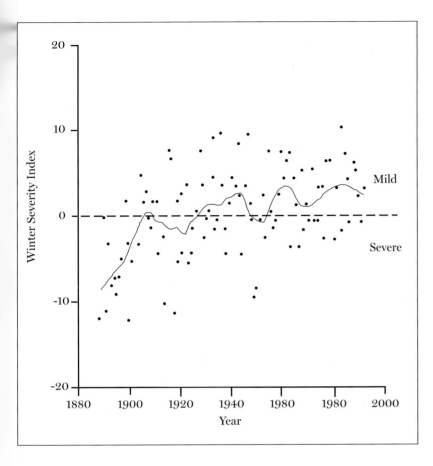

Fig. 14. *Relative winter severity index for Mammoth, Yellowstone National Park, 1888–1990.*

to show extensive changes in vegetation in response to recent climatic trends, but subtle shifts seem reasonable and inevitable. Indeed, the overall lesson is that the vegetation changes documented visually, regardless of other factors involved, must always be interpreted within the framework of known climatic events and trends, particularly the Little Ice Age and subsequent warming of the historic period.

Soils commonly have a major but subtle role in the patterns of vegetation across the landscape. This is because soils represent a combination of geologic and climatic factors interacting over time. The parent bedrock for a given soil determines the mineral nutrient content. Climate influences the weathering process of the bedrock and determines soil moisture. As soils form, the vegetation contributes to further soil formation. The result is soil-deprived (edaphic) control over vegetation in a given locale. The extensive, comparatively sterile lodgepole pine forests of the Yellowstone Plateau reflect the underlying nutrition-poor soils derived from the rhyolite lava flows of the Yellowstone caldera. In contrast, the more productive northern range soils were derived largely from andesites.[10] In the comparative photographs, edaphic controls may explain the presence of a meadow that persists generally in shape regardless of disturbance such as fire (pls. 55.1–3, 79.1–3, 89.1–3).

The Biological Landscape: Vegetation and Change

Over the past two decades numerous paleoecological records have become available for describing past plant communities. These records show that vegetation has changed on almost all temporal and spatial scales in response to natural environmental variations. Species have responded individually to climatic variations, and as a result plant communities have generally been transient assemblages.

BRUBAKER (1988)

Vegetation serves as the expression of change in biological time. Roughly 95 percent of Yellowstone National Park is covered by vegetation that grows in patterns according to soils, climate, and the frequency of disturbance.[1] Patterns change over time. Short-term changes in vegetation are relatively easy to recognize, as when spectacular wildflower summers occur in contrast to the more modest displays of drier years. The growth of trees over several years is also relatively obvious. But when human attention shifts from plants as individuals to patterns of vegetation, the changes are often less apparent. Events such as fire command attention, but the gradual renewal thereafter takes longer to be recognized. Comparative photographs allow us to telescope vegetation changes in time.

The scenes shown in the sets of photographs vary strikingly. To identify patterns among them, rather than losing ourselves in sometimes fascinating detail, we examine the changes recorded in the comparisons by major vegetation categories (appendix 2). For each we look first at the shifts observed after approximately a century, and then at conditions after the fires of 1988 as shown by the retakes of 1990 through 1993. Comments include differences in the extent of changes with elevation. Finally, we compare changes observed inside the park to those in areas outside it, because the collection contains 22 sets of photographs taken nearby.

The 1988 fires gave us the opportunity to test some of our earlier interpretations of the forces that drove vegetation changes (plant succession) observed from 1871 until 1988. We use the comparisons, plus a host of recent supporting studies, to speculate on the course of plant succession following the 1988 fires.

So, what has happened?

FORESTS

From 1871 until the fires of 1988. Changes in Yellowstone's forests (approximately 80 percent of the land area of the park) differed with community type and elevation (fig. 15), as shown by 300 comparative photo sets. Overall, the vast tracts of conifer forest between about 2,300 and 2,600 m (7,500-8,500 ft) that so characterize the central and southern portions of the park changed little in appearance or extent during the century (preceding 1988). Lodgepole pine dominates these forests, with subalpine fir and Engelmann spruce occurring in the moist, older stands, particularly along streams, lakeshores, and on north slopes. Locally, some of these forests form a near-impenetrable jungle; early travelers commented on the difficulties of crossing quantities of fallen trees and logs.[2] Most of the comparisons (appendix 2; for example, pls. 84.1-2) within this elevation zone showed tree invasion into nonforested vegetation types (forest parks, sedge meadows, riparian shrub communities), often by just a subtle shift in the forest edge as trees increased in density or area. More extensive changes occurred where forests recolonized earlier burned stands; dense stands of lodgepole pine often developed in a century or less (pls. 33.1-2, 38.1-3).

Forests dominated by subalpine fir and whitebark pine at higher elevations (above 2,600 m or 8,500 ft) also increased in area as trees colonized subalpine meadows and herblands. As on the lower elevation plateaus, increases were frequently subtle but included extensive recolonization of early burns. High elevation forests sometimes showed intriguing internal increases in tree density (pls. 17-19).

More dramatic change in the distribution, density, and composition of forests characterized many sites below 2,300 m (7,600 ft). Douglas-fir and lodgepole pine forests expanded into a wide variety of nonforested types on most slope exposures (particularly ENE to WNW slopes). In contrast, Engelmann spruce and subalpine fir increased to a much lesser extent, mainly along streams. Rocky Mountain juniper also increased on some low elevation sites. Changes took place on a wide variety of soils derived from different types of parent materials, and frequently occurred where evidence of earlier fires was visible in the original scenes (pls. 8.1-3, 53.1-3, 72.1-3). Suppression of natural fires during the past century throughout the low elevation areas of the park contributed substantially to these changes. We will have more to say on this later.

Snags (dead trees) were common in the forests of early photos. In addition to fire-killed trees, others were killed by forest insects, old age, and unknown causes; these showed as scattered gray snags (pls. 16.1-3). Clearly, a wide variety of natural forces disturbed early forest communities, just as happens today. We assume that individual fallen trees some-

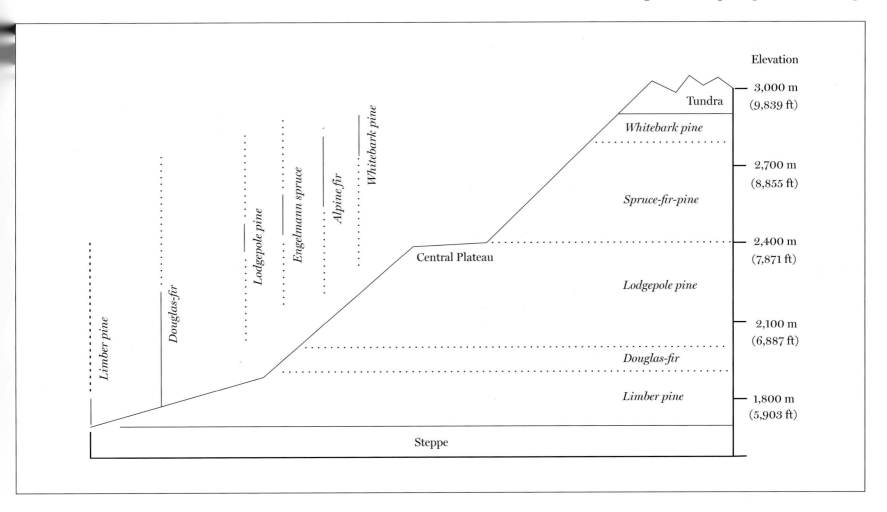

Fig. 15. *Distribution of dominant forest types along an altitudinal gradient. Dotted vertical lines show where a species is present but not important. Adapted from Whitlock (1993).*

times represented windthrow; lodgepole pine is notoriously vulnerable to this because of its shallow root system. Accordingly, we also assume blow-downs disturbed the earlier forest canopy. Individual trees, snags, and logs identifiable by characteristically shaped branches persisted for more than a century on sites from all elevations (pls. 74.1–3, 78.1–2).

The most striking change in the forests below about 2,400 m (7,800 ft) involved the reduction in area and density of aspen and its replacement by conifers, particularly along early forest/grassland boundaries. Aspen declined at other sites as well, including floodplains, wet swales, and springs on south slopes; these sites formerly occupied by aspen usually became sagebrush steppe or nonnative timothy grass meadow. In the 1871–1900 photographs, aspen nearly always appeared as dense clumps composed of short trees (actually clones of genetically identical stems; pls. 53.1, 54.1). Open stands of large mature trees were rare; only one of 22 scenes of aspen (pl. 66.1) on the northern range taken before 1901 showed a stand of mature trees—the situation so common today (appendix 2). Moreover, later comparisons documented the maturation and subsequent decline of the dense stands in the early scenes; 38 of 42 scenes first photographed after 1900 showed stands dominated by medium to tall aspen.

Stand maturation occurred in the presence of high densities of ungulates,[3] and some stands showed successful vegetative reproduction, at least on their margins, into the 1920s. These later scenes also showed the invasion of aspen understory by conifers. The photos usually did not show another important occurrence, the invasion of stands not by conifers but by nonnative timothy grass. This tough exotic not only dominated the understory but may have displaced native forbs. We think that the changes in aspen were also tied strongly to fire suppression, and an early narrative account underscores this point. Geologist Arnold Hague observed that fires had occurred frequently in the northern part of Yellowstone during the 19th century and that aspen was "the first tree to spring up upon recently burned areas. By so doing it helps conceal unsightly charred trunks, and adds bright color to the landscape."[4]

Forest changes appeared to be general for the area and not unique to the park. Sixteen comparative sets taken outside the north, east, and south boundaries of Yellowstone (pls. 1.1–2, 64.1–3) all showed increases in forest area and density, and shifts in species composition, comparable to those within the park (originals dating 1871 through 1900).

After the fires of 1988. Approximately 35 percent of the total park forest burned in 1988 (2,500 km², about 970 mi²); the extent of the fires is shown in figure 2. Fire created a fascinating mosaic of size and intensity. Mixed burns covered some 1,200 km² (460 mi²) with unburned patches and light ground-cover burns interspersed among scorched and blackened stands of trees; extensive crown fires burned an estimated 1,300 km² (500 mi²). Both mixed and crown fire resulted in stand replacement.[5] Consequently, the 160 photo comparisons of burned forests taken during the 1990s documented early postfire effects that ranged from subtle changes in understory composition to dramatic elimination of entire stands. We learned that trees sometimes required several years to die, and their dying was not always apparent at the moment of a photograph. Thus, fire occurred both as an event and as a process.

Stand-replacing fires clearly reset the biological time frame. Based upon the changes visible in the early photo comparisons and detailed studies of forest succession,[6] we expect forests to reclaim the burns but to differ in kind by climatic and site-specific factors (soils, exposure, seed availability). Rate may vary among sites depending on size of burn and available seed source. For burns on the plateaus, lodgepole pine seedlings often established in the first few years after the fires, but plant cover will be dominated for a decade or more by herbs and grasses until the pines begin to dominate. On wetter and cooler sites, lodgepole pine may eventually give way to subalpine fir and spruce. In subalpine areas, the intensively burned forests could be dominated by grasses and herbs for a longer time. As trees reestablish, those species that made up the preburn forest, especially subalpine fir, will likely dominate the postfire forests. Whitebark pine will appear especially at the higher elevations, and on some higher sites it will persist. At low elevations, Douglas-fir and lodgepole pine will likely recolonize relatively quickly.

We cannot predict the long-term response of aspen at this time; the question is complex. Some burned stands showed profuse regrowth after the fire, others showed none. Many stands may have deteriorated before the fires to a point that they will be unable to resprout and grow vigorously enough to escape browsing. On the other hand, aspen seedlings, although considered rare with the present climate of the northern Rocky Mountains, sprouted profusely where former sedge meadows burned down to mineral soil (pls. 54.1–3). Aspen as a species is unlikely to disappear in the foreseeable future; it grows widely in shrub form in the park. But its future as a tree is uncertain (see part 3, "Grazing Dynamics").

These predictions about patterns and rates of succession require assumptions about future climates and associated fire frequency, which can be a hazardous guessing game, particularly at the end of the 20th century. But given what we have seen and photographed, we expect that for-est will replace forest for the immediate future and will grow to a respectable size on many sites in less than a century (pls. 38.1–3).

Finally, it is worth noting the changes in *unburned* forests at sites during the past 15–20 years, between the initial retakes of scenes in the 1970s and those from the 1990s (pls. 14.2–3). These comparisons provided a sense of tree growth rate at different elevations and also showed that forest invasion of other vegetation types continued at all elevations (pls. 1.1–2, 10.1–3, 30.1–3, 31.1–3, 43.1–2, 90.1–3, 94.1–3, 100.1–3; also appendix 2).

SAGEBRUSH GRASSLANDS

From 1871 to the fires of 1988. Although four shrubby species of sagebrush occur in the park, big sagebrush predominates as the canopy species, with an understory of native bunchgrasses and forbs. One hundred and thirty-six comparisons of sagebrush grasslands, mostly below 2,600 m (8,500 ft), showed a complex pattern of change. Roughly one-third of all stands showed no difference in either area or density of sagebrush plants, one-third showed decreases, and one-third showed marked increases. Below about 2,300 m (7,500 ft) on the northern range, 13 of 32 comparisons with originals taken before 1901 showed extensive increases (pls. 52.1–3, 53.1–3). We believe that this too was due to fire suppression. Big sagebrush is very sensitive to burning. Volatile oils in its leaves cause plants to burn intensely, killing them outright because they do not resprout from the root crown as do so many other shrubs.

Where decreases in sagebrush grassland occurred, conifer invasion appeared mostly responsible, except along the north boundary line of the northern winter range.[7] This 4,900-hectare (12,700-acre) area (fig. 3) is mostly semi-arid grassland, some of which was part of the park as established in 1872, with the rest added in 1932 after a long history of intensive year-round livestock grazing. The substrate is composed mostly of a series of extensive mudflows, differing in age, clay content, and history of human use. These mudflows support an impoverished-appearing vegetation (pls. 2.1–3). Neither the ecology of this boundary line land addition nor its history of human activities is representative of the rest of the park, but the area is ecologically important.[8]

The photo comparisons for these lands at the north boundary suggest that big sagebrush first increased substantially on sites that were grazed intensively by livestock. This probably occurred because grass and forb cover was reduced by livestock grazing and fires were suppressed. Livestock was removed when the area was added to the park. Sagebrush began to decline. This decline probably was accelerated by native ungulates (pronghorn, mule deer, elk) foraging on the shrub, because these animals were concentrated at artificially high densities on nearby feedgrounds and with intensive hunting immediately outside the boundary. Although native perennial grasses often increased, the composition of herbaceous vegetation was altered by both inadvertent and deliberate introduction of exotics such as cheatgrass, crested wheatgrass, quackgrass, and smooth brome.

Outside the north and south park boundaries, eight comparative photo sets (original views 1871–98) also showed complex changes in sagebrush grasslands. These included both stasis (lack of change) and increased sage cover on sites grazed during the past century by livestock (pls. 1.1–2), as well as local declines where forest began to invade.

After 1988. Forty-three photo comparisons taken two to four years after the 1988 fires showed that sagebrush was virtually eliminated from the burns (pls. 9.3, 46.3, 54.3, 59.3, 66.3). This provided a graphic demonstration of fire sensitivity and confirmed our earlier supposition that sagebrush had increased in some areas as a result of fire suppression. The burned perennial grasses and herbs resprouted to produce lush, vigorous stands.[9] At the time of the retakes, sagebrush seedlings already were recolonizing small bare areas where intense fire had killed even the herbaceous vegetation. The extent of recolonization will depend on the frequency of future fires as well as on factors such as wet summers, which favor seedling establishment.

Grasslands and Meadows, Forest Parks and Tundra

From 1871 to the fires of 1988. Two hundred and twenty-one comparisons provided insight into the dynamics of grasslands and other herbaceous vegetation. Overall, we were impressed by the absence of change in basic patterns and density of vegetation (pls. 48.1–3). Our ability to determine species composition was limited, but community dominants could be identified in many originals with reasonable certainty because of distinctive growth forms or flowers.[10]

Minor changes in area or density of most types of grasslands and meadows occurred as trees and sagebrush invaded at the margins. Still in all, the same characteristically shaped meadows were often recognizable more than a century later, amid expanses of forest (pls. 99.1–3).

Grassy meadows and drier bunchgrass steppes below 2,300 m (7,500 ft) showed the greatest change; many have been invaded by Douglas-fir, lodgepole pine, and big sagebrush during the past century. Although native species dominated most sites at the time of the retakes, introduced grasses occupied others. This was particularly true of formerly cultivated hay meadows in the Lamar Valley and along Slough Creek where pasture grasses, such as common timothy and smooth brome, were seeded intentionally. In the boundary line area, nonnative (exotic) grasses and forbs reflected the ranching history prior to 1932 and additional introductions since, both deliberate (crested wheatgrass) and inadvertent (cheatgrass and a host of forbs). Fourteen of 48 early scenes (see bunchgrass steppe/meadows, table A2-1, appendix 2) showed exotic species in retakes. Common timothy was especially apparent. This tough and aggressive perennial grass has invaded even remote areas of the park, probably initially along trail systems. Even though at most sites it represented sub-

stitution of one grass for another, this shift in species composition is unfortunate in a national park.[11]

A subset of the bunchgrass steppe communities, low density steppe, characterizes many ridgetops and upper slopes on ungulate winter ranges. These generally small, frequently windswept areas support low densities of native plant species—40 percent or less canopy cover—that grow under harsh environmental conditions of shallow soils and poor moisture retention. Depending on locale, they are very heavily grazed and trampled by elk, bighorn sheep, and bison during winter and into spring, as these sites commonly green up first. Although droppings usually carpet (and fertilize) these places, most such sites have inherently low potential to produce vegetation.[12] These areas appeared in our earliest views of the northern range (18 scenes; pls. 6.1, 50.1, 58.1, 74.1) and other winter ranges in the park (pl. 82.1). They seem to have remained essentially unchanged in area and vegetation density; we view them to be part of the natural biotic effects of native herbivores on grasslands. Similarly, note that the pattern of sparse vegetation on the steep west and south slopes of Mount Everts—which furnish winter range for bighorn sheep, mule deer, and elk—has remained essentially unchanged for more than a century (pls. 7.1–3, 44.1–3).

We were particularly impressed by the lack of change in many higher elevation forest parks, subalpine meadows, and herblands (pls. 12.1–3, 65.1–3). Meadows often occur where soil characteristics retard tree invasion. Relations are complex, but either fine-textured wet soils or shallow-textured dry soils allow grasslands and forest parks to persist.[13]

Vegetation on elk bedding areas (pls. 17, 18, 19) and isolated high elevation wintering sites (pls. 3.1–3) remained essentially unchanged. Sparse vegetation where snowbanks did not melt until July showed similar patterns over time (pls. 76.1–3, 77.1–3, 94.1–3). The meager plant growth on highly erodible Absaroka volcanic substrates also showed little apparent change, despite considerable erosion over the past century (pls. 70.1–3). Tundra subjected to the harsh environmental conditions at more than 3,170 m (10,400 ft) on the east boundary appeared immune to the passage of time (pls. 71.1–3).

Differences in standing crop visible in some comparisons may reflect variation in growing conditions between years, or differences in stages of plant growth because of dates when photographs were taken (pls. 16.1–3, 17–19, 90.1–3). These plant communities are also subjected to localized disturbance; frost heaving affects tundra soils and subalpine meadows are sometimes plowed by pocket gophers when their populations reach high densities. Some of the earliest scenes showed conspicuous gopher activity (pl. 20.1).[14]

Despite the general constancy in appearance of subalpine meadows and herblands, 10 scenes showed intriguing changes. These included striking shifts in species composition from wet meadows to drier grassland types (pls. 14.1–3) and increased plant density on late-melting snowbank sites (pls. 94.1–3, 95.1–3). These changes are discussed more fully later, but note that one factor driving change at higher elevations may be the shift to warmer temperatures after the Little Ice Age.

Nine early comparisons (originals taken 1871 through 1898) outside the boundaries of the park showed similar trends in grasslands. Two taken of meadows on Republic Creek at about 2,600 m (8,500 ft) showed more forest (also a decrease in willows, pls. 64.1–3). Seven scenes photographed north of the park along the Yellowstone River valley (elevations 1,340–1590 m/4400–5200 ft; up to about 60 km/38 mi distant) showed either displacement of former native grasslands by cultivated fields or shifts in species composition on livestock ranges (pls. 1.1–2). Native grasses still predominated, but exotic species like cheatgrass were locally abundant.

After 1988. Forty-two comparisons documented responses of different types of grassland communities to fire. Neither area nor density changed in about two-thirds of the scenes; the remainder showed increases in area as trees and shrubs were eliminated by fire. Species composition was often similar to preburn conditions. As in burned sagebrush grasslands, the regrowth of burned grasses frequently showed remarkable increases in plant vigor and standing crop, particularly for the perennial bunchgrasses. This reflected a rapid recycling of nutrients postfire coupled with favorable moisture conditions.

Exceptions to the widespread increases in standing crop occurred in some burned subalpine meadows and herblands. There, standing crop as photographed two to four years postburn was lower, even though species composition roughly mirrored preburn conditions (pls. 16.1–3). This probably represented slower recovery of perennial species from burning under subalpine conditions of short growing seasons and cooler temperatures compared to lower elevations. Differences in growing seasons at the time of the retakes were probably not involved, as conditions appeared to be at least average for temperature and moisture. Grazing by elk and bison was not a probable factor in these comparisons with one exception, the meadows at the head of the Mirror Fork (pls. 90.1–3). Increasing numbers of bison used the Mirror Plateau intensively in August after 1988 and reduced the standing crop.[15]

As with unburned forests, unburned grasslands showed little change in the 15–20 years since the retakes of the 1970s. Exceptions represented continued invasion by conifers.

Willows and Other Riparian Shrubs

From 1871 to the fires of 1988. Seventy-nine scenes showed changes in riparian shrub communities located mostly below 2,600 m (8,500 ft). These communities were usually dominated by several willow species but often contained other shrubs, such as mountain alder and shrubby cinquefoil, and occasionally water birch, smooth sumac, or cottonwood. Of 37 early scenes (originals taken before 1901), 27 showed a decrease in riparian shrubs, particularly willows (pls. 11.1–3, 27.1–3, 60.1–3). The remainder showed either no change or an increase in willow (pls. 21.1–3, 83.1–3; also appendix 2). Similarly, 35 of 42 scenes first photographed from 1901 to 1944 showed decreases in willow. Photo comparisons and narrative accounts both suggested that decreases were especially pronounced on upper floodplain terraces during the prolonged, intense drought of the 1930s. Decreases occurred on ungulate winter ranges (pls. 57.1–3, 60.1–3) where willows were heavily browsed and on high elevation summer ranges (pls. 12.1–3, 13.1–3, 62.1–3, 63.1–3, 97.1–3). Willows decreased on active floodplains (pls. 62.1–3) as well as in meadows well removed from streams (pls. 97.1–3). Willow stands were replaced by coniferous forest, sedge meadows, and other meadow types. We should note here that willows were removed physically from some sites developed for hay meadows during the early operations of the park (pls. 57.1–3). However, herbivores (ungulates, beavers, insects) clearly influenced the rate of willow decline, and we will discuss their roles as well as other forces involved in the observed changes. Cottonwood appears to have been quite limited in extent originally (pls. 4.1–2, 58.1–3), and perhaps quite site-specific in occurrence (see part 3, "Grazing Dynamics," Rare plant communities).

The collection contains 14 scenes of riparian shrub communities outside Yellowstone. Nine comparisons (originals taken 1871 through 1900) of drainages north (up to 60 km, 38 mi), east (25 km, 16 mi) and south (90 km, 56 mi) of the park were mostly from sites at 2,100–2600 m (6900–8500 ft) elevation. Six showed that willows (plus alder and cottonwood at one site) also decreased outside the park (see pls. 64.1–3), two showed little change in a tall willow community, and one showed extensive human alteration (channelization, diking) of a cottonwood site. Five later scenes (originals taken 1916–1930) showed either no change or decreased willow (three of the five also had reduced alder; cottonwood decreased at one site) at elevations ranging from 1,920 to 2,410 m (6,300–7,900 ft).

Seven early scenes (originals taken 1885 through 1900) of riparian vegetation taken at sites between 2,100 and 2,600 m (6,900–8,500 ft) elevation, both inside (four scenes) and outside the park suggested that changes occurred in the dynamics of small to moderate-sized streams. At Cougar Meadows, the stream simply dried up during the past century (pls. 29.1–2). Five sites showed more gravel exposed within the original stream beds compared to the retakes, in which the overall plant cover was greater (pls. 62.1–3). These five comparisons suggest that the streams have become more channelized, with less lateral movement across their floodplains. Depending on site, several factors may be at work. It may be that these changes reflect the widespread shift to warmer, drier climates during this century. The raw appearance of the original stream deposits also could reflect the effects of local flooding, perhaps the result of particularly severe cloudbursts or earlier fires upstream. We watched runoff pulses from burned watersheds change stream dynamics in 1991 and 1993, creating more active streams with braided channels and abundant exposed substrate.[16]

After 1988. Fourteen scenes showed variable responses of willows to fire, all from sites below 2,300 m (7,500 ft) elevation. Willows decreased in 11 scenes, and either remained constant or increased in three. Decreases were particularly apparent where willows formed the overstory above dense sedge growth (pls. 9.1–3, 22.1–2). On such sites the fires burned down through accumulated layers of dry organic material and killed the willow root crowns. Elsewhere, burned willows resprouted and grew vigorously after the fires (pls. 21.1–3).

SEDGE MEADOWS

From 1871 to the fires of 1988. Sedge meadows occurred mostly below 2,600 m (8,500 ft); these were frequently dominated by one or two species such as beaked sedge, inflated sedge, or Nebraska sedge. Drier sites often contained a large component of grasses, particularly tufted hairgrass. More than two-thirds of 55 scenes showed increases in area of sedge, particularly as the result of decreased willow density (pls. 9.1–3). Additionally, six scenes provided fascinating examples of succession from open-water ponds to dense sedge-grass meadows (pls. 24.1–3, 49.1–3); these were frequently associated with early beaver activity. The remaining comparisons mostly showed no change in these highly productive communities, which, incidentally, provide important food supplies for bison in many areas of the park.

After 1988. Highly variable effects were visible in sedge communities. In five cases no change in area or density was apparent, but the burned sedges resprouted and produced lush stands. The most interesting situations occurred where fires burned down as much as 1 m (3 ft) into deep layers of peatlike material and actually killed areas of sedge. When we walked these sites in the fall of 1988, we had ash over our boot tops. In contrast, during a more usual summer we would have water in our boots. These intensely burned sites, still blackened in the retakes (pl. 9.3), were being recolonized by sedges and sometimes by aspen seedlings.

PLANT COVER ON GEOTHERMAL GROUND

Geothermal sites appeared quite variable in a given scene, with intermixed patches of bare siliceous sinter, herbaceous plant growth varying from sparse grass to dense patches of sedge, and lodgepole pines. Geothermal activity likewise varied, from warm ground to active hot springs and geysers. Twenty-nine of 35 comparisons (originals taken pre-1901) showed increased vegetation; of these, 20 showed more ground cover and nine had more lodgepole pine (pls. 34.1–3, 35.1–3, 80.1–3). Similar trends were apparent in seven later comparisons (pls. 32.1–3). These changes demonstrated that subterranean points of geothermal heat shift frequently and that cooler soil temperatures were responsible for some site-

specific vegetation increases. There is no reason to presume a generalized decrease of geothermal activity.[17] In some cases, the increased vegetation might reflect channeling of human activity to boardwalks. Climatic trends, soil development, and plant succession all likely played roles in the changes.

OTHER ITEMS OF INTEREST

Virtually every time we looked at the photographs, something new would strike us. Sometimes this was just for fun, trivial but interesting, such as the fisherman on Soda Butte Creek (pl. 62.1). Sometimes what we saw was a product of our learning; we would realize, for instance, that individual wildrye plants actually persisted for many decades (pls. 57.1–3). So did shrubs (pls. 44.1–3). We could see the edges of early fires, such as occurred on Bunsen Peak in 1886 (pl. 8.1). Comparative photographs of the ridge off Parker Peak put erosion into a biological time frame for us (pls. 70.1–3). And traces left by earlier human activity, such as the scars of abandoned roads (pls. 55.1–3, 76.1–3, 77.1–3), served to remind us to take care of Yellowstone because recovery times for some forms of physical disturbance may be measured in centuries.

YELLOWSTONE VEGETATION IN A REGIONAL CONTEXT

Elements of vegetation change and constancy documented for Yellowstone were not unique to the park or even to the surrounding area. In addition to the 22 scenes in this collection from sites outside but near the park, 10 published studies were available for comparison. These contained more than 570 different scenes of vegetation change in the northern and central Rocky Mountain region[18] and spanned a latitudinal range of about 1,100 km (680 mi) from northernmost Idaho and Montana through Wyoming and southern Idaho to the Colorado Front Range (appendix 3). George Gruell's wonderful series of comparisons was particularly relevant because these virtually surrounded Yellowstone and contained many early scenes from the national forests. Additionally, we were given access to unpublished photographs of Banff National Park in Alberta, Canada.

The other studies provided a useful and necessary perspective for the Yellowstone locale. Comparisons with other photographic studies allowed us to assess the geographic extent of particular vegetation changes and also the driving forces. A change that occurred regionally likely signaled a common cause, because special causes do not produce general effects.[19]

Basically, the changes in forest area and density documented for Yellowstone National Park were common to the northern and central Rocky Mountain region. Conifers at high elevations invaded adjacent meadows and grasslands during the past century; increases in area and density were greatest where evidence of fire was apparent in the original scenes. The most striking changes occurred at low elevations, where coniferous forest area and density showed dramatic increases, apparently also associated with reductions in fire occurrence. Changes in forest composition were often similar to those in Yellowstone; aspen declined and conifers increased. Aspen and cottonwood were replaced regionally on floodplains by various species of conifers.

Although more difficult to assess regionally, the *extent* of the forest changes also seemed roughly comparable. Coniferous forest increases in western Montana and northern Idaho were, if anything, even more dramatic than in the park. Possible exceptions involved the age distribution and recruitment of young stems to the periphery of some aspen stands, that sometimes seemed greater outside the park (see part 3, "Grazing Dynamics," introduction). But overall, in the absence of fire (and with present climate and levels of herbivory), aspen seemed clearly destined to be replaced by conifers across much of the region.

As in Yellowstone National Park, sagebrush grasslands showed complex changes. We cannot judge the overall extent of change regionally, other than to note that increases in sage and associated shrubs were common to areas outside that also used to burn frequently. As observed inside the park, big sagebrush decreased locally at sites across the region. For all its apparent hardiness, the plant is surprisingly susceptible to mortality from drought, spring frosts, excessive moisture, and insect herbivory (grasshoppers and aroga moths).[20]

Outside the park, many lower elevation native grasslands and sedge-grass meadows have been converted to hayfields. However, apart from this, grasslands at all elevations have shown a remarkable lack of change regionally, except for coniferous forest invasion and sagebrush increases at low elevations.[21] The other studies also showed low-density steppe vegetation on ridgetops and steep slopes throughout the region. These changed little over time on ungulate ranges, where they were associated with sites of low growing potential, on shallow soils and steep south slopes. Finally, comparative photos from national forests around Yellowstone National Park show increases in the density of herbaceous vegetation above about 2,700 m (8,800 ft), as do several park scenes.[22]

Regional changes in riparian shrubs and sedge meadows were more difficult to compare, because these plant communities have often borne the brunt of agricultural development and water manipulation projects (irrigation and upstream diversions). Many former willow communities have been cleared or drained, planted to exotic cultivated grasses, or subjected to intensive livestock use. Even so, diverse changes occurred in the native communities. Willows and associated deciduous species, including aspen and cottonwoods, have been replaced by conifers on floodplains and at wet sites throughout the region. However, stasis in heavily browsed willow communities was particularly apparent in the deep-snow areas of northern Jackson Hole.[23] Dramatic localized decreases of willow stands caused by land subsidence and flooding after the 1959 Hebgen earthquake showed on the Madison River both inside the park (pls. 28.2–3),

and in Bureau of Land Management photos taken to the west. Willow communities at some regional sites showed different plant structure (taller shrubs, more lateral branches, sometimes decadent upper branches) compared to those in the park. These variations in structure may result from different intensities of browsing or different species of browsers (see part 3, "Grazing Dynamics," introduction). Intense livestock utilization contributed to the decline of willows in riparian areas outside the park, particularly at lowland sites where animals have been concentrated on feedgrounds during winter and early spring. Other environmental forces have contributed, however, because declines have also occurred on livestock summer ranges where grazing was moderate. Willows declined where hydrologic regimes have been altered by fire suppression, elimination of beaver, development of irrigation projects, stream channelization, and climatic shifts.[24]

Similarly, cottonwoods on floodplains elsewhere continued to show recruitment on the peripheries of stands in some areas, in contrast to several small sites in the park. But many other areas outside showed maturation of cottonwoods, no successful young tree establishment, and replacement of cottonwoods by conifers.

Thus, in our judgment, both the nature and—to a considerable degree—the extent of most vegetation changes documented in the Yellowstone photographs seemed broadly comparable to those in areas adjacent to the park and throughout the region. Comparisons among studies such as we have attempted are necessarily subjective; we urge interested readers to look at the other studies and perhaps extend or counter our interpretations.

But comparisons with Yellowstone are limited because differences in climate and plant communities become more pronounced as one moves farther north and south of the park. For example, the Banff comparisons provided striking cases of primary plant succession at sites where ice fields melted back during this century. (We are 10,000 years too late for such photo comparisons in Yellowstone.) Ponderosa pine forests have shown remarkable increases in density throughout the region, but this tree species does not occur in Yellowstone.

Yellowstone is also unique because of the geothermal activity and early date of establishment as a national park with protective land use objectives. The latter has resulted in the persistence of nearly all native animal species, intermittently at densities approaching ecological carrying capacity (see part 3, "Grazing Dynamics"). Moreover, activities such as cultivation, livestock grazing, and forest management practices generally have been limited in the park compared to outside (see part 3, "The Human Presence"). Indeed, the photographs showed that a problem frequently encountered by those conducting comparative vegetation studies outside the park was finding sites that had not been extensively altered by the technology of Euroamericans.

PART 3

Agents of Change

Climate, Fire, and Earth Forces

Vegetational changes in the northern Rocky Mountains are a response to changes in climate, biotic interactions, and edaphic controls operating on different time scales.

WHITLOCK (1993)

Addressing agents of change is more hazardous than it might appear initially because environmental factors almost never operate separately and their influences may be complex, dynamic, and sometimes obscure. Synergistic relationships occur commonly in ecosystems where two factors acting in concert produce amplified effects on plants; effects are not merely doubled but are increased severalfold. Thus, plant mortality from cold temperatures is greater than expected if low levels of sunlight reduce photosynthesis at the same time. Similarly, extreme drought may impair a plant's ability to withstand otherwise tolerable levels of herbivory. We appreciate these complexities and realize that full understanding of all the environmental factors that interact to bring about the observed plant community changes is impossible. Nevertheless, five forces seem to merit attention as powerful influences on vegetation change in Yellowstone. Three are abiotic in kind: climate, fire, and the earth itself. Two are biotic: herbivory and human activities.[1]

RECENT CLIMATIC CHANGE

The park. The oldest coniferous trees in the park exceed 500 years of age.[2] Hence, the time scale of interest for evaluating possible climatic effects on the vegetation shown in the photographs includes the Little Ice Age, its waning near the end of the 19th century, and subsequent trends to warmer temperatures and reduced precipitation, which seemed especially sharp during the drought of the 1930s. Interactions among the other factors that have affected plant community change must have played out against (and interacted with) the backdrop of these climatic changes.

The increase in conifer establishment (for example, pls. 20.1–3, 21.1–3, 77.1–3, 84.1–2) in subalpine meadows of the park has been documented in many other mountain ranges in western North America. In the Rocky Mountains, this trend involved pulses of tree establishment that seem to have been strongly associated with warm and dry periods and the consequent reductions in snowpack. Tree invasion in Yellowstone has been occurring since the mid-1800s. Lodgepole pine establishment in drier subalpine meadows seems to be associated with warmer and wetter growing seasons since the end of the Little Ice Age. Thus, climatic shifts seem to have been the main force driving these changes. However, climatic influences may differ according to geographic locale. Fire (very infre-

quent at high elevations) and herbivory may have played secondary roles.[3]

If recent climatic changes have affected the distribution of trees at high elevations, then it is not unreasonable to expect other climate-related vegetation changes to be captured in the photo comparisons. The increased density and area of herbaceous vegetation at late-melting snowbank sites above 2,700 m (8,855 ft) may reflect a strong climatic influence (pls. 94.1–3, 95.1–3). Photo comparisons taken at high elevations south and east of Yellowstone provide more consistent and compelling examples of increased vegetation density.[4] Reduced snowpacks likely would have extended growing seasons and improved opportunities for plant establishment. For instance, long-lived herbaceous species, such as arnica, might be favored through proliferation of new stems from the spreading root systems.

The shifts of herbaceous vegetation communities in upland meadows (pls. 14.1–3) and in some sedge meadows (pls. 26.1–3, 49.1–3, 97.1–3, 98.1–3) of the park to "drier-appearing" conditions reflect changed soil-moisture relationships, which likely were climatically influenced. Increased forest cover may also play a part in changing the composition of meadows, by increasing evapotranspiration, which in turn may affect soil moisture in adjacent meadows.[5] This may have been particularly important at sites where early burns subsequently were recolonized by dense forests. The fires of 1988 provide opportunities to assess the relative strengths of such influences.

The change in willow distribution may also have been affected by climatic shifts. Willows and associated riparian shrubs declined on floodplains and meadows throughout much of the park; these were replaced by forests and herbaceous vegetation (pls. 23.1–2, 28.1–3, 60.1–3, 62.1–3, 63.1–3, 85.1–2, 93.1–3, 97.1–3, 98.1–3). Declines seemed especially pronounced during the 1930s drought,[6] and occurred outside the park as well (pls. 64.1–3). Yet willows persisted in deep-snow areas of the park, such as the upper Yellowstone River delta (pls. 100.1–3).

A regional perspective. Regionally, as mentioned earlier, two strikingly different climates occur in the Yellowstone area: summer-dry/winter-wet (southern) and summer-wet/winter-dry (northern). This pattern is determined by the interplay of regional atmospheric circulation patterns with more local topography.[7] Photo comparisons (from several collections) are limited, but they indicate that changes in riparian vegetation (pls. 36.1–3), willows in particular, have tended to be relatively more extensive at sites experiencing the summer-wet/winter-dry regime (northern winter range); and conversely, stasis has been somewhat more common at summer-dry/winter-wet sites (upper Yellowstone River, Bechler River, northern Jackson Hole). The reasons for this are not immediately clear; the drought of the 1930s may have had relatively greater effects at summer-wet sites. Alternatively, winter-wet sites may afford greater protection against browsing because precipitation occurs mostly as snow.

Willows at most low elevation areas in the park were heavily browsed, particularly during winter. The relatively recent occurrence and location of this browsing impact suggest that changes in soil moisture relationships adversely affected the willows' abilities to withstand browsing (see part 3, "Grazing Dynamics"). Changes in soil moisture may have resulted directly from the climatic events of the 20th century and, to some degree, from the effects of increased forest cover described earlier. This is not to deny that herbivores such as ungulates, beavers, and insects played powerful roles in these changes but simply to indicate that climatic/soil moisture events set the stage by making plants more vulnerable to herbivory while not killing them directly. Fire suppression also may have affected willow viability at some sites (see fire discussion, below). These complex relationships represent a good example of environmental forces acting synergistically with amplified effects on plants.

As mentioned earlier, the increased channelization of small streams shown in some comparisons might reflect the warmer temperatures and reduced precipitation of the 20th century, but stream channel changes must have been influenced as well by increased forest cover, local fires, and so forth (see discussion of riparian shrub communities in part 2, "The Biological Landscape"). It is noteworthy, however, that the climate of the Little Ice Age seems to have produced a distinctive depositional terrace known as the Lightning Terrace along rivers elsewhere in Wyoming. Deposition ceased with onset of a downcutting erosional cycle that began about 1880–1900.[8]

FIRE HISTORY AND PREHISTORY

Fire history. Fire and climate are inseparable, yet fire is itself an active and obvious agent that merits topical discussion. The Holocene climatic patterns already discussed suggest that fire should have had a role throughout the millennia. Lightning was probably the primary ignition source, sometimes aided by aboriginal peoples (see part 3, "The Human Presence"). Indeed, charcoal recovered from lake sediments indicates a long history of fire occurrence in the park.[9]

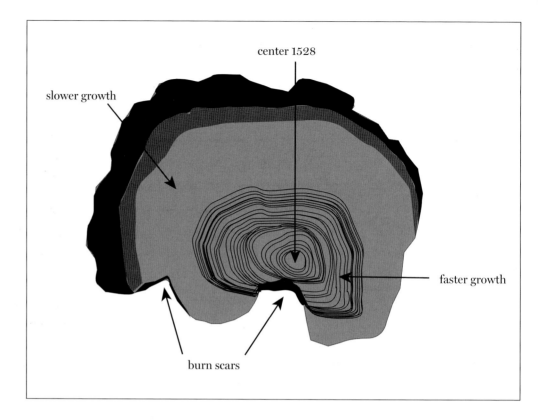

Fig. 16. *Diagrammatic cross section of a Douglas-fir tree from Yellowstone National Park. The tree was dated to 1528, making it approximately 450 years old at its death. Note variable width of tree rings and several overlapping fire scars, dated at 1575, 1762, and 1770.*

Dendrochronological techniques (tree-ring data) and fire scars have allowed the dating of trees and fire events (fig. 16). Charcoal deposits and magnetic susceptibility data recorded in lake and pond sediments have permitted some of Yellowstone's fire history to be extended about 750 years into the past.[10] This history varies geographically, just as the climate does. For the southwest part of the park, recent data indicate that large, infrequent fires occurred between about 1200 and 1660, followed by smaller, more frequent fires until about 1860 (pl. 36.1). On the Central Plateau (fig. 1), four burn periods occurred between about 1520 and 1780. Smaller fires likely maintained a mosaic of early to middle successional forest stages, but indications are that an extensive fire (or a series of smaller fires) occurred around 1700. Then, with the Little Ice Age, particularly its latter stages, fire frequency decreased, and forests grew to late successional age, with a concomitant buildup of fuels. Then came 1988!

In addition to geographic locale and climatic patterns, fire frequency over the last few centuries varied markedly by elevation. This, too, is a factor inseparable from prevailing local climate. On the northern range, particularly the lower elevations (roughly 2,000 m, 6,600 ft), mean fire intervals were much shorter, seemingly on the order of 20–30 years.

Comparable intervals occurred in grasslands and associated Douglas-fir forests at similar elevations across southwest Montana. Fires in the lower elevation forests in and out of the park seem to have been characterized by surface burns (as opposed to stand-replacing crown fires). Big sagebrush is an important fuel at low elevations, and several decades are required after a fire for sagebrush to become fully reestablished (pls. 75.1–2). The more rapid accumulation of volatile sagebrush fuels and more frequent occurrence of hot, dry burning conditions likely account for the shorter fire intervals in shrub steppe and associated forests at low elevations. Fairly extensive fires burned across northern Yellowstone about 1738, 1758, 1776, 1856, and 1870, creating the vegetation conditions shown in early photos (pl. 27.1).[11]

At higher elevations of the northern range where lodgepole pine forests grow (2,300–2,600 m, 7,500–8,500 ft), the burn interval was about 200 years. Above this, whitebark pine forests burned in stand-replacement fires at intervals exceeding 350 years.

Edaphic factors such as soil moisture and available nutrients also affect fire frequency by governing rate of tree growth and forest structure. Mean fire intervals in lodgepole pine forests growing on the more productive andesite-derived soils in the upper Lamar River seem to have been around 200 years. At comparable elevations in lodgepole pine forests on the Central Plateau, where soils derived from rhyolites are more acidic and less productive, with less moisture retention, the burn interval in recent centuries was apparently double—roughly 350–400 years.[12]

Regardless of the ignition source (mostly lightning, sometimes human), weather and fuels—forest structure, stand age, and species composition—are the most important factors affecting the presence, kind, and extent of fire. Ignition occurs frequently each year, but the vast majority of fire starts are extinguished naturally by wet weather or simple failure of fires to spread through sparse fuels. Fire intensity in subalpine forests depends on the interplay of fuels and weather. During marginal to moderate burning conditions, fuel accumulations ("fuel loads") influence the rate of fire spread and the occurrence of crown fires. During extreme conditions, such as in 1988, weather effectively overwhelms the role of fuels, and crown fires burn irrespective of levels of fuel accumulation (pl. 39.3). These very large fires are the ecologically important ones in terms of shaping landscape patterns.[13] They are also rare events in terms of human life spans, occurring at such infrequent intervals that they are outside the experience of most people, including fire ecologists.

Fire suppression. The effectiveness of historic fire suppression efforts varied by elevation and ease of access. By the 1970s, Euroamericans reduced the natural fire frequency on the northern winter range of the park for about 90 years by active suppression beginning in 1886, and perhaps by removal of Native Americans somewhat earlier (see part 3, "The Human Presence"). Fire was virtually eliminated as a natural force for about 40 years, from about 1930 until the early 1970s.

Suppression history was very different over most of the park forests at higher elevations. Fire suppression did not become effective until after World War II, particularly following the development of aerial fire fighting technology. Thus, in areas that burned naturally at intervals of two to four centuries, approximately 30 years of fire suppression probably did not add appreciably to fuel accumulations. Forests were essentially in a "natural state" at the time of the 1988 fires. We recognize that three of eight of the largest 1988 fires were not caused by lightning but by human ignition. This would call into question the "naturalness" of the outcome were it not for the hundreds of lightning strikes that occurred in and around the already active fires during late July and August. The forests would have burned in any event (although the resulting pattern might have been somewhat different), and the 1988 fires are not viewed as abnormal events.[14]

Fire suppression policies changed gradually beginning in 1972, when natural fires were allowed to burn again in a 136,000 ha (336,980-acre) area of Yellowstone. Natural fire zones were progressively enlarged (comparable zones were established on the adjacent national forests). Two hundred and thirty-five lightning fires burned 13,662 ha (33,816 acres) from 1972 to 1987, over 1.5 percent of the terrestrial area of the park. Then came 1988, when about 395,570 ha (979,133 acres) burned.[15] Despite the enormous public and political outcry, two professional review panels reaffirmed the importance of natural fire to the ecology of the park.[16] A modified fire management plan remains in effect.

The photos and the fires. Retakes of scenes following the 1988 fires confirm earlier interpretations of the importance of fire in the changes observed (pls. 8.1–3, 9.1–3, 46.1–3, 54.1–3, 82.1–3). But it is against the record of infrequent but large canopy fires at higher elevations and much more frequent burns at low elevations that we interpret the photo comparisons. Fire, and conversely the absence of fire, drove the most graphic and extensive changes captured in the photographs.

At higher elevations, evidence of fire was common in the earliest forest scenes (pls. 14.1, 31.1, 38.1, 79.1, 89.1, 91.1, 92.1). Many of the changes noted from 1871 until 1988 represented postfire succession. Many mature lodgepole pine stands visible in the earliest scenes must have become established following the extensive fires of the late seventeenth and early eighteenth centuries and consequently were about 200 years old when photographed initially. The subsequent photos did not, of course, show the inexorable accumulations of wood, duff, and other burnables under way during the past century that set the fuel stage for the 1988 forest fires.

It is difficult to overestimate the effects of fire and the recent exclusion of fire on the changes noted at lower, accessible elevations in the park, such as the northern range and portions of the Madison and Gallatin river drainages. By the 1970s, much of the northern range would have burned one to four times since park establishment (1872) were it not for suppression activities. The increased area and density of forests, increased distribution of sagebrush, and reduction of aspen were strongly linked to fire exclusion. Additionally, the replacement of willow, aspen (trees), and cottonwoods by conifers on floodplains probably resulted to a considerable extent from both the direct (prevention of burning) and indirect effects of fire exclusion. Indirect effects include possible changes in the hydrology of small streams and in soil moisture regimes from the increased abundance of forests and sagebrush.[17]

The extent to which these changes are reversible will be tested to some degree by the 1988 fires. Forests and sagebrush stands were dramatically reduced, as expected. Regeneration of aspen in tree form is more complex (see part 3, "Grazing Dynamics"). Some clones have resprouted vigorously, others have not, perhaps weakened by prolonged fire suppression and concurrent herbivory in a drier climatic regime. Still other aspen clones were lost to plant succession, replaced by conifers. This change may have been exacerbated by invading exotic grasses (see part 2, "The Biological Landscape") prior to the 1988 fires. Here again, synergisms come into play—aspen and other species must respond now in climates that differ from those of earlier establishment, during the Little Ice Age. Most tree-form aspen in the park occurs at the lower forest-grassland ecotone, where it may now find the warmer, drier climate less favorable.

The dramatic changes apparent in some scenes prompt a comment on human perceptions of "natural." Because disturbances from fire were frequent at low elevations and fire exclusion had considerable effect, the scenes so common today of lovely tall aspen trees juxtaposed against backdrops of closed-canopy Douglas-fir forests, probably were rare in the past. Tree-form aspen may have been a product of a unique combination of fortuitous circumstances that seldom occurred. If so, stands of tree-form aspen may represent a rare state rather than a formerly more constant presence. Fire disturbance seems to have been so frequent in the previous century[18] that only rarely would aspen have escaped the shrub or sapling stages to form full-sized trees. And certainly, fire maintained the Douglas-fir forests in a very different, more open state (pls. 53.1–3, 72.1–3).

Fire effects on other plant communities shown in the photo comparisons were likely powerful but more transitory. The vigorous bunchgrasses visible in the original scenes may well reflect frequent burning. Light burning is also known to stimulate willow production elsewhere,[19] and the robust stands shown in several early scenes may reflect this effect (pls. 29.1, 60.1, 96.1). As noted, the intense fires in some willow/sedge communities during 1988 killed several species of willow, rather than stimulating their growth. We do not know how common willow mortality from fire was in the past. The 1988 fires may have been unusually intense at these sites because of extreme summer drought after below-average-snowpack winters; the very dry conditions would have extended more deeply than otherwise into the root systems.

Regionally, burning is known to rejuvenate willows at both upland sites and in willow/sedge meadows by stimulating sprouting and eliminating competing vegetation. In the Jackson Hole area, a compelling case can be made from comparative photographs that fire was important in stimulating cottonwood regeneration and in eliminating invading conifers from cottonwood stands. Several authors of the photo comparison studies done outside the park (appendix 3) considered that fire, including recent fire exclusion, was the dominant force driving vegetation changes in their study areas.[20]

We cannot know what the future will bring us as regards climate change and the role of human influence on this. But the photographs should serve as baseline records for future plant succession (perhaps decades or even several hundred years hence, when the sites reburn). In a sense, the areas that burned returned to a biological starting point. The fires served as the curtain for the stage.

The Earth: The Fundamental Force

Earthquakes, erosion, crustal uplift, and shifts in geothermal activity have all produced vegetation changes within the time scale on which we focus in the photo comparisons. Because these earth forces in this locale appear to be a function of the Yellowstone hotspot (see part 2, "Assembling the Yellowstone Landscape"), we would observe that the Yellowstone hotspot also partly explains the biological face of Yellowstone.[21]

Specifically, the 1959 Hebgen earthquake affected floodplain elevations and consequently the distribution of riparian vegetation in and out of the park (pls. 28.1–3). Geologic erosion of the friable Absaroka volcanics sometimes forced us to shift camera points because the original had eroded away (pls. 70.1–3).

Perhaps most intriguing of all, crustal changes on the temporal scale of the photographs may have influenced drainage patterns and vegetation (pls. 85.1–2, 86.1–3, 100.1–3). We do not know how to interpret fully the effects of resurgent dome activity on the vegetation or to separate this influence from other forces (geothermal shifts, climate, human activities). But uplift of the magnitude recorded (1 m, 3.3 ft) and subsequent subsidence must have changed local streamflows and soil moisture characteristics, which likely altered vegetation composition and density.[22]

Finally, shifts in geothermal activity have changed vegetation locally in many geyser basins during the past century (pls. 31.1–3, 37.1–3, 42.1–2, 88.1–3). At the same time, natural change occurred rapidly in geothermal activity itself, as shown in photographs of major features. Minerva Terrace (pls. 6.1–3) at Mammoth Hot Springs changes constantly in small ways as calcium carbonate deposited from hot water seals vents or changes the water flow pattern. Yet as a long-recognized feature, with water flowing *somewhere*, it has persisted through historic time. In some instances, human activities, including vandalism, have contributed to the changed appearance of features, as at the Punchbowl and Old Faithful (pls. 38.1–3, 41.1–3). Siliceous sinter in the geyser basins accumulates much more slowly than does calcium carbonate at Mammoth, and consequently human impact lasts much longer.

Grazing Dynamics

A plant-herbivore system is not simply a vegetation suffering the misfortune of animals eating it. Rather it is an interactive system with massive feedback loops between the dynamics of the plants and the dynamics of the animals. Any disruption of those loops changes the system profoundly.

CAUGHLEY (1989)

Around the world, grazing systems have been examined intensively during the past 20 years. Work on long-evolved grazing systems, such as the Serengeti Plain, has shown that mammalian herbivores determine the genetic and species composition of the grassland vegetation to a substantial degree. Moreover, herbivory may actually increase plant productivity by accelerating the flow of nutrients through the ecosystem.

Moose browsing is known to change the species composition, structure, nutrient availability, and long-term dynamics of forests. Selective browsing by beaver plus their construction of dams and ponds causes profound, landscape-level changes along streams. The humble spruce budworm periodically defoliates and kills extensive tracts of coniferous forest in North America, dramatically altering forest composition and succession. The message from studies of these and other species is that mammal and insect herbivores interact powerfully with the vegetation; they are by no means passive components of ecological systems.[1]

Our work has focused on the effects of large mammals, particularly elk and bison, on the vegetation in Yellowstone National Park, but it is abundantly clear that herbivory by smaller species, including forest insects and pocket gophers, also has a profound influence on the vegetation. The effects of herbivory are often visible in the photo comparisons. We describe several important components of the Yellowstone grazing system, emphasizing facets and species that relate to interpreting the photographs.

The concept of carrying capacity in the grazing systems of free-ranging large mammals is more complex than it seems. Consider the simplest situation, in which a population of large herbivores, such as elk, increase in an area where predators, if present, are not regulating herbivore numbers. The equilibrium reached between herbivores and their food supply represents the maximum sustainable population level, ecological carrying capacity.[2] The animal side of this equilibrium is often reached through a sequence of higher losses of young, rising ages of sexual maturity, a lowered birth rate, and increased adult mortality. The plants show reciprocal changes: a much reduced standing crop, shifts in species composition, and changes in structure and chemical makeup. In harsh environments such as Yellowstone, the equilibrium between plants and animals is more accurately a "dynamic equilibrium," because plant growth and winter severity (which influence the number of large herbivores) fluctuate markedly between years. Thus, ecological carrying capacity is a fluctuating capacity in the short term and may exhibit longer-term trends as environmental parameters change.

Range and game managers generally mean something else by carrying capacity. A game manager's objective is often to maximize the sustained harvest of wildlife; most range managers aim for maximum yields from livestock. Cropping a population of large herbivores to produce a sustained yield reduces density to below the (unharvested) level of ecological carrying capacity. The maximum sustained yield is harvested from a density in the region between one-half and three-fourths of ecological carrying capacity. This point on the continuum of possible herbivore/vegetation densities has been called economic carrying capacity (somewhat unfortunately, because dual use of "carrying capacity" has produced confusion). Economic carrying capacity is characterized by a lower animal population and a higher standing crop of edible vegetation, and is the only carrying capacity usually recognized by range managers.

In marked contrast to the range management perspective, ecological carrying capacity is the dynamic equilibrium level most pertinent to large herbivores in national parks, including Yellowstone. The number of animals in a population fluctuating around ecological carrying capacity may be thought of as being "naturally regulated," in the sense that the dynamic equilibrium is not imposed by human cropping, artificial feeding, or other manipulation.[3]

What does all this mean for interpreting comparative photographs? First, because of the intensity of interaction between herbivores and vegetation, we expect to see effects from herbivory—animal populations must leave their mark on the landscape in some fashion. Second, because of the relationship between economic and ecological carrying capacity levels, we might expect to see more pronounced influences on the vegetation inside the park compared to outside. If densities of herbivores have changed substantially over the period covered by the photos, then we must be particularly careful about interpreting changes in the appearance of the vegetation.

Two examples serve to illustrate this last point. First, beaver populations were reduced widely by trappers from the 1820s to the early 1900s.

Within the park as we now know it, trapping was likely more sporadic, with major impact from the late 1820s to about 1840 and probably during the 1870s to early 1880s. The virtual elimination of these herbivores locally must have resulted in noticeable changes in the appearance of streams and streamside vegetation, and this effect may be reflected in our earliest photographs. Second, a host of explorers and frontiersmen traveling through the broader Yellowstone region during the first half of the 19th century, beginning with Lewis and Clark, reported astounding populations of bison, elk, pronghorn, and deer. These animals were eliminated from large areas outside the park during settlement by Euroamericans in the last quarter of that century. It was well into the first part of the 20th century before populations of all except bison recovered across the region (and now game managers usually strive to maintain populations closer to economic than to ecological carrying capacity). These historical changes have implications for interpreting the photographs, particularly comparisons involving conditions inside versus outside the park. The long-established grazing systems of the native species were destroyed before their effects on the vegetation could be captured in photographs.[4] Vegetation outside the park then developed for over a half-century without influence from these native grazers. Several livestock species were substituted for the native ungulates outside the park, but livestock grazing systems may differ appreciably from those of native herbivores.[5]

THE YELLOWSTONE GRAZING SYSTEM

Eight species of ungulates occur in and around Yellowstone, and although the habitats selected and diets preferred differ among species, their grazing regimes share important characteristics. Most migrate seasonally, food supplies are restricted during winter, and food quality changes markedly by season.[6] This review concentrates on elk and bison. Herbivory by small mammal species inhabiting the area has not been studied much in the park, but they represent important components of the grazing system. We focus on pocket gophers and beaver, because their activity is recorded in the photographs.[7]

Elk. Elk are the most abundant ungulates in Yellowstone, but their numbers vary greatly by season. Most elk in and around the park migrate from restricted low elevation winter ranges to expansive high elevation summer ranges located along hydrographic divides (fig. 17). Not all members of population units that winter outside summer inside; some move to other summer ranges. During late summer of the past decade, 25,000–31,000 elk were estimated to summer in the park.

Elk wintering on the lower Lamar, Gardner, and Yellowstone rivers have come to be known as the northern herd and the area they occupy is called the northern winter range or simply the northern range (fig. 17). The northern range is about 153,000 ha (591 mi²) in area. About 65 percent of the northern range lies within the park. The northern Yellowstone elk represent the park's single largest ungulate population, and the man-

agement of these animals has been extremely controversial. The controversy centers on whether the National Park Service should crop the elk in the park to maintain a particular equilibrium between elk and vegetation, or whether the park ecosystem has sufficient integrity for numbers to be regulated naturally to a considerable extent (recognizing that animals habitually wintering outside the park will be hunted).

This ongoing controversy necessitates a brief management history. The winter population of 12,000–16,000 elk that occurred in the 1930s to mid-1950s was reduced (mainly by National Park Service personnel) to around 4,000 animals by 1968. A moratorium on park removals began in 1969, to test the concept of natural regulation. The population rebounded, and winter numbers (post–hunting season) averaged 15,520 elk from 1982 to 1995. The upswing was associated with a sequence of nine near-average and mild winters unprecedented in historic time for Yellowstone (from 1980 through 1988, see fig. 13) and an expansion into additional winter range north of the park.[8] The extensive elk reductions of the 1960s provided a very useful perspective on the elk grazing system and an important test of the effects of elk herbivory (see part 3, "Grazing Dynamics," Herbivory in the Photo Comparisons).

For added perspective on the northern range grazing regime, note that of the eight ungulate species occupying the area, elk are by far the most numerous. Maximum counts for 1994 were 1,985 mule deer and 665 bison. Bighorn sheep were estimated to number 300, moose 400, and pronghorn 500. White-tailed deer and mountain goats hardly qualify as populations because their numbers are so low—probably less than 50. However, mountain goats have gradually begun to colonize the northern fringes of the park from introductions made by the State of Montana half a century ago in the mountains to the northwest and north.[9]

Although elk occupy portions of the northern range throughout the year, greatest densities occur from November through April. Elk are driven progressively into the valleys by deepening snows that produce increasingly severe environmental conditions. As winter progresses, the animals concentrate more and densities increase. Winter food supplies are essentially fixed after the killing frosts in late August to early September, in marked contrast to the forage available during the growing season on spring and summer ranges. This winter food supply, of relatively low nutritional quality, is composed of cured leaves and stems of dormant grasses, the twigs and some leaves of dormant shrubs, and the needles of conifers. Food quantity and quality are greatest during spring and summer when the forage consists of rapidly growing plants offering high concentrations of nutrients. Elk are amazingly versatile creatures. They occupy all vegetation types in the park at some season of the year and eat a wide variety of grasses, herbs, shrubs, and trees year-round. Elk herbivory affects the species composition of plant communities as well as the abundance and stature of individual plant species. Recent studies in Yellowstone indicate that ungulate herbivory accelerates the aboveground production of plants

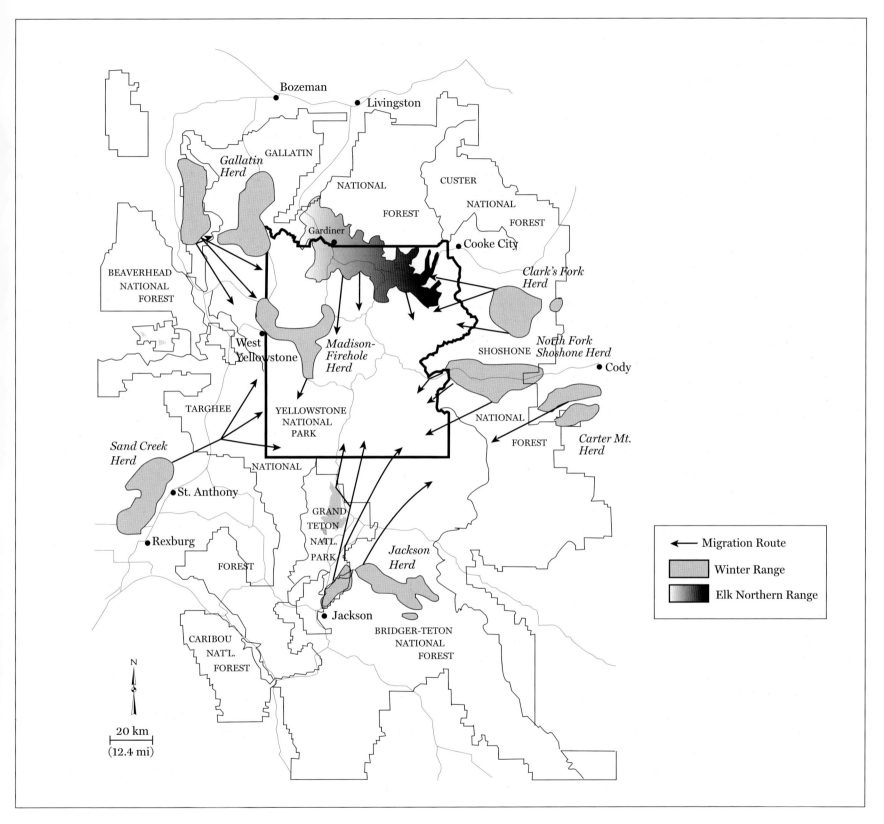

Fig. 17. *Distribution of elk herds in and adjacent to Yellowstone National Park. Arrows indicate shifts of elk from winter to summer ranges. Adapted from Singer and Mack (1993).*

in grasslands and increases the nutrient cycling through the grazing system.[10]

Bison. Bison occupy a unique niche, their biological role accompanied by a spiritual one, a heritage from Native Americans and a vanished frontier. We confine ourselves here to biology, but management issues inescapably must recognize the complications brought about by the spiritual element.

Yellowstone is one of two places where wild bison were not exterminated during the latter part of the 1800s (the other being Wood Buffalo National Park, Canada). Historically, the bison in the park represented a population contiguous with other bison in the Yellowstone River valley to the north. Other bison populations were not far removed—southward in Jackson Hole, east of the Absaroka Mountains on the park's east boundary, and to the west and southwest of the park in intermountain valleys. Populations external to the Yellowstone Plateau are gone now, leaving the park bison as an "island" population. By the winter of 1994–95, park bison numbered more than 4,000.[11]

Establishment of the park did not prevent poaching. By about 1900, only 22 bison were counted in the remote Pelican country (fig. 18). Accordingly, bison were brought in from captive populations in 1902; in 1907 the Buffalo Ranch was established in the Lamar Valley. The wild bison survived to mix and interbreed with the Buffalo Ranch bison; their descendants are the Yellowstone bison of today. In 1936, bison from these mixed bloodlines were trucked from the Buffalo Ranch to reestablish bison on the vacant Mary Mountain winter range (Firehole and Hayden valleys). From 1936 until the early 1980s, bison wintered in three separate and fairly distinct habitats and were referred to as the subpopulations of Lamar (northern range), Mary Mountain, and Pelican (fig. 18).

As an understandable outgrowth of the Buffalo Ranch operation, bison numbers were controlled by periodic reductions on the northern range and by more sporadic removals in the interior. Reductions ceased after 1966 as part of the moratorium discussed above in reference to elk. The parkwide population numbered about 400 bison in 1967, about 2,000 in 1981, and about 3,500 in 1991.[12] Northern range bison numbers increased from less than 100 in 1967 to about 900 in early winter 1988–89. By spring 1989, 569 were shot north of the park by licensed hunters. Numbers have varied since.

The bison grazing regime is similar in basic ways to that of the elk. In this mountain habitat they are seasonally migratory. They forage almost entirely on grasses and grasslike plants (mostly dense-growing, highly productive sedges) throughout the year, functioning as huge mowing machines that take large quantities of comparatively low quality food. Theirs is a built-in rest rotation grazing pattern during the growing season of spring and summer: mow a site and move on, to return and mow again when the vegetation has regrown in a few weeks. They are always on the move: take-a-bite, take-a-step. Effects of bison herbivory on the grass-

lands are similar to that of elk (see part 3, "Grazing Dynamics," Herbivory in the Photo Comparisons). With bison, herbivory also includes recognition of effects such as wallowing, travel trails, and tree rubbing.

Gregariousness is a major component of the bison grazing regime. Year-round, they appear to be the most gregarious large mammal in North America. The particular habitat and season of year governs group size, because it takes extensive suitable forage to allow them to aggregate. In winter, as for the elk, deepening snows progressively exclude them from the peripheries of the wintering valleys. But unlike for elk, bison densities do not progressively increase throughout the winter. As environmental severity worsens, they break their social bonds and begin to scatter. One or a few bison can survive the winter where a larger aggregation cannot. On the other hand, if conditions permit, bison move to more favorable locations rather than breaking their social bonds.

This brings us to a brief description of the present (1995). The degree to which the bison population is naturally regulated within the park has changed dramatically. By the winter of 1981–82, the bison that wintered in the Pelican Valley appeared to have fully occupied their habitat. That winter, snow depths and densities were somewhat above average and the bison began to learn to use the snow-packed road system and move westward, to Hayden Valley. Since then, movements have escalated to change seasonal distributions drastically as the bison have learned to use more favorable locations. By using roads instead of breaking trail in deep snow, the bison save huge amounts of energy in traveling; they gain access to previously unavailable winter forage; they escape winter mortality in the harsher locations and they also avoid new-calf mortality during heavy spring snowstorms. Numbers have doubled since the winter of 1981–82. The changes represent an ecosystem change, because the patterns and locations of herbivory have changed and greatly intensified in some locations. The food base for dependent meat eaters such as grizzly bears has decreased because of less winterkill, and other more subtle effects are just becoming apparent. For bison, human activity has thus changed the system parameters. We have not yet seen the outcome of this situation, which is still in flux, but it is apparent that the changes cannot continue in an open-ended fashion within the park.[13]

Pocket gophers. Pocket gophers live throughout the grasslands, herblands, and sagebrush steppe of the park (pls. 12.1–3, 94.1–3). Populations fluctuate considerably, and judging from the extent of soil disturbance, gophers sometimes reach extremely high densities, estimated at 252 per hectare (102 per acre) for one study. Densities vary according to habitat, season, and between years. Accounts of early explorers mention extensive gopher activity in the park. W. A. Jones (1875:22) commented: This prairie [Pelican Valley] is the home of great numbers of field mice and moles [pocket gophers] which have burrowed up the ground to such an extent that it is traveled over with difficulty. The same is true of a great deal of the open country in the Yellowstone basin." Pocket gophers have a

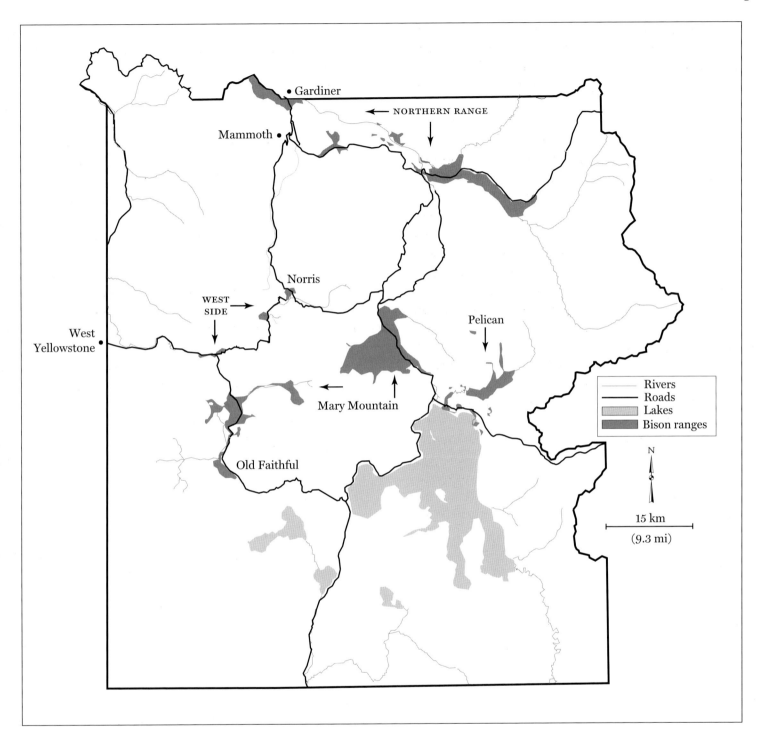

Fig. 18. Bison wintering valleys in Yellowstone National Park. Areas shown are the traditional locales, with the addition of some west side areas used in conjunction with the population distribution changes of recent years. Meagher (unpub.) and Yellowstone GIS.

major effect on soil, plant succession, and plant species composition in grass and grassland-shrub communities.[14]

Beavers. Beavers are found throughout the park and are associated with willow (primarily) and aspen communities along streams and lakeshores. Although considered common, they do not generally appear to establish large, long-lasting colonies here. In many locations they den in the stream banks rather than constructing dams and houses; only the willow cuttings make their presence obvious. At many locations, particularly along headwater streams, their presence appears to be ephemeral (pls. 45.1–3). An alternative to a bank den is when a dam is built across a mountain stream, a small pond forms, perhaps one litter of kits is born to disperse by their second year, the pond silts in during spring runoff, and the beavers move on. During their generally brief tenure at a site they consume most of the available food, usually a limited quantity of willow (which then regrows as hydrological conditions permit). In the park, few substantial long-term dams have been built that are comparable to those seen in Jackson Hole and elsewhere in the general region.

Much of Yellowstone National Park would not be termed good beaver habitat, as beaver appear to prefer (and reach their greatest densities in) relatively flat, fertile valleys with large quantities of food supplies. One has only to watch the spring runoff with snowmelt and the resulting terrific fluctuations in water levels in headwater streams to grasp this. A stream that is knee-deep when forded in the fall may be over one's head in spring, a churning, tumbling, icy mass that can be lethal.

Beaver seem to have fluctuated substantially in abundance (for Yellowstone) since the earliest accounts from the 1830s. Fur trappers certainly penetrated the Yellowstone Plateau and saw enough beaver sign to set traps. Trappers and Native Americans undoubtedly had impacts during the historic period (see part 3, "The Human Presence"). People may well have caused local extinctions; pockets of beaver activity would have been especially vulnerable. After the heyday of the fur trapper era (about 1840) the plateau was probably little visited by Euroamericans until perhaps the 1860s, when the major interest was gold. Beavers likely increased somewhat in the interim, to be trapped again (legally and illegally). Trapping probably had a localized impact from the early years of the park into the early 1900s. Archival records suggested that beaver increased considerably on the northern range around 1900. Colonies were abundant in aspen stands on the northern range during the early 1920s; several colonies are shown in the photo comparisons (pls. 45.1–3, 49.1–3). The animals declined subsequently and populations remained comparatively low into the 1950s.

Field surveys in 1979–80, 1988–89, and 1994 indicated that beaver were distributed widely throughout the park, including the northern range, during those decades. A compilation of records as part of the first survey confirmed the ephemeral nature of many sites and suggested cyclic occupation of perhaps 20 to 40 years, depending on the hydrology of a particular location and the regrowth of food supplies. The 1988–89 and 1994 field surveys documented 27 and 28 stream segments or lakes, respectively, with active beaver presence. Locales overlapped considerably between surveys. Of these, 13 in 1988–1989 and 14 in 1994 were classified as high quality habitat, likely occupied continuously. All these locations have relatively extensive stands of willow.

Beavers have been a major influence on the hydrology of streams in the park, although the effects may sometimes have been relatively transient. Whether transient or longer-term occupants, beavers have affected the structure and abundance of streamside and pond vegetation, particularly aspen and willow.[15]

Insects and Other Invertebrates. The sheer quantity of a host of invertebrates guarantees that they have an important role in the grazing system. Grasshopper populations may reach a density of $36-42/m^2$ ($30-35/yd^2$) in the Lamar Valley; their estimated biomass may sometimes exceed that of the ungulates by a factor of three.[16] Myriad species of biting flies, dung beetles, and soil nematodes perhaps are more fundamental components of nutrient cycling pathways. But most obvious in their effects on the vegetation are pine bark beetles and western spruce budworms. The grazing systems of forest insects differ markedly from those of mammals, especially the ungulates, and are characterized by wild fluctuations in insect abundance over time. Pine bark beetles and western spruce budworms periodically reach epizootic levels and kill susceptible trees across vast sections of the park. Insect populations then decline to low levels until additional cohorts of susceptible trees mature and the conditions once again favor an outbreak (drought, in the case of the bark beetle). Large-scale pine bark beetle outbreaks occurred across western Yellowstone Park during the 1970s and 1980s, and western spruce budworm caused extensive mortality of Douglas-fir in northern Yellowstone during the same decades (pl. 73.2). Forest insects exert powerful short- and long-term effects on forest composition, rates of succession, and nutrient cycling. They also may affect fire return intervals.[17]

The role of predators. We cannot leave this outline of the park's grazing system without mentioning the present and past roles of predation on ungulates, mainly elk, mule deer, and pronghorn. Predation on and scavenging of these species is now common for native carnivores, which include coyotes, cougars, and grizzly and black bears.[18] Additionally, human predation—the annual sport harvest—on elk, in particular, is intense as the animals migrate from the park each autumn; hunters took an average of 1,823 elk per year (range 527 to 4,515) from the northern herd from 1982 through 1995. Yet the combined carnivore and human predation has not prevented the dominant ungulate, elk, from being resource limited.

The present system differs from that of earlier days because aboriginal hunters are absent and gray wolves are in the process of reestablishing their presence. Just what this means in terms of predation rates and ungulate population levels is difficult to judge.[19] On the one hand, it may mean that predation today is lower, particularly on the dominant ungulates, and that their populations are consequently at higher levels and more frequently or intensively resource limited. On the other hand, current human predation outside the park combined with that from native carnivores inside may more than compensate for the absent predators. Whatever the earlier effects, the Yellowstone ecosystem now differs to some degree because of the absences. These differences do not mean (to us at least) that ungulate grazing systems unavoidably self-destruct in the absence of predators or that cropping by humans is necessary in Yellowstone.

Impact of climatic trends. Climatic trends may also have affected levels of ungulate herbivory. Warmer temperatures combined with reduced snowfall seem to have produced a trend to milder winters in Yellowstone during the past century (fig. 14). Therefore, ecological carrying capacity for elk, bison, and most other ungulates probably increased during the time frame of the photographs, accompanied by localized changes in distribution. Substantial changes have occurred in the distribution and abundance of arctic animals in response to seemingly small climatic fluctuations on the scale of decades.[20] Similar changes could be expected to affect ungulate populations in harsh, high elevation areas like Yellowstone National Park. Unfortunately, the historical accounts of winter ungulates' densities are too sparse to be of much help on this issue, and the animals being described were influenced by forces such as intense market hunting. However, we believe that winter ranges probably have become more accessible during the past century and ungulate densities might be somewhat greater as a result.[21] This possibility further complicates the photo interpretations.

HERBIVORY IN THE PHOTO COMPARISONS

Herbivory is a dynamic, interactive, often subtle process that happens over a span of time. Even though photographs represent fixed samples of the process, these comparisons provide considerable insight into change—and lack of change.

Coniferous forests. The effects of insect and ungulate herbivory on coniferous forests were visible in the original scenes and retakes. Trees dead from what appear to be forest insect attacks are apparent in the earliest scenes at both high and low elevation sites (pls. 16.1, 44.1; appendix 2, table 3). Conifers that were horned, rubbed, shaped, or "highlined" by ungulates (having had lower branches heavily browsed) also appear in both the early photos and retakes (pls. 27.1–3, 34.1–3, 40.1–3, 52.1–3, 74.1–3, 80.1–3, 81.1–2, 88.1–3). Highlined trees may be more conspicuous in some of the retakes because of the increased density and distribution of forests, particularly at low elevations, as well as because of increased ungulate numbers.[22]

Aspen. The most contentious effect of herbivory on the northern range concerns aspen as a tree (it grows in shrub form throughout the park). The tree form of aspen appears to have declined about 50 percent during this century, from 4–6 percent of the 82,600 ha (204,455-acre) northern range until about 1930 to about 2 percent now.

The life history of aspen is complex and involves fire frequency (and suppression), climate, and herbivory; the *interactions* among these factors may be most important. Early photographs show low, dense stands of aspen that almost surely originated after fire (pls. 53.1, 54.1, 59.1, 72.1). Early fire suppression efforts became effective shortly thereafter at sites occupied by most stands. As indicated by the photos, beaver herbivory on aspen was intense in the early 1920s (pls. 49.1, 57.1), to the point that beaver control was recommended (but not implemented).[23] Photographs show that many aspen stands matured in spite of beaver and ungulate herbivory. Evidence of ungulate browsing on aspen also occurs in early scenes, but by the 1930s concern was expressed that elk browsing had suppressed aspen reproduction. Importantly, the severe reductions in elk numbers (about 75 percent of the population removed) during the 1950s and 1960s generally failed to reduce utilization or to increase vegetative reproduction of aspen. That is, there was no measurable feedback between elk densities and aspen browsing levels. However, several aspen stands that burned on the northern range inside and outside the park from 1939 through 1977 regenerated successfully.

Work on aspen since the fires of 1988 has provided additional perspective. The age distribution of the mature aspen on the northern range showed that most stems sprouted from about 1870 to 1890 (confirming their appearance in the early photographs). This clumped age distribution indicated that recruitment into older aged trees was episodic even before the park's establishment. The pulse of regeneration was associated with extensive fires, moister climates, and probably reduced numbers of elk and beavers (market hunting of elk, trapping of beavers). Little regeneration has occurred since.

Just how should aspen be expected to respond following the 1988 burns? Aspen sprouted in quantity in the first two years after the fires of 1988, but all sprouts that project above the winter snows were heavily browsed. The evidence seems to indicate that escape from browsing and maturation of aspen stems into large trees will be uncommon, as was the situation historically. Aspen will likely remain heavily browsed by a wide range of herbivores. But, as noted earlier, our expectations for the life history of aspen may be badly skewed. Aspen persisting in shrub form may be the norm in areas subjected to the present climatic regime (of which frequent small fires were a component) and browsed by a full complement of native herbivores; maturation into large-stemmed trees may be very uncommon. While interruption of the pattern of frequent fires, coupled with shifts to drier climates, may have led to irretrievable (and to a degree unnatural) deterioration of existing aspen clones, the historic distribution of the species cannot (and will not) be reestablished. The regionwide photo comparisons indicate that aspen has undergone (and may continue to undergo) much the same reduction across the northern and central Rockies. The future of aspen in tree form on the northern range is not clear; the interactions of the factors involved obviously are complex, and the rare synchrony of necessary factors may be of ultimate importance.[24]

Sagebrush steppe. With few exceptions, the effects of herbivory on sagebrush grasslands were difficult to discern in the photographs. Ungulate trails and wallows were conspicuous in some sagebrush steppes, and ungulate browsing played a role in the decline of sagebrush communities along the north boundary of the park (see part 2, "The Biological Landscape"). Additionally, range studies have shown that ungulates maintained smaller crowns on shrubs along upper slopes and ridgetops on the northern range; this effect can be observed in some photos (pls. 2.1–3, 5.1–3, 47.1–3). Insect herbivory also may have affected sagebrush mortality rates at several sites. But overall, the photographs suggest that the effects of abiotic forces such as fire and drought were more important than herbivory in affecting sagebrush.[25]

Bunchgrass steppe and other grassland types. In general, the effects of ungulate and insect herbivory were difficult to discern in photos of most grassland types. A major exception involved bison and the recent population changes generated by the winter road system (pls. 90.1–3). Other exceptions involved conspicuous ungulate trail systems (pls. 5.1–3, 6.1–3, 88.1–3), buffalo wallows, and the maintenance of the low-density vegetation by grazing on ridgetop sites (see part 2, "The Biological Landscape"). Ungulate grazing also produced lower standing crops of vegetation and reduced crown cover of many shrub species on upper slopes across the northern winter range. The vegetation on ridgetops and upper slopes remains in stable condition because early spring grazing is followed by an absence of late spring and summer grazing, as ungulates move to other sites. Early spring grazing has less effect on production and survival than once supposed, provided that further grazing during the growing season is minimal. Ungulate herbivory probably has been a strong influence on the spread of several exotic grasses throughout the park, particularly common timothy.[26]

The small herbivore showing the most conspicuous effects on grasslands is surely the northern pocket gopher; soil disturbance from this fossorial rodent's tunneling and mound building was clearly visible in both early photos and retakes (pls. 20.1–3). Pocket gophers seemed to be an especially powerful influence on plant density and species composition of subalpine meadows and herblands within the park and on adjacent national forests.

Locally, grizzly bear digging disturbs grasslands of all types. The bears frequently displace large stones and boulders in their search for food (which has been known to foil biologists in their efforts to match camera points for retaking comparative photos!). Bears also dig for rodents in the grasslands, creating torn-up patches of bunchgrass clods. (Bison horning and pawing to start a wallow site does this too, but the tearing up is distinctive.)

Regardless of the obvious activity of plant eaters, drought and fire seemed to overwhelm the effects of herbivory on the standing crop of grassland vegetation shown in the photos, just as with sagebrush steppe. Note too, that drought has a widespread effect on all vegetation of the affected region; fire affects only the locales that burn.

Riparian shrubs. Plant communities dominated by willows declined inside and outside the park during the past century. Prior to the 1930s, willows may have totaled about 1 percent of the northern range vegetation. They appear to have decreased by roughly 50 percent. The interactions of climate, fire, and herbivores in these changes are at least as complex as for aspen. Willow mortality occurred at both high and low elevations in the park and seemed especially pronounced on upper floodplain terraces during the drought of the 1930s. However, willows persisted in deep-snow areas and also colonized active floodplains and some localized wet sites. Herbivores contributing to the decline included elk, moose, beaver, and at least one insect.[27] Elimination of ungulate browsing by exclosures on the northern range produced increased height and cover of ungrazed willow, but usually no substantial increase in *number* of plants. Willows persisted with heavy browsing outside exclosures but at reduced canopy and height. There appeared to be relatively little relationship between elk numbers and willow browsing intensity. Willows showed minor increases in height locally, but they did not increase in abundance following the elk reductions.

Further complexities of interpretation. The addition of moose to the park fauna further complicates interpretations. Moose were not reported in Yellowstone during the fur-trapping era of the 1830s. They were present but still very rare by the 1860s. A detailed historical review turned up no reports of moose *wintering* on the northern range until about 1913. They were commonly observed year-round before the 1988 fires but have been less common since. The moose is an inhabitant of the spruce-fir (boreal) forest type over the long term. Numbers may increase strikingly with the addition of willow habitat, but the recent decline underscores their basic dependence on older growth forest.[28]

These enormously complicated relationships, which involve considerations of the timing, location, and direction of changes in willow distribution, indicate that herbivores were a powerful influence, but they also suggest more general underlying forces at work. We suspect that fire suppression at low elevations and the climatic events of the past century (which also may have affected natural fire frequency) set the stage for riparian shrub changes by altering soil moisture and interspecific competitive relationships in many plant communities. Herbivory by ungulates, beavers, and insects accelerated the decline, but was not a fundamental force. Some changes in willow communities were to be expected with the arrival of wintering moose, bringing along their particular fondness for willow. Similar changes to willow communities occurred as moose colonized Jackson Hole during the early 20th century (see note 27). We recognize that our information on willow ecology is incomplete; perhaps the fires of 1988 will provide additional insights. Soil moisture regimes may change at many burned sites, and the associated lateral movement of streams on floodplains in burned areas could be accelerated, which would produce gravel and sandbars suited to willow colonization.[29]

Rare plant communities. Additional comments about uncommon plant communities and rare plants in grazing systems are prompted by our photo comparisons, by research in Yellowstone before and after the era of heavy ungulate cropping (especially of elk), and by studies of herbivory elsewhere. These remarks are directed at concerns about cottonwood communities (pls. 4.1–2, 58.1–3) as well as relatively rare shrubs such as water birch, chokecherry, and serviceberry. These plant communities are uncommon in the park; cottonwood may occupy 12 ha (about 30 acres) or 0.0001 percent of the northern range vegetation. The amount of the other rare shrub species is even less. The relationships described here are equally applicable to aspen and willow.

These plants are highly palatable to Yellowstone ungulates that browse, and they share the attribute of being so uncommon as to be quantitatively insignificant in the diets of the dominant generalist ungulate, the elk. This means there is essentially no feedback in the grazing system between the utilization of these species and the size of the elk population: the plants are consumed at low as well as high elk densities.[30] It may be that some of these species—cottonwood, for example—are the ecological equivalent of whitetail deer in the park. That is, the park does not furnish significant suitable habitat, and these species are at the fringe of their ecological niche. If so, a rare juxtaposition of factors may be necessary to allow these species to establish in the first place.

In the grazing system outlined, it seems certain that the uncommon plants persist only under physiologically optimum growing conditions where they are best able to compensate for tissue removals and, at least occasionally, escape herbivory.[31] Escape may be either direct, as where individuals grow out of reach or become chemically unpalatable, or indirect in the sense that some plants produce seed banks that remain poised to take advantage of infrequent conditions favorable for establishment. In the case of the Yellowstone grazing system, we suspect that frequent burning provided these plants with the needed edge in the past. Whether the plants will persist or increase remains unclear (as noted, disrupting the fire regime at low elevations in a drier climate may have wrought irreversible change). What seems clear is that these plant taxa, separately and combined, are quantitatively too uncommon to provide useful guidelines for reducing ungulate populations in the park. Calls to reduce elk populations to a level sufficient to relieve utilization on aspen, willows, and cottonwood, if carried out to the necessary level, would result in near extirpation of the elk (as was demonstrated during the 1960s).

The Yellowstone grazing issues are complex, as reflected in the length of this chapter, and have been attended by a long history of controversy. Controversy reflects the state of our knowledge, and new information accrues almost daily. Even so, we do not expect the ungulate management questions to be answered during our lifetimes. Indeed, the system is so dynamic that long-term answers need not be expected or may not even be possible. We are certain, however, that management philosophies and range condition criteria designed to guide the operation of fenced preserves and ranches, or to provide ungulate harvests elsewhere for hunters, are simply inappropriate for Yellowstone.

Agents of change could be grouped in three relatively simple categories: environmental, human, and large grazing mammals. We cannot prevent the influence of environmental agents of change, such as geology, climate, and fire, even if we wished to do so. And the human presence is with us, although we may sometimes compensate for human effects. Large mammals and their presumed biological role perhaps become the simplest, easiest avenue on which to focus. Fascinating as the grazing system is, and as much as we learn, herbivory may have the least effect of the three on Yellowstone in the future.

The Human Presence

Human presence and activities are an integral part of the biological scene of Yellowstone. At first, humans were here because they could make a living, seasonally and then throughout the year. The numbers of people and the amount and kinds of activities they brought with them initially left scarcely a noticeable trace. Over the centuries the human presence has escalated to the point of human activity being so intensive that some present-day visitors choose the times they come to miss the crowds, or even avoid the park altogether. To discuss the park fairly as a natural area, we must look at the role of humans and the implications of their activities since their arrival.

PREHISTORY: AFTER THE ICE

People apparently arrived in the Yellowstone country even as the last of the ice melted, about 12,000 years ago. As suitable terrain became ice-free, plants and animals colonized it. Humans probably followed quickly, likely as small groups penetrating ice-free valleys and subsisting as foragers or hunting as opportune. At first, their presence may have been seasonal only.

The ancestors of these first Yellowstone people apparently crossed the Bering land bridge from Asia by about 12,000 years ago, because the Bering Strait again severed the land connection after this time. The human population apparently expanded rapidly as people colonized from the high arctic to the tip of South America. Dental, genetic, and linguistic evidence suggests at least two and perhaps three groups of colonizers, all probably small in numbers. The earliest wave of human immigrants were the probable ancestors of the people who first inhabited the Yellowstone area.[1]

There is considerable archeological evidence from lower elevations near the park to place human presence in the greater Yellowstone area more than 11,000 years ago.[2] As the climate warmed at the end of the Pleistocene (see part 2, "Setting the Stage," Long-Term Climatic Trends), the higher elevations became more hospitable to humans. More than 9,000 years ago a foothills-mountain subsistence economy developed in the greater Yellowstone area, with people sufficiently flexible to exploit a variety of seasonal food sources. The accumulated evidence suggests exploitation by small mobile bands, family groups perhaps. The people who used the Yellowstone Plateau were likely a part of this general land use pattern, staying seasonally or year-round depending on conditions and food sources.

Evidence suggests that people first penetrated the high country in search of lithic materials (cherts, agate, silicified limestone, obsidian), but they probably did not stay and left limited sign of their presence. However, human occupation on the Yellowstone Plateau dates to more than 10,000 years ago, as evidenced by an Agate Basin–type Paleoindian point made of material quarried from Obsidian Cliff (pls. 25.1–3). Recent archeological work indicated that the Fishing Bridge peninsula of Yellowstone Lake was occupied by Native Americans roughly 10,000 years ago. Numbers of people in the area were sufficient to leave a variety of stone tools dating to 10,000–8,000 years before the present. Blood residue analysis techniques applied to some of these tools indicated that these early people used a variety of animal foods, including large mammals such as bear, bison, deer, and elk. However, small animals such as rabbits apparently were quite important.[3]

The numbers of people, the foods that were their primary subsistence, and the details of their occupation must have varied with climatic changes (see part 2, "Setting the Stage," Long-Term Climatic Trends). Human occupation also probably changed somewhat in character over time as people developed new techniques and as their populations increased. However, a fundamental consideration in the use of the park area by early people would have been comparable to that which applies to the wildlife found here in numbers today. That is, human foraging and hunting activities must have been reasonably energy-efficient; the energy expended to acquire food must not have been greater than the energy derived from the food source. In this context, it may have been more energy-efficient sometimes to live near the food source, to the extent climatic conditions permitted, than to travel long distances on foot. People eventually occupied the Yellowstone Plateau throughout the year, moving from campsite to campsite as they utilized various seasonal food sources. They undoubtedly lived as hunters and gatherers. These people probably had a localized impact on a food source at times, but their lifestyle and technology would have dictated that they lived more as an interactive part of the ecosystem, with generally transient effects.[4]

The presence of native peoples on the Yellowstone Plateau probably was continuous after 10,000 years ago until the 1870s.[5] As numbers of humans increased toward the historic period, their hunting and trapping activities may have had more impact but were likely still quite localized. They probably set fires for reasons ranging from warfare to forage enhancement for wildlife. However, the conditions in which they could have set fires successfully were also conditions conducive to lightning-caused fires. Thus, their role in affecting vegetation patterns and plant succession cannot be separately assessed.[6]

ARRIVAL OF EUROAMERICANS

The terms *prehistoric* and *historic* are convenient time designations, although in reality the two obviously constitute a continuum in time. For our purposes, we begin the historic period with 1800, because the first Euroamericans apparently arrived here about 1807.[7] Fur trappers, miners, and explorers followed prior to establishment of the park in 1872. A few Native Americans were resident until the late 1870s. The second superintendent of the park referred to the Sheepeaters, members of the Shoshone-Bannock group, as living here in 1878 (Haines 1977). These people exploited the resources of the Yellowstone Plateau, living in small bands and utilizing bighorn sheep, as their name indicates. Temporary shelters have been found, widely distributed. Their lifestyle would have fit the forager-hunter-gatherer strategy. They were well adapted to their locale and the resources within it. Procurement of bighorn sheep required as much hunting ability as did procurement of any large mammal, but methods undoubtedly differed.

Additionally, tribes from the surrounding plains traversed the plateau seasonally on hunting expeditions after they acquired horses, apparently early in the 18th century. Physical evidence marking these activities is minimal: campsites and quarries; hunting blinds and game driveways; the Bannock Indian Trail, deeply indented in some places and used heavily from about 1840 to 1878; and fur traps cached at Beaver Lake (pls. 24.1–3).[8] Many travel routes already existed as game trails, probably from the time the ice melted. Some enterprises, such as beaver trapping and later elk and bison market hunting, had at least transient impacts on wildlife populations.

After park establishment in 1872, the human presence and evidence of it increased gradually. By present-day standards, some early activities were amazingly insensitive. For instance, roads crossed geothermal areas and sometimes infringed on named features. A telegraph line crossed close by Old Faithful Geyser (pl. 41.1). Hotels were built close to major tourist attractions (pls. 40.1–3). Wood was cut and rock was quarried for use within the park. Road camps were placed at frequent intervals. A comprehensive list of site-specific activities would be enormous. Most of these resulted from some combination of the technology of the time and economic expediency, coupled with absence of today's perspective on the purpose of our first national park.

An extensive perusal of published, unpublished, and park archival sources suggests that many of these site-specific operations sat rather lightly on the land, such as the slaughter house on Indian Creek (pl. 15.1) and the horse pasturing in the Cougar Meadows (pl. 29.1). Other works, abandoned road alignments for example, left scars still visible to the casual eye today (pls. 76.1–3, 77.1–3). The decade of the 1930s seemed to be when the idea of "using the park to run the park" peaked. Costs and transportation were key to this. For instance, wild hay was cut in quantity (pl. 87.1) for horses used in the park, and sometimes for wildlife feeding operations.

In 1872 an estimated 300 visitors came to Yellowstone National Park. By World War II annual visitors numbered just over half a million, and by the 1970s tourism was reaching 2 million annually.[9] As tourism increased, so did numbers of employees. Real and potential impacts within the park also increased. However, human use was not evenly distributed (nor is it now). Including roads, at most 2–3 percent of the park was developed, and people and their activities were concentrated accordingly.

Into the 1970s, many human-caused impacts could be evaluated on the basis of site-specific actions as compared to ecosystem effects, although these two categories overlap and may be interrelated sometimes. The presence of people does not necessarily equate with functional changes, meaning alterations in energy pathways through the system. For example, thousands of people geyser-watching at Old Faithful on a mid-summer day present a congested scene, but their effect is different ecologically from what would result if the same number of people caught and ate native fish. The latter represents a shunt in the food chain that, if done on a large scale, has ecosystem effects.[10]

Our task is to distinguish between site-specific impacts and *ecosystem changes* caused by the arrival of Euroamericans. A number of topical human activities within the park during the historic period unquestionably had ecosystem effects. From the earliest days of the park, fish seemed not to be regarded as wildlife, resulting in both individual and commercial exploitation, the removal of fish and eggs to stock hatcheries, and the widespread introduction of nonnative fish species (40 percent of the park's lakes were fishless originally).[11] Predator control effectively exterminated the wolf as resident in the park and probably altered the population relationships between coyotes and red foxes (among other effects).

Nonnative plant species began to invade or were planted deliberately; lightning-caused fires were controlled. Both affected vegetation communities and distributions. In a more subtle and less visible way, the establishment of open pit garbage dumps and the availability of roadside food handouts from tourists changed the seasonal distribution and behavior of bears. The population numbers of large ungulates, mainly elk, bison, and pronghorn, were lowered, sometimes drastically, by humans (through illegal market hunting before 1900 and removals carried out by park personnel later), thus changing the grazing systems of the time (see part 3, "Grazing Dynamics").[12]

By the 1960s, human activities outside the park began to generate concerns. For many years the park had been part of a much larger and contiguous wilderness area. Now that began to change. Logging on the Targhee National Forest along the park's west boundary left a 58 km (36 mi) straight line (intermittent sometimes) where no forest abuts park forest south of West Yellowstone. This north-south line is visible in satellite photographs. Mining and development increased. As adjacent communities grew, people often came to view the park's primary function as one of supporting their livelihoods. The more tourists, the better. Subtle external effects included gradual accumulations of airborne pollutants caused by human activities far removed from the park.[13]

For many years Yellowstone was relatively protected from external impacts by its location. Fortunately, the park encompasses the headwaters of most of its rivers and streams; is bordered yet on the north, east, and south by large tracts of national forest wilderness; and has been long shielded by a comparatively harsh climate. Too, no large metropolitan areas existed nearby. But the protection afforded by relative isolation began to erode during the late historic period.

Since 1976

We separate the past two decades from the rest of the historic period because in recent years the *scale* of human activity has become much more important in considering ecosystem changes. The annual number of park visitors approached three million early in the 1990s, and about 5 percent of the park is considered developed.[14] We humans of whatever persuasion and good intentions are a very dominant species. Even when people are onlookers, as opposed to consumptive users, in sheer numbers we now have a direct effect on the ecosystem by changing animal behavior and therefore distribution. Usually such changes are unforeseen and inadvertent. Too much hiking activity displaces foraging grizzly bears from an area, for instance, and in effect removes some of the habitat from their use. Even when the human activity is focused on a development,

bear use of adjacent lands may be affected adversely.[15] Over time, this could result in fewer bears. A reverse situation exists with bison because of human use of park roads in winter. Bison numbers have increased hugely, in large part because this stolid-tempered beast has adapted to using the snow-packed roads to move to more favorable locations, saving much energy and escaping much of the negative impact of winter on the population.[16] From the standpoint of ecosystem relationships, more is not necessarily better.

Additional unforeseen ecosystem alterations will likely occur because we do not know enough and because the changes may be slow and often subtle, at least initially. Three examples are important. Air quality is showing subtle but pervasive changes. A fire lookout who has worked here more than 40 years commented that from his high vantage point, sparkling summer mornings are much less frequent. Even when the morning is clear, there is a discernible touch of haze on the horizon that he did not see during his earlier years. A major nonnative fish problem surfaced, literally, during the summer of 1994. Lake trout were discovered in Yellowstone Lake. The locations from which lake trout have been caught since, and the variety of age classes represented, indicate that they were introduced illegally perhaps a dozen years ago or more but that there were not enough of them to make their presence known sooner. The future of the Yellowstone Lake cutthroat trout has been jeopardized.

The third example involves nonnative plants. Numbers (both species found and plants present) have escalated enormously since the early 1980s. Species such as spotted knapweed have the capability of greatly reducing native forage plants—a topic of concern for ungulate populations. Experimental work with common timothy has demonstrated that this grass is extremely aggressive when grazed, displacing native species as it spreads. Although it is a forage used by ungulates, its ability to invade and take over could result in much more of a monoculture compared to the present biodiversity of the native grasslands. In the future, should a plant disease infect the common timothy, the nearly single-species grasslands could have much less resiliency, and the total ungulate forage base could decrease.[17] Ecosystem changes of the kinds described can span one or more human generations to become apparent.

In perusing historical sources, we are shown the patterns of increasing visitation, expanded development within the park to accommodate this, increasing external influences, and some resulting ecosystem changes. Human numbers and desires combined with sophisticated technology have a potential for future ecosystem change far beyond that of the past.

Epilogue

YELLOWSTONE AS A NATURAL AREA PARK

I wish to emphasize the lesson we learned in Yellowstone: we have much to learn.

WALLACE (1990)

What do the photo comparisons teach about Yellowstone? The photos provide lessons in biological time. Within that time frame, the Yellowstone landscape has been characterized by dynamic change as well as long-term stasis, and the landscape patterns have been determined by a hierarchy of interacting physical and biological forces. At biological time scales, physical forces, particularly fire, have caused the most dramatic and abrupt shifts in ecological processes.[1] The effects of recent climatic changes have been subtle and more gradual but overall more pervasive. By comparison, the influences of native herbivores seem much less important in driving change.

Changes caused by modern (technological) humans as shown in the photographs have been limited mostly to site-specific impacts. Some system changes have been reversible with time and removal of the human cause of change. Fire suppression fits this category. All native species still occupy the park, although a gray wolf population was absent for three-quarters of a century. This absence is in the process of being corrected; the reintroduction of an experimental population began early in 1995. Other human-caused changes seem practically irreversible to us now, such as the introduction and spread of certain nonnative plants.[2]

The lack of change is important also. We note that the relative stasis of grasslands, subalpine meadows, and tundra in Yellowstone must not be overlooked (recognizing always that subtle changes in species composition cannot be detected in the photographs). This apparent lack of change indicates that grasslands have been in equilibrium with the physical forces as well as the suite of herbivores. In essence the feedback loops that characterize the grazing system appear to have remained intact over time and the system has been resilient to disturbance.[3]

Given the perspective of time that the comparative photographs provide, we think that Yellowstone National Park has survived as a relatively intact natural area. This is not wholly because of human foresight in setting aside a national park. To a remarkable extent, the park survives in spite of us, largely because of powerful natural processes that operate on a time scale often longer than our own.

We make this comment in the context of the development of the national park idea and not to detract from the efforts of those who have cared so passionately for the well-being of Yellowstone. The legal framework, social purpose, and scientific understanding of the park idea all represent the evolution of human values and knowledge. This evolution has progressed immensely since the establishment of Yellowstone National Park in 1872, when the governing idea was represented by a simple phrase: "set apart . . . for the benefit and enjoyment of the people." By 1916, with the passage of the National Park Service Act, the phrasing had progressed to "conserve the scenery and the natural and historic objects and the wildlife therein and to provide for the enjoyment of the same in such manner and by such means as will leave them unimpaired." The agency and the public have wrestled since to define this charge.[4]

What should be the philosophy of management of a natural area and the role of human intervention? The topics are loaded with semantic debates, particularly as regards the current meaning and relevance of the concept *natural*. A recent review of park management goals worldwide has outflanked many of the difficulties: "The management of a national park will be determined by whether the aim is to conserve biological and physical states by suppressing processes or whether it is to preserve processes without worrying too much about the resultant states."[5] There are three options: (1) to conserve specified animal and plant associations, intervene; (2) to give full expression to the processes of the system, do not intervene; or (3) some of both. The third option seems to us to describe best the practical, achievable, and realistic, with emphasis on the fullest possible expression of processes. By defining acceptable limits to the ecological processes of interest, we produce an operational definition of *natural* that is appropriate for the beginning of the 21st century.[6]

What does all this mean for management of Yellowstone National Park? The most important message from this photographic study is that the Yellowstone landscape is, above all else, magnificently dynamic—there is no "correct" or "pristine" fixed state to which the park ecosystem should be held, even if this were possible.[7] We underscore this last point. Although the photographs span the time of settlement by Euroamericans and establishment of the park, they cover only a bit more than one century, a mere instant in postglacial time. We feel certain that if pairs of comparative photographs of Yellowstone were available from 800 years ago,

A.D. 1194 to compare with A.D. 1294, for example, changes would be as dramatic as those we documented. In this sense the past serves only as a limited guide to the future because the intensity and frequency of the processes driving ecosystem dynamics change.[8]

We cannot overemphasize the idea that Yellowstone is a dynamic ecological system; change *must* occur. Changes may be subtle and slow, or dramatic, happening overnight. We must expect and accept natural events such as the 1988 fires as essential. If the trend to a warmer, drier climate continues, we can expect an increase in fire frequency. Additionally, trees will continue to invade meadows, streamflow patterns and riparian vegetation will change, and the numbers and distribution of ungulates will be altered. The ungulate grazing system is marvelously dynamic; we expect that warmer, drier climates will cause riparian vegetation in some locations to become even more susceptible to browsing-induced changes. But the Yellowstone ecosystem is highly resilient and able to absorb change and disturbance.

This message has not been well understood by (or presented to) the American people. The most recent example of failure occurred during the fires of 1988. Outraged calls for fire suppression represented, in effect, tacit cries to maintain an inherently transitory biological state to which people had become accustomed. Moreover, the perennial shouts of "overgrazing" on the park's ungulate ranges represent similar attempts to restore a particular biological state or condition that is perceived to be more desirable or "better" than the current state. However, the record demonstrates that often we have not known enough to compensate or mitigate for problems we have caused. Hence our message is *be careful*; the system is more complex than it may at first appear.

How successful can we hope to be at conserving the biological processes that shaped large natural areas such as Yellowstone, and what limits must (and can) be imposed on process dynamics in the future? What changes should we accept and when should we do battle? Difficult questions. Nowhere in history is there a guide for management of national parks with the pressures of the changing modern world, and we cannot provide definitive answers here.

However, at this point in our effort to maintain and understand the park, it appears that modern humans may have altered some parameters of the ecosystems (by introducing nonnative species, altering species distributions, and affecting species population levels) but the *processes* continue, although the pathways may have changed in detail. Although we recognize their presence, the effects of human activity that originate beyond the park (potential global climatic change, for example) are beyond our scope. While human activity may result eventually in further changes in parameters (and a less hospitable environment for our own burgeoning numbers), it seems unlikely that the forces that shape broad climatic patterns over geological time can be changed by us.

From a human perspective, management of large natural areas for their ecological baseline value, and the preservation of the processes that this entails, appears to be an overwhelming need in our own self-interest. Conservation of the *processes* driving landscape dynamics should be the goal of the park, not conservation of particular biological states.

Appendix 1

COMMON AND SCIENTIFIC NAMES OF ANIMALS AND PLANTS

Common Name	Scientific Name
INVERTEBRATES	
beetle	*Disonycha plurigata*
beetles, dung	Scarabæidæ
beetle, pine bark	*Dendroctonus ponderosæ*
budworm, western spruce	*Choristoneura occidentalis*
cankerworm, fall	*Alsophila pometaria*
grasshoppers	Orthoptera
moth, aroga	*Aroga websteri*
nematodes	Nematoda
REPTILES	
rattlesnake	*Crotalus viridis*
BIRDS	
eagle, bald	*Haliæetus leucocephalus*
FISH	
trout, Yellowstone cutthroat	*Salmo clarkii bouvieri*
trout, Eastern brook	*Salvelinus fontinalis*
trout, lake	*S. namaycush*
MAMMALS	
bear, black	*Ursus americanus*
bear, grizzly	*U. arctos*
beaver	*Castor canadensis*
bison	*Bison bison*
cougar	*Felis concolor*
coyote	*Canis latrans*
deer, mule	*Odocoileus hemionus*
deer, white-tailed	*O. virginianus*
elephant, African	*Loxodonta africana*
elk	*Cervus elaphus*
fox, red	*Vulpes vulpes*

Common Name	Scientific Name
MAMMALS (CONT.)	
goat, Rocky Mountain	*Oreamnos americanus*
gopher, northern pocket	*Thomomys talpoides*
moose	*Alces alces*
pronghorn	*Antilocapra americana*
rabbit, cottontail	*Sylvilagus nuttallii*
sheep, bighorn	*Ovis canadensis*
wolf, gray	*Canis lupus*
VASCULAR PLANTS	
alder	*Alnus* spp.
alder, mountain	*A. incana*
arnica	*Arnica* spp.
arrowgrass	*Triglochen* spp.
aspen	*Populus tremuloides*
aster	*Aster* spp.
balsamroot, arrowleaf	*Balsamorhiza sagittata*
barley, foxtail	*Hordeum jubatum*
bentgrass, redtop	*Agrostis stolonifera*
bentgrass, Ross's	*A. rossiæ*
birch, water	*Betula occidentalis*
bistort	*Polygonum bistortoides*
bluegrass	*Poa* spp.
bluegrass, Sandberg's	*P. sandbergii*
bluebell, broad-leaved	*Mertensia ciliata*
brome, mountain	*Bromus carinatus*
brome, smooth	*B. inermis*
buckwheat, wild	*Eriogonum* spp.
bulrush	*Scirpus* spp.
cattail	*Typha* spp.
camas, death	*Zigadenus* spp.
canarygrass, reed	*Phalaris arundinacea*
cheatgrass	*Bromus tectorum*

Common Name	*Scientific Name*	Common Name	*Scientific Name*

Vascular Plants (cont.)

Common Name	Scientific Name
chokecherry, common	*Prunus virginiana*
cinquefoil	*Potentilla* spp.
cinquefoil, slender	*P. gracilis*
cinquefoil, shrubby	*P. fruiticosa*
clematis	*Clematis hirsutissima*
clover	*Trifolium* spp.
coneflower, western	*Rudbeckia occidentalis*
cottonwood	*Populus spp.*
cow-parsnip	*Heracleum lanatum*
dandelion, mountain	*Agoseris glauca*
dock (sorrel)	*Rumex occidentalis*
dock, curly	*R. crispus*
Douglas-fir	*Pseudotsuga menziesii*
elephant's head	*Pedicularis groenlandica*
fescue, Idaho	*Festuca idahoensis*
fescue, alpine	*F. brachyphylla*
fir, subalpine	*Abies lasiocarpa*
flax, wild	*Linum perenne* var. *lewisii*
fleabane	*Erigeron* spp.
gentian, fringed	*Gentianella* spp.
gooseberry, mountain	*Ribes montinegum*
grama, blue	*Bouteloua gracilis*
greasewood	*Sarcobatus vermiculatus*
groundsel	*Senecio* spp.
hairgrass, tufted	*Deschampsia cæspitosa*
harebell	*Campanula rotundifolia*
hopsage, spiny	*Grayia spinosa*
horse-brush	*Tetradymia canescens*
hound's tongue	*Cynoglossum officianale*
jacob's ladder	*Polemonium* spp.
junegrass	*Koeleria macrantha*
juniper, common	*Juniperius communis*
juniper, Rocky Mountain	*J. scopulorum*
knapweed, spotted	*Centaurea maculosa*
knotweed, Douglas	*Polygonum douglasii*
larkspur	*Delphinium* spp.
lupine	*Lupinus* spp.
lupine, silvery	*L. argenteus*
magnolia	*Magnolia* spp.
milkvetch, Olympic Mountain	*Astragalus australis* var. *olympicus*
monkeyflower, yellow	*Mimulus guttatus*
mule's ears	*Wyethia* spp.

Vascular Plants (cont.)

Common Name	Scientific Name
mullein	*Verbascum thapsus*
needlegrass	*Stipa* spp.
needle-and-thread	*S. comata*
oak, red	*Quercus coccinea*
oak, white	*Q. alba*
oniongrass	*Melica* spp.
paintbrush	*Castilleja spp.*
phlox	*Phlox* spp.
pine, limber	*Pinus flexilis*
pine, lodgepole	*P. contorta* var. *latifolia*
pine, ponderosa	*P. ponderosa*
pine, whitebark	*P. albicaulis*
pinegrass	*Calamagrostis rubescens*
pond-lily	*Nuphar polysepalum*
prickly pear	*Opuntia polycantha*
quackgrass	*Agropyron repens*
rabbitbrush, common	*Chrysothamnus nauseosus*
rabbitbrush, green	*C. viscidiflorus*
reedgrass	*Calamagrostis* spp.
ricegrass, Indian	*Oryzopsis hymenoides*
rose	*Rosa* spp.
rush	*Juncus* spp.
sage, threetip	*A. tripartita*
sagebrush	*Artemisia* spp.
sagebrush, big	*A. tridentata*
sagebrush, fringed	*A. frigida*
sagebrush, Rocky Mountain	*A. scopulorum*
sagebrush, silver	*A. cana*
saltbush	*Atriplex* spp.
sedge	*Carex* spp.
sedge, beaked	*C. rostrata*
sedge, inflated	*C. vesicaria*
sedge, Nebraska	*C. nebrascensis*
sedge, Ross's	*C. rossii*
serviceberry	*Amelanicher alnifolia*
spike-rush	*Eleocharis* spp.
spruce, Engelmann	*Picea engelmannii*
spurge, corrugate-seeded	*Euphorbia glyptosperma*
stickseed	*Hackelia* spp.
stickseed, many-flowered	*H. floribunda*
stonecrop	*Sedum lanceolatum*
sumac, smooth	*Rhus trilobata*

Common Name	Scientific Name

Vascular Plants (cont.)

sycamore	Platanus spp.
thistle, Canada	Cirsium arvense
thistle, elk (Evert's)	C. scariosum
timothy, alpine	Phleum alpinum
timothy, common or nonnative	P. pratense
toad-flax	Linaria spp.
verbena, Yellowstone sand	Abronia ammophila
walnut	Juglans spp.
wheatgrass	Agropyron spp.
wheatgrass, bluebunch	A. spicatum
wheatgrass, crested	A. cristatum
wheatgrass, slender	A. trachycaulum
wildrose	Rosa spp.

Common Name	Scientific Name

Vascular Plants (cont.)

wildrye	Elymus spp.
wildrye, giant	E. cinereus
willow*	Salix spp.
willow, Booth's	S. boothii
willow, Eastwood's	S. eastwoodiæ
willow, Farr's	S. farriæ
willow, Geyer's	S. geyeriana
willow, Wolf's	S. wolfii
winterfat	Krascheninnikovia lanata
yampah	Perideridia montana
yarrow	Achillea millefolium

*Willows are taxonomically complex. At least 25 species occur plus hybrids (J. Whipple pers. comm. 1995).

Appendix 2

SUMMARY OF VEGETATION CHANGES SHOWN BY PHOTO COMPARISONS

TABLE A2-1

Summary of vegetation changes shown by 323 photo comparisons in Yellowstone National Park, prior to the fires of 1988

			CHANGES IN AREA/DENSITY (% OF SCENES)[a]			
Vegetation	Dates of Originals[b]	Number of Comparisons	No Change	Increase	Decrease	Comments
Coniferous forest	1871–1900	148	6	92	2	Mostly Douglas-fir & lodgepole pine <2300 m; lodgepole with subalpine fir 2301-2600 m; lodgepole/whitebark pine/subalpine fir >2601 m. Eighteen percent of the scenes showed only minor increases.
	1901–1943	152	16	81	3	Species as above.
Aspen	1871–1900	23	0	0	100	All stands were <2400 m. Of 22 scenes on the northern range, 21 show dense stands of short trees in originals, probably of fire origin.
	1901–1944	42	5	0	95	All on northern range ≤2400 m; 38 show medium to tall trees in originals; four show dense stands of small trees.
Sagebrush steppe	1871–1900	54	28	37	35	Mostly <2600 m and involving big sagebrush, some threetip and silver sagebrush above 2300 m. Eleven scenes below 2300 m show extensive increases. Many decreases occurred when forests invaded sagebrush stands below 2300 m.
	1901–1943	82	43	22	35	Eleven of 23 scenes of decreases occurred in former livestock grazing areas along the north park boundary, below 1800 m.
Bunchgrass steppe/ meadows	1871–1900	48	46	44	10	Below 2300 m. About 30% contained exotic species, mostly timothy grass, at retakes. Nineteen of 21 increases occurred on thermal ground.

a. Area and/or density of subject vegetation changed.   *b*. Dates of original photographs arrayed in two categories, 1871–1900 and from 1901 on.

		CHANGES IN AREA/DENSITY (% OF SCENES)				
Vegetation	Dates of Originals[b]	Number of Comparisons	No Change	Increase	Decrease	Comments
	1901–1943	76	76	17	7	Below 2300 m. Seventeen percent show timothy in retake. Nine scenes show increase on thermal ground.
Low density steppe[c]	1871–1900	22	91	0	9	Below 2400 m. Eighteen scenes on the northern range; one in Hayden Valley; and three along Firehole River. No changes on 20 ridgetop sites. Cover increased on two stream terraces.
Forest parks	1871–1900	22	64	18	18	2301–2600 m. Four scenes show change from native sedge or forb dominance to native grasses.
	1901–1935	24	67	21	12	Elevations as above.
Subalpine meadows/ herblands/ tundra	1871–1900	16	63	25	12	Above 2600 m. Four scenes show increased plant cover on snowbank sites.
	1901–1935	13	85	15	0	Above 2600 m. Two scenes show increased plant cover on snowbank sites.
Sedge meadows	1871–1900	23	35	65	0	Mostly below 2600 m. Increases occurred as willows decreased. Three scenes show pond succession to sedge meadows.
	1901–1944	32	25	69	6	Below 2600 m. Three scenes show pond succession to sedge meadow.
Riparian shrubs (willow)	1871–1900	37	22	5	73	Mostly below 2600 m. Decreases involved several willow species, shrubby cinquefoil, and mountain alder.
	1901–1944	42	10	7	83	Changes as above.
Plant cover on thermal ground[d]	1871–1900	35	6	83	11	Of 29 scenes showing increased cover, 20 involved herbaceous plants, nine were lodgepole pine.
	1901–1943	7	0	71	29	Of five scenes showing increases, four were herbaceous plants, one was lodgepole pine.

c. These "low potential" ridgetop and upper slope sites represented small areas that were heavily grazed by native ungulates; also called "zootic climax" vegetation (Houston 1982).
d. Sites in and around geyser basins and hotsprings, especially deposits of siliceous sinter.

TABLE A2-2

Summary of 1988 fire effects noted in photo comparisons in Yellowstone National Park

CHANGES IN AREA/DENSITY (% OF SCENES)[a]						
Vegetation	Elevation (m)	Number of Comparisons	No Change	Increase	Decrease	Comments
Coniferous forest	≤2300	103	0	0	100	
	2300–2600	24	0	0	100	
	>2600	33	0	0	100	
Aspen	≤2400	8	0	12	88	Decreases represented mortality of overstory trees. Six of seven scenes show resprouting. Increases represented aspen seedlings in a sedge meadow.
Stagebrush steppe	≤2300	35	0	0	100	
	2300–2600	7	0	0	100	
	>2600	1	0	0	100	
Bunchgrass steppe/ meadows	≤2300	27	67	33	0	There was often greatly increased standing crop, with vigorous growth.
Forest parks	2300–2600	8	63	37	0	Changes as above.
Subalpine meadows/ herbland/ tundra	>2600	7	71	29	0	Changes as above.
Sedge meadows	≤2300	8	50	12	38	Decreases occurred where fire burned through layers of peat.
	2300–2600	1	100			
Riparian shrubs	≤2300	14	14	7	79	Willow mortality occurred where root crowns burned in sedge meadows.

a. Scenes rephotographed in the 1990s; analysis is of burned vegetation only. Although no changes in area or density occurred in many grasslands and sedge types, many herbaceous perennials (especially grasses) showed pronounced increases in vigor and standing crop following a burn.

TABLE A2-3

*Summary of the occurrence of highlined trees in 102 photo comparisons for
Yellowstone Park winter ranges*

	HIGHLINED APPEARANCE[a]				
Period and Winter Range	Y/Y	N/N	N/Y	Y/N	Total
Pre-1900 (1871–1896)	14 (37)	14 (37)	10 (26)	0	38
Northern Range	9	3	3	0	15
Firehole-Madison [b]	4	11	6	0	21
Hayden-Pelican	1	0	1	0	2
1900–1944	43 (67)	7 (11)	11 (17)	3 (5)	64
Northern Range	34	2	2	2	40
Firehole-Madison [b]	8	4	7	1	20
Hayden-Pelican	1	0	2	0	3
Gallatin	0	1	0	0	1

a. Number of comparisons where highlined trees appear in both the original photo and retake = Y/Y, none in either = N/N, etc. (percent). Retakes mostly from 1970s.

b. Includes Gibbon River and Cougar Creek areas.

Appendix 3

REPEAT PHOTOGRAPHY IN THE ROCKY MOUNTAIN REGION

*Ten published repeat photography studies showing vegetation changes in
the central and northern Rocky Mountain region*

Author	General Area	Number of Comparisons	Dates of Originals	Dates of Retakes
Gruell 1973	Teton Wilderness, Wyoming	10	1872–1928	1969–1971
Gruell 1980a, b[a]	Bridger-Teton National Forest, Wyoming	85	1872–1942	1968–1972
Gruell 1983	Montana and northern Idaho	86	1871–1941	1979–1982
Johnson 1987	Southern Wyoming	56	1869–1871	1974–1985
Wyoming State Historical Society 1976	Bighorn Mountains, Wyoming	36	1900	1975
Bureau of Land Management 1979	Missouri Breaks, Montana	71	ca. 1880-1932	1977
Bureau of Land Management 1980	Southwest Montana	57	ca. 1865-1947	1978–1979
Veblen and Lorenz 1991	Front Range, Colorado	69	1870-1921	1982–1988
Brock and Brock 1993	Central Idaho	77	ca. 1880-1940	1992 ?
Wright and Bunting 1994	Southern Idaho	34	1923-1965	1986–1990

a. Contains several scenes published in Gruell 1973 and six scenes published in Gruell 1979. Several of Gruell's comparisons are also housed as part of this comparative
photo collection in Yellowstone.

Notes

Prologue

1. The *ecosystem* is arguably the most important conceptual model developed to describe the organization of nature. Functionally, an ecosystem is composed of producers (green plants), consumers (herbivores, carnivores), and decomposers (bacteria, fungi), interacting with one another and their nonliving environment. Energy to drive the system comes from sunlight captured through photosynthesis by plants. The transfer of energy and cycling of nutrients through the components of an ecosystem represent the basic *ecological processes*. Ecosystems vary in size depending on the scale of interest. A single lake, decaying log, or thermal pool may represent a functioning ecosystem. At the landscape scale, it is useful to recognize a Yellowstone National Park ecosystem or the "greater Yellowstone ecosystem" (a mosaic of national parks, national forests, wildlife refuges, and other lands). For the Yellowstone Park ecosystem, an idealized management goal is to maintain the ecological processes that link native species of plants and animals (the *food web*) as free as possible from the influence of present-day humans (see epilogue).

The species that constitute an ecosystem usually change in abundance or occurrence over time. This fundamental process, ecological succession, occurs when established ecosystems are disturbed. For example, fire is an important natural force that disturbs ecosystems and initiates plant and animal succession.

Introduction: The Art of Repeat Photography

1. Rogers et al. (1984) discuss the worldwide use of repeat photography and the many factors that affect such efforts.

2. We used a variety of cameras and films over the years. Cameras: 3¼ x 4¼, Crown Graphic, lens not recorded; 4 x 5 Crown Graphic, 135 mm f/4.7 lens; 35 mm Nikon FM, Nikkor 50 mm f/1.4 and 35 mm f/2 lenses; Rollei 35, Tessar 40 mm f/3.5 lens. Film: The 1970s retakes were made with Kodak Plus-X, Panatomic-X, and Tri-X; the 1990s retakes, with Kodak Plus-X, Panatomic-X, and TMAX 100.

3. Common and scientific names of animals and plants mentioned in the text are listed in appendix 1.

4. Johnson (1987) provides a good description of the equipment and procedures used by early photographers. Some of the early photographers of the Yellowstone region have been described in biographical detail, complete with photographs of their equipment and the pack trains that supported them. F. J. Haynes (Tilden 1964) and W. H. Jackson (Jackson 1947) are among these. Unfortunately, no one has described J. P. Iddings's labors on behalf of the U.S. Geological Survey. Given the huge cameras of the time, made of glass and varnished wood, the wet-plate glass negative development techniques of the era, and the necessary travel by saddle horse and with pack animals, the clarity and detail of the scenes recorded are nothing short of phenomenal. L. Whittlesey (pers. comm.) is preparing a manuscript that discusses all of the Yellowstone early-day photographers; undoubtedly Iddings will receive his due.

5. The comparative photograph collection and negatives in the park's possession are retained permanently as a part of the Yellowstone National Park photo archives.

We rephotographed most of the scenes, but the collection contains several comparisons produced by former U.S. Forest Service biologist George Gruell and former National Park Service biologist Bill Barmore. Also, this tally treats 14 records as individual scenes when they actually represent components of mosaic views.

Assembling the Yellowstone Landscape: Geology

1. The geological literature for Yellowstone is extensive, beginning with the 1872 report of the Hayden Survey, forerunner of the U.S. Geological Survey. After many subsequent studies by the USGS and others, the Survey began extensive and intensive new research in the 1960s. Keefer (1971) synthesized the geological knowledge to date in a nontechnical monograph. This was followed by roadside guides by Fritz (1985) and Fournier et al. (1994). See Good and Pierce (1996) for the most recent synthesis.

2. Worldwide research in the last few decades has produced major insight into plate tectonics and the character of the planet and its internal forces. Hypotheses regarding the formation of the Yellowstone hotspot are presented by Pierce and Morgan (1992) in their detailed description of its track. Smith and Braile (1993) focused on geophysical data. The

hotspot created a geoid dome some 600–800 km (300–400 mi) across that centers on the caldera. This feature is similar to oceanic geoid domes that are crowned by volcanic islands on the surface.

3. After Keefer's 1971 publication, a third caldera, the smallest, was recognized for the Yellowstone Volcanic Field. This is the Island Park caldera, shown as II on figure 9. Christiansen (1984) and Smith and Braile (1984) discussed explosive volcanism and caldera formation in detail. Although caldera formation happened very quickly, pre- and postvolcanism spanned hundreds of thousands of years. Earthquakes and surface volcanic flows would provide ample indication of renewed activity.

4. Simply put, we are closer to hell than we realized only a few years ago! This partial melt body, presumed to be magmatic, is responsible for the geothermal features found in Yellowstone National Park. Approximately 10,000 hot springs, geysers, fumaroles, and mud pots give the park the greatest concentration of geothermal activity in the world. Surface waters circulate deeply to heat and perhaps to combine with some magmatic water to supply the thermal features (Christiansen 1984; Smith and Braile 1984, 1993).

5. The syntheses of Pierce and Good (1992) and Pierce and Morgan (1992) provided a graphic sense of the interplay of the forces of uplift and ice formation. Continuing uplift between glacial periods is indicated by such features as the comparative length of the most recent glaciers on the outer slopes of the crescent of uplift, lateral migration of streams, tilting of stream terraces away from the park, and the divergent-convergent patterns displayed by terrace pairs.

6. The glacial story is the result of the work of many authors. General overviews are provided in Keefer (1971) and Fritz (1985). Pierce (1979) traces the glaciation of the northern half of Yellowstone in much detail. A synthesis of the Jackson Hole glaciation (Pierce and Good 1992) leads the reader to more detailed papers, and proposes some differences of interpretive detail. Dates used reflect the more recent work. See also Good and Pierce (1996).

7. Turbidity and silt in the Yellowstone River and its tributaries have received much attention. Pierce and Morgan (1992) pointed out that the uplift of the Absaroka Mountains caused by the track of the hotspot results almost annually in snowmelt carrying everything from fine particles to boulders. They noted that climbing is dangerous because of loose and detached fragments of bedrock. Sedimentation studies indicated that most load contribution in the Yellowstone River came from Soda Butte and the upper Lamar River. Both head in the Absaroka volcanics. Mount Everts with its Cretaceous shales was the other significant source (Shovic et al. 1988). Meyer's (1993) intensive study of Soda Butte Creek showed the interrelationships of the highly erodible volcanic bedrock with events such as large fires and climatic conditions.

8. The description by Pierce and Morgan (1992) gave local slopes of 27° and 31° in Absaroka stream heads. Overall peak-to-valley relief was as much as 2,000 m (6,560 ft).

SETTING THE STAGE: CLIMATE AND SOIL

1. The present climate is described in greater detail, including maps and diagrams showing the distribution of precipitation, in Houston (1982) and Despain (1990). Despain called attention to contrasting climatic regimes. Whitlock and Bartlein (1993) and Whitlock (1993) examined the derivation of the two climates, their changes over postglacial time, and the consequent long-term differences in vegetation. See also Whitlock et al. (1995).

2. The reconstruction of paleoclimates of the Rocky Mountains has been revised extensively during the past 20 years. This interpretation is drawn from Porter et al. (1983), Burke and Birkeland (1984), Baker (1983), Barnosky et al. (1987), Mahaney and Spence (1990), Pielou (1991), Whitlock et al. (1991), Whitlock and Bartlein (1993), Elias (1993), and Whitlock (1993).

3. Whitlock (1993) discusses pollen data. Evidence from insect fossils permits a more detailed paleoclimatic reconstruction (Elias 1993). Rapid and relatively large climatic fluctuations are major factors determining the presence of many life forms and the speed with which they may vanish.

The amount of climatic change at the glacial/Holocene transition signaled a huge change in biological communities. Pielou (1991:269–90) observed that the amount and timing of change varied geographically. The temperature and precipitation changes noted here appeared applicable to the Rocky Mountains. Climatic change may have had a significant role in the megafaunal extinctions, but a satisfactory explanation has yet to be made (Pielou 1991:266).

4. These changes are inferred mainly from pollen profiles, described in Whitlock and Bartlein (1993) and Whitlock (1993).

5. See Douglas and Stockton (1975) for tree-ring analyses. Houston (1982) presented much greater detail from available climatic research pertinent to the last century.

6. The Mammoth station has the longest-existing weather records for Yellowstone National Park. The hazards of relying upon just one weather station to infer trends and the comparability of the Mammoth records to other climatic records were explored in Houston (1982:102–6). The trend of increasing temperatures is consistent with that at many other stations worldwide (Hansen and Lebedeff 1987). The relationship of solar cycle length to temperature trend is reported by Friis-Christensen and Lassen (1991).

7. Recall the drought and fires of the summer of 1988, masked here by trends shown on a scale of decades and longer. These trends govern longer-term vegetation patterns and the changes that take place in depen-

dent wildlife. It is the shorter term changes and events that draw major attention within human time. See Balling et al. (1993) for additional comments on historic climatic trends and model predictions associated with increased CO_2.

8. A winter severity index was developed by Picton (1979). The indices were constructed for December to March periods by algebraic summation of the signs (+ or -) of the monthly deviations from the long-term monthly mean values of temperature and precipitation. The signs of all precipitation values were reversed because snow hinders ungulate feeding. A minor modification of Picton's calculations included adding additional signs for each standard deviation exceeded by a particular monthly value. The trend line was produced by LOWESS smoothing with f = 0.15. The index is still a crude expression of severity (snow density is not incorporated and environmental conditions may vary markedly across the northern range), but the graph serves to underscore the dynamics of climatic trends with respect to the large ungulate component of the Yellowstone ecosystem.

Recognize also that different ungulate species respond differently to the same set of conditions because of anatomical, behavioral, and physiological differences. Effects will vary further depending on the interrelationship of population levels and winter severity.

9. Little Ice Age effects are described by Bray (1971) and Pielou (1991) among others. Despain (1990) calls attention to the possibility that forest composition will differ following disturbance now because of changes in climate.

10. Despain (1990) discusses the soils of Yellowstone and their properties at length. Knight (1994:33) provided an excellent summary of soil types and the association of soils and vegetation in Wyoming.

The Biological Landscape: Vegetation and Change

1. Yellowstone contains 8,995 km² (3,472 mi²); about 95% is land and 5% is water (including Yellowstone Lake at about 4% of the park area). Vegetation categories of park land area (8,545 km²) discussed are forests (aspen is .002% of the forest) > 80%; sagebrush grassland 6.0%; grassland and meadow, forest park and tundra 7.0%; sedge meadows and willows (willows are a small fraction of 1%) < 1%; and geothermal vegetation < 0.2%. The remaining approximately 5% of the land surface is nonvegetated (eg., rock, developments, and roads).

Despain (1990) discusses patterns of vegetation in more detail and relates these patterns to influences from soils and climate. For example, the extensive lodgepole pine forests of the Yellowstone Plateau reflect acidic, nutrient-poor soils derived from rhyolitic lavas. In contrast, andesitic soils of the Lamar and Yellowstone river valleys are richer; this and a drier climatic regime fostered extensive grasslands with sagebrush—the northern winter range. Note that Renkin and Despain (1992) use 83

percent forest. Percentages may vary somewhat among references consulted because of map resolution and sources used.

2. Early travelers used natural travel routes, such as wildlife trails and stream courses. A sampling of early narratives provides a graphic sense of travel. Among the more interesting are Russell's journeys of 1834–43 (Haines 1955), Cook-Folsom-Peterson (Haines 1965), and Strong (1876). According to archive records, park personnel began to maintain a trail system of major routes in 1908 (local trails were undoubtedly cut earlier for convenience).

3. See Houston (1982) and references therein for details on ungulate numbers.

4. Hague (1886) traversed the park during the 1880s for the U.S. Geological Survey. His publications and manuscripts characterize him as a careful observer of the natural scene. Many of the early photographs used here were taken during these surveys.

Despain (1990) discussed growth forms and requirements of aspen. Engstrom et al. (1991) found that aspen pollen occurred only in trace quantities on their northern range study sites over the last 100–150 years, and that no large-scale decline in aspen pollen was noted.

5. Extrapolated from Despain et al. (1989) and Renkin and Despain (1992). Both high-intensity ground burn and crown fire kill the overstory and are referred to as stand-replacement fires.

6. Plant succession in general and forest succession in detail are discussed by Despain (1983, 1990).

7. The complex geology and ecology of the boundary line area, near Gardiner, Montana, was described in detail by Houston (1982). This area is part of the northern winter range, which extends from Dome Mountain, some 20 km (12 mi) north of Gardiner, south and eastward 80 km (50 mi) along the Yellowstone and Lamar rivers across the northern part of the park (fig. 3).

8. Along with a host of exotic plants, natives such as blue grama, prickly pear, and spiny hopsage grow in the boundary line area. The comparatively mild winter climate makes the area suitable for rattlesnakes, cottontail rabbits, and pronghorn. See Houston (1982) for more details.

9. This lush growth is partly a response to post-fire nutrient enhancement that occurs mostly in the first one to two years. Release from shrub competition may also be a factor.

10. Tweedy's (1886) account of plant species and their relative abundance in the park's grasslands was based on his 1884 and 1885 collections and others made as early as 1871. After allowing for taxonomic changes and the arrival of exotics, his description is appropriate now; i.e., we have no reason to believe that large-scale shifts in species composition have occurred in most park grasslands (exotic species excepted).

11. Introduced common timothy is found widely on both summer and winter ranges and on sites where minimal wildlife use occurs at any season. It apparently continues to expand its distribution, sometimes intermixing with the native alpine timothy. To date, there is no evidence for hybridization (J. Whipple, pers. comm.). Eventually the exotic seems to displace the native species. For instance, the park's herbarium contains specimens of alpine timothy collected 30 years ago on the Buffalo Plateau, but it cannot now be found on this lightly grazed summer range. Dr. Linda Wallace (pers. comm.) has found that the strain of introduced timothy has proven to be extremely resilient in experiments designed to simulate high-intensity grazing.

12. The term *zootic climax* has been used for these sites (Houston 1982) because of the tremendous influence of native ungulates. But whatever the sites are called, from an ecological perspective we do not consider that they represent range problems or deterioration.

13. Knight (1994:193) devoted an entire chapter to meadow and snow glade formation and their persistence over time. Particular snow drift patterns also favor meadows over forest.

14. See section on pocket gophers in part 3, "Grazing Dynamics." Gruell (1973) discussed pocket gopher activity in more detail for Big Game Ridge on the south boundary.

15. Meagher (1993) documented major changes in numbers and distribution as bison learned to use the winter roads that were packed and groomed for snowmobile travel.

16. Meyer (1993) and Meyer et al. (1995) discussed the effects of the 1988 fires, climatic changes, and the interactions of these forces on the hydrology and geomorphology of Soda Butte Creek. All major postfire erosion/sedimentation events he examined were related to brief but strong summer thunderstorms striking steep-sloped mountain basins that had burned intensely. He estimated that 30 percent of the late Holocene alluvial fan material was deposited in fire-related events, as shown by much charcoal. From these materials he identified five major fire-related depositional periods between 5500 B.C. and 1200 A.D.

17. Earthquakes apparently play major roles in rejuvenating the underground "plumbing" of geysers and hot springs, because fissures and vents gradually seal with deposits of siliceous sinter. Earth movements keep these open, create new ones, and surely influence lesser changes such as the locations of warmer-than-normal soil. An increase in geothermal activity was documented following the 1959 Hebgen Lake earthquake and subsequently, after other major shocks felt in Yellowstone. The myriad lesser events recorded by seismographs, but rarely felt by humans, undoubtedly exert a constant influence (Good and Pierce 1996).

Despain (1990:103) described the fascinating geothermal plant communities found in the park. Plants show adaptations to geothermal conditions; corrugate-seeded spurge, for example, grows flat on the warm ground and flowers in January. Ross's bentgrass, one of two plant species known to be endemic to Yellowstone, occurs exclusively in the geothermal environments of the Upper, Midway, and Lower geyser basins along the Firehole River. (Yellowstone sand verbena is the other plant species known only from Yellowstone National Park.)

18. Based on floristics, Daubenmire (1943) described the northern Rockies as extending from central Alberta and British Columbia south to an east-west line through the center of Wyoming. The central Rockies extend from Wyoming south to just within the northern borders of Arizona and New Mexico.

19. See Caughley (1976).

20. Knight (1994) discussed the ecology of big sagebrush in Wyoming, including the complex interplay of mortality factors in the lowland environments.

21. Johnson (1987) concluded that "the management and environmental influences of the past 100 years have brought about no significant change in plains vegetation" since the early 1870s in southern Wyoming.

22. See Gruell (1973, 1980*a*, 1980*b*).

23. Gruell (1980*a*, 1980*b*) and Houston (1987) evaluated the condition of willows in Jackson Hole, Wyoming. Heavily browsed though they are, there seems to be no decrease in the numbers of shrubs nor area they occupy. Also, regionwide, willows and cottonwoods have been maintained along irrigation ditches.

24. The complex changes in riparian communities in the western United States and the role of livestock and other forces in driving change are discussed in Vavra et al. (1994). Knight (1994) discusses the issue for Wyoming.

CLIMATE, FIRE, AND EARTH FORCES

1. See Daubenmire (1974) for more detailed discussion. Crawley (1983), Myers (1993), and Precht et al. (1973) explored linkages and provided topical examples of synergistic relationships and interactions among environmental factors and vegetation.

2. W. Romme (pers. comm.) aged a lodgepole pine at 550 years, the oldest he has found. Lodgepole pine commonly reaches 250 years. Barrett (1994) dated stand-replacing fires. Whitebark pine commonly reaches 300–450 years of age, so the oldest individuals likely reach approximately 500 years.

3. Treeline has fluctuated considerably in elevation during the past 10,000 years, the Holocene. Rochefort et al. (1994) concluded that "the generally synchronous reconstruction of past treeline fluctuations indicates that temperature is the predominant force determining treeline location on a broad geographic scale." The expectation is that trees will continue to expand into the subalpine areas of Yellowstone, even with a

wide range of alternative future climates (Romme and Turner 1991). Jakubos and Romme (1993) studied the timing of lodgepole pine establishment in dry subalpine meadows in Yellowstone.

4. See Gruell (1980a) for a comparative photo record showing increased densities of herbaceous vegetation in subalpine areas. Gruell (1980b) discussed climatic factors involved in the changes, again demonstrating the role of interaction and complexity.

5. Knight (1994:182, 186) discussed the relationship of forest type and leaf area to evapotranspiration and streams.

6. Houston (1982) discussed this at greater length.

7. See Whitlock (1993) and Whitlock and Bartlein (1993) for detailed discussions. Whitlock and Bartlein (1993) pointed out that the climatic patterns have changed progressively in time for both regimes, with modern plant communities having established in the Yellowstone region between 5,000 and 4,000 years ago.

8. Albanese and Wilson (1974).

9. See Baker (1976). Balling et al. (1992, 1993) showed significant statistical correlations between wildfire (lightning-caused) and historical climatic change. The likelihood of fire in Yellowstone National Park has increased in conjunction with increasing summer temperatures and decreasing January–June precipitation. Millspaugh (1994) found charcoal present throughout the sedimentary record from Cygnet Lakes on the Central Plateau. The record begins about 14,000 years ago, indicating the occurrence of fire in the region since the ice melted.

10. Charcoal and magnetic susceptibility records applicable to the Central Plateau (Millspaugh and Whitlock 1995) agreed with dendrochronological data of the last 400 years (Romme 1982, Romme and Despain 1989). The sediment records were then used to extrapolate further back in time. (Magnetic susceptibility measurements are a new technique that analyzes sediments for inwash from adjacent burned areas.)

11. Houston (1973) estimated a 25-year return interval for fires in the Douglas-fir/sagebrush/grasslands of the northern range; Barrett (1994) found a 30-year mean interval. Arno and Gruell (1983) found similar return intervals in comparable habitat outside the park. For fire frequency data from higher elevations on the northern range, see Barrett (1994).

12. See Barrett (1994) for details of burn intervals on the northern range andesitic soils. Romme and Despain (1989) defined the burn interval for the Central Plateau. However, prior to extensive fire on the Central Plateau ca. 1670–1700, burn intervals apparently were shorter (Millspaugh and Whitlock 1995). The Little Ice Age, with cooler temperatures and increased precipitation, allowed a greater increase in fuels prior to 1988.

13. Bessie and Johnson (1995) modeled fire behavior in the subalpine forests of the southern Canadian Rocky Mountains from information on fuel accumulation and weather conditions. They make a compelling case that the extent of area burned over time is determined primarily by weather variation among years, rather than by fuel variation associated with stand age. In other words, fire is less an attribute of the forest community in subalpine areas than was previously thought. The large, ecologically important fires are driven primarily by the rare occurrence of extreme burning conditions. The Bessie and Johnson fire behavior models probably apply to Yellowstone, if they are modified slightly to account for the slower rates of forest growth on rhyolite soils (J. Agee, pers. comm.). The models also imply that the effects of any unnatural fuel accumulations in Yellowstone forests, as might have resulted from earlier fire suppression, were inconsequential in terms of the area burned during 1988.

14. See Romme and Despain (1989).

15. Schullery (1989) reviewed fire history and fire policy, emphasizing the events of 1988.

16. In the fall of 1988 a panel of research scientists convened in Yellowstone National Park to review the fires of 1988 (Christiansen et al. 1989). The second review was conducted by an interagency group of fire professionals and ecologists, the Fire Management Policy Review Team (1988; also called the Philpot Report).

17. See Houston (1973) for more detail.

18. See Romme et al. (*Ecology* 1995).

19. Lyon (1971) found that burning stimulated willow growth in Idaho. Effects vary among species of willow and according to intensity of burn.

20. Gruell (1980a, 1980b) identified the role of fire in maintaining cottonwood stands and preventing or greatly retarding conversion to conifers.

Knight (1994:52) summarized the roles of fire and hydrological forces in producing mosaics of riparian vegetation across Wyoming. Fire apparently was a strong influence on cottonwood stands. Gruell (1980a, 1983) and Johnson (1987) both stressed fire as a dominant force in their photographic comparisons.

21. A fascinating example of geological and biological forces interacting on a time scale that would show in comparative photographs occurs on the coast of Hudson Bay. Grazing by geese maintains a highly productive plant community, but the system is unstable in both time and space because of isostatic uplift (crustal rebound from removal of ice masses after the last ice age) at a rate of 0.5 to 1.2 m (about 1.5 ft to over 3 ft) per century (Hik et al. 1992).

22. Cannon et al. (1995) discussed the complexities of the most recent phase of uplift in the Sour Creek resurgent dome of the Yellowstone caldera (III on fig. 9). W. Romme (pers. comm.) wrote: "The crustal uplifting in the early 1980s raised the water level in the southern end of Yellow-

stone Lake sufficiently to flood and kill many small groves of lodgepole pine that were growing along the lakeshore. The Molly Islands also were affected by a greater frequency of high water that impaired bird reproductive success."

GRAZING DYNAMICS

1. Herbivory is the study of plant-animal interactions. The subject matter is extremely broad and involves more than just consideration of the actual consumption of vegetation by animals. Other effects of herbivores, which include trampling, trailing, and urine and dung deposition, are considered part of herbivory, as are studies of the biochemical responses of plants to grazing and the dynamics of plant and animal populations (Crawley 1983). Sources for the studies mentioned are: moose in boreal forests (Pastor et al. 1988; McInnes et al. 1992); beavers (Naiman et al. 1988); effects of spruce budworm on forests (Morris 1963); Serengeti (McNaughton 1985). Our introductory material was modified from Woodward et al. (1994).

2. The explanations we present, with some modification, are from Macnab (1985). Caughley (1976) developed and explained the relationships between ecological and economic carrying capacities and sustained yield harvests of ungulates. Ungulate populations achieve dynamic equilibrium only in the short term (perhaps decades), because disturbances of most established grazing systems are inevitable and the system then shifts to different levels. In some systems, predators can clearly affect the level of the equilibrium between plants and herbivores. Finally, populations of ungulates growing from low densities may overshoot their ecological carrying capacity levels before equilibria are achieved. The sequence of population irruption, crash, and stable equilibrium (in some environments) has been examined by Riney (1964) and Caughley (1970). Sinclair (1995) discussed African elephants and large mammal grazers in the Serengeti from the perspective of a multiple stable equilibrium hypothesis.

The interplay of forces acting to limit ungulate population size is complex. Sinclair and Arcese (1995) explored the *predation sensitive foraging* hypothesis, where food supplies and predation jointly limit ungulate population growth. Under this hypothesis, intraspecific competition and predation interact to establish an equilibrium for the prey population at a level slightly below ecological carrying capacity. This situation develops as food becomes limiting because animals take greater risks to obtain it, and as a result some are killed by predators. This concept makes sense for the Yellowstone ungulates and the applicability of the hypothesis merits field evaluation.

3. We use the term *natural regulation* in the same sense that David Lack (1954) employed it in his influential book *The Natural Regulation of Animal Numbers,* namely that "wild animals fluctuate irregularly in numbers between limits that are extremely restricted compared with what their rates of increase would allow" (Lack 1954). This implies to us that animal numbers are likely regulated in some density-dependent fashion, in contrast to population levels being imposed by human cropping (Sinclair 1989). It does not mean that factors regulating populations in Yellowstone are necessarily the same, or act with the same intensity, now as they did in earlier ("pristine") times. Actually, few ungulate populations in Yellowstone are clean examples of naturally regulated populations; most are cropped to some degree as they move beyond park boundaries. For these populations the park does not provide ecologically complete habitat. There may be ungulate populations in Yellowstone with segments that reside entirely within the park and that are naturally regulated over long periods (Cole 1983; Houston 1982; Meagher 1973).

We also recognize that all populations over time will fully occupy their habitat if able to do so and will emigrate or expand their range if suitable habitat permits. This is how animals first occupied the Yellowstone Plateau after the ice melted. Emigration and range expansion may be gradual processes that function as part of the ongoing natural regulatory mechanisms for some species in some circumstances. In other cases stress dispersal may be involved (Meagher 1989, 1993). In these instances the above-described natural regulation mechanisms may govern a population for a period in a given locale, but over a longer time frame, if the parameters change, so will the population and its distribution. Even so, the density-dependent mechanisms are part of the overall complex process (which may include density-independent factors as well). The key element in the debate is the existence of natural feedback mechanisms vs. factors imposed by the actions of people today.

4. Fragmentary accounts suggest that ungulates, especially bison, could have enormous impact on the vegetation. Osborne Russell was encamped with a party of trappers on the Yellowstone River near the confluence with Clark's Fork during the winter of 1836–37. The trappers had to feed cottonwood bark to their horses because "the Buffaloe have entirely destroyed the grass throughout this part of the country" (Haines 1965:51). Charles Goodnight recounts the extent of bison mortality following depletion of their food after a spring drought delayed greenup in 1867 along the divide between the Concho and Colorado rivers in northern Texas: "[The bison] had remained until the grass was gone, and had died from starvation by thousands and thousands. The dead buffaloes, which extended for a hundred miles or more, were so thick they resembled a pumpkin field, and their carcasses had hatched millions and billions of what is known as screw flies" (Haley 1936:161). This is a graphic illustration of the effects of environmental fluctuation, what we could call a "biological crunch."

5. The distribution, dynamics, and abundance of livestock are controlled to a great extent by humans through husbandry practices. In particular, the provision of supplemental food during winter, in the form of hay cut earlier from irrigated and fertilized pastures, maintains livestock

densities at higher levels than would be possible otherwise. Livestock may have greater potential to affect native vegetation grazed at other seasons of the year than would be expected from native ungulates subjected to the winter food "bottleneck."

6. See Houston (1982), Meagher (1973), and Singer and Norland (1994).

7. Streubel (1989) provided a readable and informative book on the smaller mammals of Yellowstone.

8. The management history of the northern Yellowstone elk from the time of the earliest accounts through 1979 has been described by Houston (1982). Numbers and population history since are contained in Mack and Singer (1993a, 1993b), Singer (1991), Singer and Mack (1993), and Lemke et al. (1998). Cole (1969a) proposed a moratorium on elk removals in the park (elk were routinely trapped or shot by National Park Service rangers) to test the extent to which natural regulation would affect elk numbers, and later expanded the concept as potentially applicable to several Rocky Mountain national parks (Cole 1971). Houston (1971) emphasized natural regulation in the context of ecosystems of parks; Coughenour and Singer (1991, 1996) further discuss the concept of "overgrazing" and evidence for nutritional limitation of elk numbers on the northern range. A volume presenting recent research on the vegetation and ungulates of the northern range is in preparation (Vohs 1996).

The size of the northern winter range increased from around 109,000 ha to about 153,000 ha from the 1970s to the 1990s as elk numbers increased and animals occupied larger areas north of the park (Lemke et al. 1998). Maximum winter counts depend upon the conjunction of suitable elk distribution, snow cover, and flying weather. A given winter may not provide good counting conditions, hence there are gaps in the data of the early 1980s, or counts throughout that are known to be low (Lemke et al. 1998). Minimum winter populations averaged 15,520 ± 2,324 (SD) elk for 9 annual censuses conducted from 1981–82 through 1994–95, the poor counts of 1988–89 and 1990–91 excluded. This represents the actual number of elk counted, minus those killed subsequently during late season hunts (Lemke et al. 1998). Actual numbers would be higher because not all elk present are observed during censuses. The posthunt population estimate is important because that is the density of elk affected by the Yellowstone winter. The mean observed rate of population increase (r) was 0.0012 for the past 14 years (through the winter of 1994–95) and did not differ significantly from zero (Lemke et al. 1998). Thus, the population appears to have achieved dynamic equilibrium with the available forage resources and hunting removals in the changeable Yellowstone environment. Annual hunting removals have been variable and averaged 1,823 ± 1022 (SD) elk from 1981–82 through 1994–95. Houston (1982) and Lemke et al. (1998) explain census terminology, methods of calculation, and hunt seasons. All this can be confusing, and understandably, authors less immersed in the subject have sometimes been inconsistent with the elk numbers they show.

9. Each species has a best time/season for maximum counts; good counts are not possible every year. Moose in this habitat do not present a good subject for aerial counts by either fixed-wing aircraft or helicopter. An estimated 60 percent of the northern range bighorn sheep died during an epizootic of infectious keratoconjunctivitis (pinkeye) caused by a *Chlamydia* sp. organism during the winter of 1981-82 (Meagher et al. 1992). Some population recovery occurred, but counts have been variable since 1988. None of the available field survey data suggested a bighorn sheep population increase comparable to that seen in elk, bison, pronghorn, or mule deer. Also, in contrast to species that have shown recent increases, moose apparently declined appreciably on the northern range following the 1988 fires. Tyers' (1993) field data underscored the importance of old-growth forest to moose in this habitat; large areas of coniferous forest used by northern range moose burned in 1988. However, one can anticipate that in time their numbers will increase just as happened after moose arrived on the northern winter range in the early 1900s (Houston 1982). Yellowstone National Park does not represent good white-tailed deer habitat. Occasional animals are seen widely distributed every summer; they winter in low densities north of the park. A few are seen near the north boundary most winters, and occasionally farther within the park toward Tower. Mountain goats are in the process of establishing a presence in the park (Varley 1994, 1995).

10. The elk grazing regime is amazingly complex. They "know" what they are taking through nutritional cues and select for the best available forage at all seasons. Houston (1982) provided a foundation for understanding how elk utilize their habitat. More recently, Frank et al. (1994), Frank and McNaughton (1991, 1992, 1993), Merrill et al. (1994), and Coughenour (1991) have provided insight into the elk role in nutrient flux through the system. Landscape ecologists are modeling the system, providing more insight into the interaction of elk numbers and the patterns of herbivory on a population-landscape scale (Pearson et al. 1995; Turner et al. 1993, 1994; Wallace et al. 1995). As this work continues it leads to more questions, all of which demonstrate that the simplistic numbers game of so many elk to so many acres of grass will tell us little about the functioning of natural systems.

11. Bison have been reestablished in Jackson Hole. Their history is detailed in Grand Teton National Park (1994).

12. The history of the Yellowstone bison, the reductions, and subpopulations and their numbers through 1968 are in Meagher (1973).

13. Stress dispersal and range expansion are documented in Meagher (1989). The role of the snow-packed winter road system and the details of changes are in Meagher (1993). Current numbers are from ongoing aerial surveys.

During the extraordinarily severe winter of 1996–97, large numbers of bison moved to and beyond park boundaries. By April 1997 nearly 1,100 had been trapped and shipped to slaughter or shot to protect the brucellosis-free status of Montana cattle. Additional bison died inside the park because of the harsh conditions. The winter's outcome was evaluated during summer 1997; it appears that 1,900–2,000 of the early winter population of approximately 3,500 bison survived.

14. See Cole (1969*b*) and Gruell (1973) for effects of gophers at higher elevations such as Big Game Ridge on the park's south boundary. Laycock (1958) looked at grassland effects in Jackson Hole. Youmans (1979) studied habitat relationships in Pelican Valley, noting that soil moisture limited distribution. Gruell (1973) and Chase et al. (1982) provided broad discussions of pocket gopher activities, densities, effects, and environmental relationships in various habitats. Interestingly, Burns (1980) considered them a geomorphic agent on tundra in Colorado. See Huntly and Reichman (1994) for a broad review of the effects of fossorial mammals, including pocket gophers, on vegetation.

15. Haines (1965:27) quoted Osborne Russell's encounter with a small band of Snake Indians in the Lamar Valley during July 1835: "They said there had been a great many beaver on the branches of this stream [Lamar River] but they had killed nearly all of them and being ignorant of the value of fur had singed it off with fire in order to drip the meat more conveniently." Haines (1977) described several poaching episodes during the early years after the park's establishment.

Hill (1982) and Naiman et al. (1988) describe the history of beaver exploitation more widely in North America and discuss the animals' influence on streams. Profound effects on streams occur as a result of water impoundment behind beaver dams, including changes in water chemistry, sediment deposition, and nutrient cycling. Beaver herbivory influences the development of riparian soils and alters the direction of plant succession. These effects may be transitory or longer lasting, depending on occupancy over time. Warren (1926) documented the extensive beaver colonies on the northern range during the 1920s. Jonas (1955) documented the change to a lower population level. The 1979–80 survey was made by S. Fullerton (unpub. data). The 1988–89 survey is reported by Consolo-Murphy and Hanson (1993), the 1994 survey by Consolo-Murphy and Tatum (1995).

16. See Bergstrom (1964) and Houston (1982).

17. Despain (1990) provided a detailed account of the pine bark beetle epizootic, with maps showing the extent of tree mortality and an introduction to the ecological literature on the insect. He also traced the history of management concerns, noting a request to Congress in 1924 for money to control spruce budworm. These concerns were equivalent to those regarding the suppression of natural fire. Yeager (1934) expresses the attitude of the early 1930s nicely in his fictionalized account of life for a Yellowstone ranger.

The effort to control natural spruce budworm outbreaks on the northern range led to spraying of DDT in the 1950s in the Hellroaring area. At least one knowledgeable ranger, a fine fly fisherman, stated that the fish would be killed, and indeed they were. Swenson et al. (1986) implicated the spraying of DDT at that time in the decline of area bald eagles; populations have recovered since.

Romme et al. (1986) and Knight (1994:177) examined the ecological effects of bark beetles. Beetles accelerated the rate of forest succession and may have increased the primary productivity of forests.

18. These comments on predation and resource limitation are drawn largely from Houston (1982). Sinclair and Norton-Griffiths (1979) describe the extent of resource limitation among herbivores in the enormous Serengeti ecosystem, a grazing system not unlike Yellowstone in many respects. Predation by the several meateaters has been studied more intensively in recent years to provide a database for future comparisons once a wolf population is reestablished. Refer to Gese (1995) for data on coyotes and Murphy (1998) for cougars. See Gunther and Renkin (1990) and French and French (1990) for documentation of grizzly bear predation on elk calves.

19. Reintroduction of wolves to Yellowstone began in January 1995 with the translocation of 14 animals from Canada to holding enclosures in the Lamar Valley, from which they were released later. Sixteen additional wolves were brought to holding enclosures in January 1996 for later release. Stay tuned; this topic changes in detail constantly. The informed opinions of wolf biologists and the projections from population models differ in their predictions of the likely reduction of prey species levels, mainly for elk. Ten percent was the opinion indicated by four consultants (Lime et al. 1993); Boyce (1993) predicted 10–30 % reduction within the park from his model. We do not know what effect wolves will have on prey distributions, but fundamental energy relationships will govern this. That is, the prey cannot spend so much energy (including obtaining decreased quantity and/or quality of forage) avoiding the predators as to jeopardize its own survival. The real test of ideas, informed opinions, and models will be the active presence of the wolf.

It appears unlikely that aboriginal peoples exerted any great predatory effect (see part 3, "The Human Presence"), except perhaps for roughly the century prior to park establishment, when horse-owning Native Americans traversed the plateau seasonally. The Eagle Creek archeological site just north of the park, located on the migratory elk travel route, may provide insight as excavation work continues.

20. See May (1979).

21. The Little Ice Age was most severe in this area during the latter part of the nineteenth century (see part 2, "Setting the Stage"). After our field research years in Yellowstone National Park, we have no doubt about ungulate response to snow depths and winter severity. For example, Meagher (1973:17) estimated that the bison population at the time of park

establishment might have been approximately 1,000, recognizing that some likely migrated beyond park boundaries. Since 1973, an increased database and understanding of bison responses to winter severity (Meagher 1993) suggest that ecological carrying capacity may have fluctuated around 2,000 in the present-day climatic regime (had the bison not adapted to using the snow-packed, energy-efficient winter roads of the park interior).

22. Highlining of trees has been viewed by some range managers as evidence of range deterioration in the park and elsewhere. We examined the photos for the occurrence of highlined trees. One hundred and fifty two comparisons were available from the major ungulate winter ranges in the park. Of these, 102 allowed an assessment of the effects of ungulates on tree morphology (appendix 2, table 3). Fourteen (37 percent) of 38 comparisons taken before 1900 (1871–76) on the northern range, in the Madison-Firehole areas, and in Hayden and Pelican valleys showed high-lined trees in both the original photos and the retakes. Forty-three (67 percent) of 64 later comparisons (originals taken 1900–1944) showed high-lined trees in originals and retakes. Increased highlining, including the effects of rubbing and horning, seemed to be associated with recolonization of some areas by bison (recall that bison were exterminated from the northern range and Hayden Valley–Firehole before 1900, and were greatly reduced in the Pelican area).

We do not consider the occurrence of highlined trees to be a useful index to the condition of range resources in the park. Highlined trees occurred in the earliest photos. Such effects have become more conspicuous over time as extensive conifer invasion occurred, with climatic change (Jakubos and Romme 1993), and as a consequence of fire suppression. Highlining seems to be inevitable for palatable conifers growing on ungulate winter ranges, and is exacerbated by mechanical impacts as ungulates move in and out of forest edges and isolated stands of trees. Once a highline forms it persists for decades, since trees tend not to grow new branches on the lower portion of the trunk. A single hard winter when elk numbers are high could create a browse line that will persist for many years.

23. Warren (1926) initially recommended beaver control. Descriptions of the beaver population trends on the northern range suggest that the animals underwent an irruption and crash similar to that reported for ungulates (Caughley 1970; endnote 2). Perhaps the question should have been why Warren saw so much beaver activity, rather than why beavers have declined.

The history of aspen studies and the evidence available through 1979 was reported in Houston (1982). Much of the concern for aspen developed from observations of ungulate exclosures (fenced plots from which ungulates were excluded). These studies showed that vegetative suckers sprouting inside exclosures sometimes matured into larger stems, but even given full protection, stem densities and growth rates often did not approach those suggested in the early photographs.

24. Romme et al. (*Ecology* 1995) studied the interrelationships of aspen, fire, climate, and ungulate browsing. They concluded that the establishment of aspen as trees was complex, more so than their study could define. Kay (1990, 1993) held to an opposite perspective, that elk were the major cause of aspen decline. Research continues, see Romme et al. (1995 unpubl. manuscript) for post-1988 fire seedling establishment since the 1988 fires.

25. See Houston (1982). Knight (1994: chap. 6, also p. 238) discussed sagebrush ecology and insect herbivory.

26. Changes in the bison population are discussed in Meagher (1993). The remaining interpretations are discussed in Houston (1982). See also Singer and Renkin (1995). Knight (1994) discussed grassland ecology and responses of grasslands to grazing.

27. Defoliation by a small native beetle killed stands of willow on the northern range during the 1970s. Houston (1982) discussed the relationship between elk browsing and willow growth. See Singer et al. (1994) for a more recent perspective. Chadde and Kay (1991) held to the view that elk were responsible. The situation appears to be much more complex than they suggest; understanding changes in stream hydrology related to the Little Ice Age, followed by warmer and drier climates, seems fundamental to understanding the changes in riparian plant communities.

Studies in the Jackson Hole area over 29 years demonstrated that these same species of willow not only tolerated heavy winter browsing annually on dormant plants but thrived at sites where soil moisture was optimum (Gruell 1980a, 1980b; Houston 1968, 1987, 1992).

28. See Tyers (1993) and note 9, this chapter.

29. The snowmelt spring runoff of 1991 and 1993 occurred rapidly on some drainages. For example, the summation of the two seasonal events on upper Blacktail Deer Creek of the northern range flooded the local bottom area and deposited cobbles and silt to form new substrate. The main channel of the creek had shifted eastward when the water level dropped.

30. See Romme et al. (*Ecology* 1995) for elk-aspen relationships in Yellowstone National Park. Analogous relationships for incidentally consumed forage species have been identified in other grazing systems. In Olympic National Park, herbivory on a rare endemic milkvetch remained high even at greatly reduced densities of mountain goats (Schreiner et al. 1994). The milkvetch was of essentially no consequence in the grazing system of the nonnative goats. In New York, the uncommon white oak received disproportionately heavy defoliation in forests dominated by red oak (Futuyma and Wasserman 1980). White oaks were maintained at low densities because an insect herbivore, the fall cankerworm was a dietary generalist whose populations were maintained at high levels by the more common species of oak.

31. Rare plants may also persist in refugia where ungulate herbivory is reduced or absent. For willows in Yellowstone these include deep-snow areas, steep streambanks, and rock crevices.

THE HUMAN PRESENCE

1. The time of arrival of the earliest human colonizers in North America has been, and still is, much debated (Stanford and Day 1991; Hoffecker et al. 1993). Evidence to date indicates that anatomically modern humans first appeared in eastern Siberia about 22,000 years ago, so humans could not have colonized North America earlier. Turner (1992) used genetically determined dental traits to trace origins to east Asia. Dental traits, in combination with other genetic and linguistic characteristics, also indicated that the earliest immigrants colonized most extensively.

Hoffecker et al. (1993) refined the probable human chronology because of new studies of global sea level changes that have occurred in the past 17,000 years. Although the land bridge existed earlier, colonization of Beringia may not have been possible much before 12,000 years ago. Wood for fuel may have been a critical factor for human occupation, but the harsh environment would not yet support tree growth, even in river valleys. Human arrival in North America about 12,000 years ago would be consistent with Clovis period dates. That is, people descended from the earliest immigrants left Clovis period evidence from more than 11,000 years ago. New dating (Hoffecker et al. 1993:51) places Clovis evidence as clustering around 11,200-10,900 years ago.

2. Cannon (1992) reviewed regional and local archeological evidence for human presence as well as the faunal assemblage. Mummy Cave east of the park and the Meyers-Hindman site to the north are nearby human-occupied sites dating to more than 9,000 years ago. Both sites indicated long-term occupation. Frison (1992) and Davis and Greiser (1992) provided considerable Clovis and Folsom site evidence for Wyoming and Montana, respectively. Part of an obsidian Clovis point was found in 1959 in Gardiner, Montana, during excavation for a new post office (Haines 1977). The source of the obsidian is not known, and our inquiries indicate that the fragment probably has disappeared.

3. Cannon (1992) estimated that only about 2 percent of the park has been inventoried for archeological sites. See Haines (1977: chap. 2) for an overview of earlier work. Since 1989, archeological research effort has increased, often being site-specific because of road work or other development plans.

Each obsidian source is geochemically unique, so artifacts can be identified as to source; other techniques allow dating. To date, 59 quarry or quarry-associated loci have been identified at Obsidian Cliff (Davis and Johnson 1993), indicating intensive and long-term use by people. Trade among later native groups must have been considerable; Obsidian Cliff

was the main obsidian source for Hopewellian people in the upper Mississippi and Ohio River valleys (Cannon 1993). These people were the Mound Builders of roughly 2000 years ago.

Cannon et al. (1995) presented a fascinating overview of the complex environmental and geomorphic factors relating to early human occupation of the Fishing Bridge area. Blood residue analysis (one of the newest archeological research tools) is discussed briefly. See Cannon (1995) and Cannon and Newman (1994) for more detail. Cannon (pers. comm., 1995) indicated that positive blood residue analyses for bear, rabbit, and bison had been obtained from Yellowstone Lake locations, from lithic materials that dated to 8,500–10,000 years ago. These results indicated use of these mammal species by early peoples, although means of procurement and nature of use are unknown.

4. Kay (1994) dissents. He proposes an overkill hypothesis, arguing that aboriginal peoples had a major role in keeping ungulate numbers low. Frison (1991, 1992) discussed the foothills-mountain economy. Connor (1993) used the term *cold* hunter-gatherer lifestyle in discussing mountain adaptations. Janetski (1993) pointed out the importance of diverse resources and ecological zones in a seasonally harsh environment. The recent excavation of an 800-year-old bison butchering site near Yellowstone Lake attests to the ability of these people to hunt effectively in the ecological niche they occupied (Cannon 1992). The site does not suggest communal hunting, as occurred with bison drive sites even in mountain valleys at lower elevations (Arthur 1962). But it fits nicely with the use of the locale by scattered bison that occurs even now, particularly in winter–spring.

The role of humans in megafaunal extinctions in North America at the end of the Pleistocene has been much debated. Owen-Smith (1988) and Haynes (1991) provided considerable ecological insight into the relative roles of climate change and human hunting. The extinctions seem to have represented a complex of interactive factors, with humans often in a terminal role but at somewhat different times and places. Pielou (1991:266) noted that "the great wave of extinctions at the end of the Pleistocene has yet to be convincingly explained." Barnosky (1989) placed the Pleistocene mammal extinctions in context with earlier such events in the geologic record. In his perspective, climatic change and arrival of new species apparently interacted in all such events. Although humans had a role as the new species, the Pleistocene extinctions did not represent an extraordinary occurrence.

5. In 1835 Osborne Russell (Haines 1955) described the superbly wrought bows and quill work of people known as the Sheepeaters. An ecological perspective on these hunters contrasts markedly with that of Euroamericans, who often viewed the Sheepeaters as "poor" because they lacked horses and guns. Horses would have been a liability for people who wintered on the plateau, and their procurement methods apparently were quite efficient without the use of guns (Frison 1991, 1992).

The resident Sheepeaters apparently left the park as they became increasingly distanced from other Shoshone-Bannock groups. Haines (1977) gives a date of 1871, but considering the superintendent's comment above (p.249), a few must have lingered for a few years. Norris (1881:35–36) observed that shelters and "countless drive-ways and coverts in every stage of decay are still found in favorable localities throughout the Park." Haines (1977:chap. 2) provided an overview of use of the park area by the more recent native groups. Territories of these people were quite dynamic in the period shortly before European peoples arrived. The Sheepeaters had apparently arrived on the Yellowstone Plateau as recently as 1800. They represented the northeasternmost expansion of Shoshone peoples, who apparently had dispersed north and east across the Great Basin during prehistoric times.

6. Gruell (1985) analyzed the role of native peoples in setting fires. There seems no question this was done for various purposes, but the activity may have been minor in much of Yellowstone compared to other locales because of relatively fewer people, in smaller groups, who utilized a mountain food-based economy. Recall too the climatic influence of the Little Ice Age during the previous few centuries. Even now, in a year when it is too wet to burn, a dozen lightning-caused fire starts may burn only a few acres total.

7. Haines (1977) provided a comprehensive and readable history of Yellowstone National Park, and leads the reader to myriad topical sources. His account places John Colter on the Yellowstone Plateau during the winter of 1807–8.

8. See Haines (1977) for detail. In addition to published sources and manuscripts, Aubrey Haines had an unrivaled knowledge of the park's archives, an official branch of the National Archives. Quantities of original park records are stored within the park. Note that the Bannock Trail followed what was probably a prehistoric travel route in large part, which became much more obvious in some locations because of use by the Bannock people.

9. During the 1930s annual park visitor numbers increased from about one-quarter million to one-half million (Haines 1977). The travel season was short, early June through August. Technology was comparatively limited and dictated such practices as open pit garbage dumps; these were not eliminated until about 1970.

10. See Houston (1971) for a discussion of ecosystems and their ability to function in national parks.

11. See Varley (1981), Varley and Schullery (1983), and Gresswell and Varley (1988).

12. Houston (1982) and Meagher (1973) discuss these programs in detail.

13. Klein (1989) estimated that 60 percent of the lead he found in Lewis Lake came from mine smelters outside the park, between 1880 and 1985.

14. Five percent is the number used at present (1994) by the park's planning office, but this is an administrative rather than a biological determination. This area is still a small percentage of the park but receives the bulk of visitor use. For example, the land area actually removed (paved over, built upon) from the ungulate forage base is still around 1 percent. However, the number of people using the developments has grown greatly. This has increased the overall impact by fostering more hiking, fishing, driving, wildlife viewing, and so forth. Larger numbers of automobiles on the roads and greater backcountry use has done much to exacerbate the exotic plant presence.

15. Gunther (1990) studied the relationship between grizzly bear use and human activity (hikers, anglers, horseback travel) in Pelican Valley. Mattson (1990) examined the influences of human activity on grizzly bear use of winterkill ungulate carcasses.

16. Meagher (1993) documented the changes in the bison population; these are still in flux. This example is particularly difficult for administrators to address, because just decreasing the number of winter visitors would not remove the influence of the roads.

17. The fire lookout commenting on air quality was J. McKown. The U.S. Fish and Wildlife Fisheries Assistance Office in Yellowstone National Park is collecting the data on lake trout. Research work on common timothy is being conducted by L. Wallace.

Epilogue: Yellowstone as a Natural Area Park

1. We note that these powerful disturbances are essential to retain components of the Yellowstone ecosystem, as in many other natural areas. Romme and Knight (1982) described the role of fire disturbance in maintaining the diversity of birds in Yellowstone; many species are more abundant in early seral stages, including the mountain bluebird. In turn, diversity of plant communities has been shown to contribute to stability (Frank and McNaughton 1991). See Lewin (1986) for an introduction to the idea that disturbance has been essential to maintaining species diversity in many African conservation areas.

2. Control or elimination of alien species may become feasible. Recent advances in molecular biology and genetics suggest that development of highly specific, genetically engineered toxins or agents of biological control may soon become operational tools, at least for selected problems and specific sites.

3. The reality of equilibrium states is a hotly contested topic in ecology, and much of current ecological theory does not support the concept of equilibria. However, we follow Hik et al. (1992:404) in believing that the concept of an equilibrium state "remains a useful descriptive term to

describe situations where the balance between positive and negative feedbacks is relatively constant and the system is resilient to disturbance within a defined time frame."

In our own time in Yellowstone we have witnessed the ability of systems to "repair" themselves. That is, systems or parts of systems, may revert in a relatively short time when the human-induced change is removed. Examples are the increased numbers and dispersion of grizzly bears on natural foods after closing of open pit garbage dumps. Bald eagles have recovered in numbers after the negative influence of DDT spraying in the 1950s. The pronghorn population recovered in the early 1980s after a period of reduction of numbers during the park's range management phase. The northern Yellowstone elk reoccupied their habitat and reestablished historic migration patterns. The list could continue, but we should add that time alone will not compensate for some changes in systems after human interference. New equilibria may be the result. However, these cases demonstrate the ability of systems to recover if allowed to do so, within some limits at least. The ability of an ecosystem to absorb change and disturbance and still maintain relationships among populations is a measure of system resilience (Holling 1973). Ecosystems such as Yellowstone that evolved in harsh environments where disasters are relatively common (drought, floods, fires, severe winters) likely will be highly resilient.

4. Many authors have presented the national park idea and its evolution, dichotomy of mission, compromises, and so forth. We suggest the volume edited by Boyce and Keiter (1991) for perspectives and many additional references on the debate over the purpose of national parks managed primarily for their natural area values. Sellars (1997) traced the history of science and resource management in the National Park Service. A reader would conclude from the historical documentation that the agency management emphasis was on human use rather than resource conservation: if the scenery was lovely, all was well.

The National Research Council (1992) reviewed the state of science in the national parks and in essence called for an agency cultural change: "The call for change made in this report is not new. But given the consistent lack of response to so many previous calls for change . . . it is time to move toward a new structure—indeed, toward a new culture—for science in the national park system" (88). The recommendations in this report . . . will require substantial alterations in the philosophic and substantive structure and function of the Park Service" (111).

5. Quote from Shepherd and Caughley (1987:191). To continue: "Specifically, there are three options: (1) If the aim is to conserve specified animal and plant associations that may be modified or eliminated by wildfire, grazing or predation, then intervene to reduce the intensity of wildfire, grazing or predation. (2) If the aim is to give full rein to the processes of the system and to accept the resultant, often transient, states that those processes produce, then do not intervene. (3) A bit of both—if the aim is to allow the processes of the system to proceed unhindered unless they produce 'unacceptable' states, then intervene only when unacceptable outcomes appear likely."

6. The word *natural* and the concept of natural areas are laden with semantic difficulty; some biologists consider natural to be an anachronistic term that is not particularly useful (e.g., Soule 1990). We think the term still has scientific merit as well as important heuristic value. Scholars of natural philosophy consider that naturalness can be seen meaningfully as a relative quality, i.e., the extent to which ecological processes are functioning without major change or disruption by modern humans is a measure of relative naturalness (Rolston 1989, 1994; Hoerr 1993). The concept is too important philosophically and scientifically to abandon.

7. Describing the dynamics of Yellowstone in terms used by landscape ecologists is difficult. Fire disturbances have been so large and infrequent in the extensive lodgepole pine forests that we agree with Romme (1982) that these ecosystems are best considered "a non–steady state system characterized by cyclic long-term changes in structure and function." In contrast, the history of frequent, smaller fires in the lower elevation Douglas-fir/sagebrush/grassland steppe areas may have produced a landscape more appropriately described as a "shifting-mosaic steady state" (Bormann and Likens 1979), where the spatial distribution of postfire succession was always changing in patches, but the mosaic produced remained relatively constant over time given an appropriate climatic regime.

8. These same cautions should be applied to the narrative accounts of conditions in the Yellowstone area, which span less than two centuries. These rich accounts provide useful insight, but the information remains fragmentary enough that it must be interpreted with great care and considerable ecological insight. Historical accounts, like the photographs, may become traps for unwary park managers if these are seen as a route to restoring particular biological states.

Literature Cited

Albanese, J. P., and M. Wilson. 1974. Preliminary description of the terraces of the North Platte River at Casper, Wyoming. In *Applied geology and archeology: the Holocene history of Wyoming*, ed. M. Wilson, 8–18. Geological Survey of Wyo., Report of investigations. Cheyenne.

Arno, S. F., and G. E. Gruell. 1983. Fire history at the forest-grassland ecotone in southwestern Montana. *J. Range Manage.* 36:332–36.

Arthur, G. W. 1962. The emigrant bison drives of Paradise Valley, Montana. In *Symposium on buffalo jumps*, ed. C. Malouf and S. Conner, 16–27. Montana Archeological Society Memoir 1.

Baker, R. G. 1976. *Quaternary vegetation history of the Yellowstone Lake basin, Wyoming.* U.S. Geological Survey Prof. Paper 729-E.

———. 1983. Holocene vegetational history of the western United States. In *Late-Quaternary environments of the United States*, vol. 2, ed. H. E. Wright, 109–27. Minneapolis: University of Minnesota Press.

Balling, R. C., Jr., G. A. Meyer, and S. G. Wells. 1992. Relation of surface climate and burned area in Yellowstone National Park. *Agri. Forest Meteorology* 60:285–93.

———1993. Climate change in Yellowstone National Park: Is the drought-related risk of wildfires increasing? *Climatic Change* 22:34–35.

Barnosky, A. D. 1989. The late Pleistocene event as a paradigm for widespread mammal extinction. In *Mass extinctions: Processes and evidence*, ed. S. K. Donovan, 235–54. New York: Columbia University Press.

Barnosky, C. W., P. M. Anderson, and P. J. Bartlein. 1987. The northwestern U.S. during deglaciation: Vegetational history and paleoclimatic implications. In *North America and adjacent oceans during the last deglaciation*, vol. K-3, ed. W. F. Ruddiman and H. E. Wright, 289–321. Boulder, Colo.: Geological Society of America.

Barrett, S. W. 1994. Fire regimes on andesitic mountain terrain in northeastern Yellowstone National Park, Wyoming. *Int. J. Wildland Fire* 4(2):65–76.

Battle, D. C., and E. N. Thompson. 1972. *Fort Yellowstone historic structures report.* Denver, Colo.: National Park Service, Denver Service Center.

Bergstrom, R. C. 1964. *Competition between elk and phytophagus insects for food in the Lamar Valley, Yellowstone National Park.* Ph.D. diss., University of Wyoming, Laramie.

Bessie, W. C., and E. A. Johnson. 1995. The relative importance of fuels and weather on fire behavior in subalpine forests. *Ecology* 76:747–62.

Bonney, O. H., and L. Bonney. 1970. *Battle drums and geysers.* Chicago, Ill.: Swallow Press.

Bormann, F. H. and G. E. Likens. 1979. *Pattern and process in a forested ecosystem.* New York: Springer-Verlag.

Boyce, M. S. 1991. Natural regulation or the control of nature? In *The greater Yellowstone ecosystem: Redefining America's wilderness heritage*, ed. R. B. Keiter and M. S. Boyce, 183–208. New Haven, Conn.: Yale University Press.

———. 1993. Predicting the consequences of wolf recovery to ungulates in Yellowstone National Park. In *Ecological issues on reintroducing wolves into Yellowstone National Park*, ed. R. S. Cook, 234–69. National Park Service Sci. Monogr. NPS/NPYell/NRSM-93-22.

Boyce, M. S. and R. B. Keiter, eds. 1991. *The greater Yellowstone ecosystem: Redefining America's wilderness heritage.* New Haven, Conn.: Yale University Press.

Bray, J. R. 1971. Vegetational distribution, tree growth and crop success in relation to recent climatic change. In *Advances in ecological research*, vol. 7, ed. J. B. Cragg, 177–233. New York: Academic Press.

Brock, G., and L. Brock. 1993. *Snapshots in time: Repeat photography on the Boise National Forest 1870–1992.* Boise, Id.: U.S. Forest Service, Boise National Forest.

Brubaker, L. B. 1988. Vegetation history and anticipating future vegetation change. In *Ecosystem management for parks and wilderness*, ed. J. K. Agee and D. R. Johnson, 41–61. Seattle: University of Washington Press.

Bureau of Land Management. 1979. *Historical comparison photography: Missouri Breaks, Montana*. Billings, Mont.: Bureau of Land Management.

———. 1980. *Historical comparison photography: Montana foothills and Dillon Resource Area*. Billings, Mont.: Bureau of Land Management.

Burke, R. M. and P. W. Birkeland. 1983. Holocene glaciation in the mountain ranges of the western United States. In *Late-Quaternary environments of the United States*, vol. 2., ed. H. E. Wright, 3–11. Minneapolis: University of Minnesota Press.

Burns, S. F. 1980. Alpine soil distribution and development, Indian Peaks, Colorado Front Range. Ph.D. diss., University of Colorado, Boulder.

Cannon, K. P. 1992. A review of archeological and paleontological evidence for the prehistoric presence of wolf and related prey species in the northern and central Rockies physiographic provinces. In *Wolves for Yellowstone? A report to the United States Congress*. Vol. 4. Research and analysis, ed. J. D. Varley and W. G. Brewster, 1-177 through 1-265. Yellowstone National Park, Wyo.: National Park Service.

———. 1993. Paleoindian use of obsidian in the Greater Yellowstone Area. *Yellowstone Sci.* 1(4):6–9.

———. 1995. Blood residue analyses of ancient stone tools reveal clues to prehistoric subsistence patterns in Yellowstone. *Cultural Resource Manage.* 18(2):14–16.

Cannon, K. P. and M. E. Newman. 1994. Results of blood residue analysis of a late Paleoindian projectile point from Yellowstone National Park, Wyoming. *Current Res. Pleistocene* 11:18–21.

Cannon, K. P., K. L. Pierce, and G. M. Crothers. 1995. Caldera unrest, lake levels, and archeology: The view from Yellowstone Lake. *Park Sci.* 15(3):28–31.

Caughley, G. 1970. Eruption of ungulate populations, with emphasis on Himalayan thar in New Zealand. *Ecology* 51:53–72.

———. 1976. Wildlife management and the dynamics of ungulate populations. In *Applied biology*, vol. 1, ed. T. H. Coaker, 183–246. New York: Academic Press.

———. 1989. New Zealand plant-herbivore ecosystems past and present. In *Moas, mammals and climate in the ecological history of New Zealand*, ed. M. R. Rudge, 3–10. (Supplement) *New Zealand J. Ecol.* 12.

Chadde, S. W. and C. E. Kay. 1991. Tall-willow communities on Yellowstone's northern range: A test of the "natural regulation" paradigm. In *The greater Yellowstone ecosystem: Redefining America's wilderness heritage*. ed. R. B. Keiter and M. S. Boyce, 231–62. New Haven, Conn.: Yale University Press.

Chambers, J. M., W. S. Cleveland, B. Kleiner, and P. Tukey. 1983. *Graphical methods for data analysis*. Boston, Mass.: Duxbury Press.

Chase, J. D., W. E. Howard, and J. T. Roseberry. 1982. Pocket gophers. In *Wild mammals of North America: Biology, management, economics*, ed. J. A. Chapman and G. A. Feldhamer, 239–55. Baltimore, Md.: Johns Hopkins University Press.

Christiansen, N. L., J. K. Agee, P. F. Brussard, J. Hughes, D. H. Knight, G. W. Minshall, J. M. Peek, S. J. Pyne, F. J. Swanson, J. W. Thomas, S. Wells, S. E. Williams, and H. A. Wright. 1989. Interpreting the Yellowstone fires of 1988. *Bioscience* 39:678–85.

Christiansen, R. L. 1984. Yellowstone magmatic evolution: Its bearing on understanding large-scale explosive volcanism. In *Explosive volcanism: Inception, evolution, and hazards*. Studies in Geophysics, 84–95. Washington, D.C.: National Academy Press.

Cleveland, W. S. 1979. Robust locally weighted regression and smoothing scatterplots. *J. Amer. Statistical Assoc.* 74:829–36.

Cole, G. F. 1969a. *Elk and the Yellowstone ecosystem*. Research note. Yellowstone National Park, Wyo.: National Park Service.

———. 1969b. *The elk of Grand Teton and southern Yellowstone national parks*. Yellowstone National Park, Wyo.: Yellowstone Library and Museum Association.

———. 1971. An ecological rationale for the natural or artificial regulation of native ungulates in parks. *Trans. North Amer. Wildlife Conf.* 36:417–25.

———. 1983. A naturally regulated elk population. In *Symposium on natural regulation of wildlife populations*, ed. F. L. Bunnell, D. S. Eastman, and J. M. Peek, 62–81. Moscow: University of Idaho.

Connor, M. A. 1993. Stability and change in mountain adaptations: The view from Jackson Hole, Wyoming. Abstract. Jackson, Wyoming: Rocky Mountain Anthro. Conference.

Consolo-Murphy, S., and D. D. Hanson. 1993. Distribution of beaver in Yellowstone National Park, 1988–1989. In *Ecological issues on reintroducing wolves into Yellowstone National Park*, ed. R. S. Cook, 38–48. National Park Service Sci. Monogr. NPS/NRYell/NRSM-93-22.

Consolo-Murphy, S., and R. B. Tatum. 1995. Distribution of beaver in

Yellowstone National Park, 1994. Report of 1994 beaver survey. Yellowstone National Park, Wyo.: National Park Service file memo.

Coughenour, M. B. 1991. Biomass and nitrogen responses to grazing of upland steppe on Yellowstone's northern winter range. *J. Appl. Ecol.* 28:71–82.

Coughenour, M. B. and F. J. Singer. 1991. The concept of overgrazing and its application to Yellowstone's northern range. In *The greater Yellowstone ecosystem: Redefining America's wilderness heritage*, ed. R. B. Keiter and M. S. Boyce, 209–30. New Haven, Conn.: Yale University Press.

——. 1996. Elk population processes in Yellowstone National Park under the policy of natural regulation. *Ecol. Appl.* 6:573–93.

Cox, D. R. 1969. Some sampling problems in technology. In *New developments in survey sampling*, ed. N. L. Johnson and H. S. Smith, 506–27. New York: John Wiley.

Crawley, M. J. 1983. *Herbivory: The dynamics of animal-plant interactions*. Berkeley: University of California Press.

Culpin, M. S. 1994. *The history of the construction of the road system in Yellowstone National Park, 1872–1966*. Historic Study vol. 1. Denver, Colo.: National Park Service.

Daubenmire, R. 1943. Soil temperature versus drouth as a factor determining lower altitudinal limits of trees in the Rocky Mountains. *Bot. Gazette* 105:11–13.

——. 1968. *Plant communities: A textbook of synecology*. New York: Harper and Row.

——. 1974. *Plants and environment*. 3rd ed. New York: John Wiley and Sons.

Davis, L. B., and S. T. Greiser. 1992. Indian Creek Paleoindians: Early occupation of of the Elkhorn Mountains' southeast flank, west-central Montana. In *Ice age hunters of the Rockies*, ed. D. J. Stanford and J. S. Day, 225–83. Niwot: University Press of Colorado.

Davis, L. B. and A. M. Johnson. 1993. Quarry research implications of the 1989 Obsidian Cliff flow plateau reconnaissance, Yellowstone National Park, Wyoming. Abstract. Jackson, Wyoming: Rocky Mountain Anthro. Conference.

Despain, D. G. 1983. Nonpyrogenous climax lodgepole pine communities in Yellowstone National Park. *Ecology* 64:231–34.

——. 1990. *Yellowstone vegetation*. Boulder, Colo.: Roberts Rinehart.

Despain, D. G., A. Rodman, P. Schullery, and H. Shovic. 1989. Burned area survey of Yellowstone National Park: The fires of 1988. Yellowstone National Park, Wyo.: National Park Service unpub. rpt.

Dirks, R. A., and B. E. Martner. 1982. *The climate of Grand Teton and*

Yellowstone National Parks. National Park Service Occasional Paper 6. Washington, D.C.: U.S. Government Printing Office.

Dorn, R. D. 1992. *Vascular plants of Wyoming*. Cheyenne, Wyo.: Mountain West Publishing.

Douglas, A. V. and C. W. Stockton. 1975. *Long-term reconstruction of seasonal temperature and precipitation in the Yellowstone National Park region using dendroclimatic techniques*. Tucson: University of Arizona, Lab. of Tree-Ring Res.

Elias, S. A. 1993. Insect fossil evidence on the rate of environmental change at the Wisconsin-Holocene transition in the Rocky Mountains: Archeological implications for the Yellowstone. Abstract. Jackson, Wyo.: Rocky Mountain Anthropology Conference.

Engstrom, D. R., C. Whitlock, S. C. Fritz, and H. E. Wright. 1991. Recent environmental changes inferred from the sediments of small lakes in Yellowstone's northern range. *J. Paleolimnology* 5:139–74.

Fire Management Policy Review Team. 1988. *Report on fire management policy*. [Philpot Report.] Washington, D.C.: U.S. Dept. Agriculture and U.S. Dept. Interior.

Fournier, R. O., R. L. Christiansen, R. A. Hutchinson, and K.L. Pierce. 1994. *A field trip guide to Yellowstone National Park, Wyoming, Montana, and Idaho: Volcanic, hydrothermal, and glacial activity in the region*. U.S. Geological Survey Bull. 2099.

Frank, D. A. and S. J. McNaughton. 1991. Stability increases with diversity in plant communities: Empirical evidence from the 1988 Yellowstone drought. *Oikos* 62:360–62.

——. 1992. The ecology of plants, large mammalian herbivores, and drought in Yellowstone National Park. *Ecology* 73:2043–58.

——. 1993. Evidence for the promotion of aboveground grassland production by native large herbivores in Yellowstone National Park. *Oecologia* 96:157–61.

Frank, D. A., R. S. Inouye, N. Huntly, G. W. Minshall, and J. E. Anderson. 1994. The biogeochemistry of a north-temperate grassland with native ungulates: Nitrogen dynamics in Yellowstone National Park. *Biogeochemistry* 26:163–88.

French, S. P., and M. G. French. 1990. Predatory behavior of grizzly bears feeding on newborn elk calves in Yellowstone National Park, 1986–88. *Int. Conf. Bear Res. Manage.* 8:335–41.

Friis-Christensen, E., and K. Lassen. 1991. Length of solar cycle: An indicator of solar activity closely associated with climate. *Science* 254:698–700.

Frison, G. C. 1991. *Prehistoric hunters of the high plains*. 3rd ed. New York: Academic Press.

———. 1992. The foothills-mountains and the open plains: the dichotomy in Paleoindian subsistence strategies between two ecosystems. In *Ice age hunters of the Rockies*, ed. D. J. Sanford and J. S. Day, 323–42. Niwot: University Press of Colorado.

Fritz, W. J. 1985. *Roadside geology of the Yellowstone country*. Missoula, Mont.: Mountain Press Publishing.

Futuyma, D. J., and S. S. Wasserman. 1980. Resource concentration and herbivory in oak forests. *Science:* 210:920–21.

Gennett, J. A. and R. G. Baker. 1986. A late Quaternary pollen sequence from Blacktail Pond, Yellowstone National Park, Wyoming. *Palynology* 10:61–71.

Gese, E. 1995. Foraging ecology of coyotes in Yellowstone National Park. Ph.D. diss., University of Wisconsin, Madison.

Good, J. D., and K. L. Pierce. 1996. *Interpreting the landscape: Geology of Grand Teton and Yellowstone National Parks*. Moose, Wyo.: Grand Teton Natural History Association.

Grand Teton National Park. 1994. *The Jackson bison herd: Long-term management plan and environmental assessment*. Public rev. draft. Washington, D.C.: U.S. Government Printing Office 1994-577-049/05172.

Gresswell, R. E. and J. D. Varley. 1988. Effects of a century of human influence on the cutthroat trout of Yellowstone Lake. *Amer. Fisheries Soc. Symp.* 4:45–52.

Gruell, G. E. 1973. *An ecological evaluation of Big Game Ridge*. U.S. Forest Service, Intermountain Region.

———. 1979. Wildlife habitat investigations and management implications on the Bridger-Teton National Forest. In *North American elk: Ecology, behavior, and management*, ed. M. S. Boyce and L. D. Hayden-Wing, 63–74. Laramie: University of Wyoming.

———. 1980a. *Fire's influence on wildlife habitat on the Bridger-Teton National Forest, Wyoming*. Vol. 1. *Photographic record and analysis*. U.S. Forest Service Res. Paper INT-235.

———. 1980b. *Fire's influence on wildlife habitat on the Bridger-Teton National Forest, Wyoming*. Vol. 2. *Changes and causes, management implications*. U.S. Forest Service Res. Paper INT-252.

———. 1983. *Fire and vegetative trends in the northern Rockies: Interpretations from 1871–1982 photographs*. U.S. Forest Service General Tech. Rept. INT-158.

———. 1985. Indian fires in the interior West: A widespread influence. In *Proc. Symp. Wilderness Fire*, Missoula, Mont., Nov. 15–18, 1983, 68–74. General Tech. Rept. INT-182. Ogden, Ut.: U.S. Forest Service, Intermountain Forest and Range Exper. Sta.

Gunther, K.A. 1990. Visitor impact on grizzly bear activity in Pelican Valley, Yellowstone National Park. *Int. Conf. Bear Res. Manage.* 8:33–56.

Gunther, K. A. and R. A. Renkin. 1990. Grizzly bear predation on elk calves and other fauna of Yellowstone National Park. *Int. Conf. Bear Res. Manage.* 8:329–34.

Hadly, E. A. 1990. Late Holocene mammalian fauna of Lamar Cave and its implications for ecosystem dynamics in Yellowstone National Park, Wyoming. M.S. thesis, Northern Arizona University, Flagstaff.

Hague, A. 1886. Vegetation of the Yellowstone Park. Monograph no. 32. Part 2. Draft manuscript. National Archives, Washington, D.C.

———. 1887. Notebook no. 1. Unpublished field notebook 3894-G. National Archives (USGS), Denver, Colo.

———. 1888. Notebook no. 1. Unpublished field notebook 3894-I. National Archives (USGS), Denver, Colo.

Haines, A. L., ed. 1955. *Osborne Russell's journal of a trapper*. Portland: Oregon Historical Society. (Reprint 1965, Lincoln: University of Nebraska Press.)

———, ed. 1965. *The valley of the Upper Yellowstone*. Norman: University of Oklahoma Press.

———. 1977. *The Yellowstone story*. 2 vols. Yellowstone National Park, Wyo.: Yellowstone Library and Museum Association.

Haley, J. E. 1936. *Charles Goodnight: Cowman and plainsman*. New York: Houghton Mifflin.

Hamilton, W. L. 1987. Water level records used to evaluate deformation within the Yellowstone caldera, Yellowstone National Park. *J. Volcanology and Geotherm. Res.* 31:205–15.

Hansen, J., and S. Lebedeff. 1987. Global trends of measured surface air temperatures. *J. Geophysical Res.* 92:13,325–72.

Haynes, G. 1991. *Mammoths, mastodonts, and elephants: Biology, behavior, and the fossil record*. Cambridge, Eng.: Cambridge University Press.

Hik, D. S., R. L. Jefferies, and A. R. E. Sinclair. 1992. Foraging by geese, isostatic uplift and asymmetry in the development of salt-marsh plant communities. *J. Ecol.* 80:395–406.

Hill. E. P. 1982. Beaver. In *Wild mammals of North America: Biology, management, economics*, ed. J. A. Chapman and G. A. Feldhamer, 256–86. Baltimore, Md.: Johns Hopkins University Press.

Hitchcock, C. L., and A. Cronquist. 1976. *Flora of the Pacific Northwest*. Seattle: University of Washington Press.

Hoerr, W. 1993. The concept of naturalness in environmental discourse. *Natural Areas J.* 13:29–32.

Hoffecker, J. F., W. R. Powers, and T. Goebel. 1993. The colonization of Beringia and the peopling of the New World. *Science* 259:46–51.

Holling, C. S. 1973. Resilience and stability in ecology and systems. *Ann. Rev. Ecol. Systematics* 4:1–23.

Houston, D. B. 1968. *The Shiras moose in Jackson Hole, Wyoming.* Technical Bull. no. 1. Moose, Wyo.: Grand Teton Natural History Association.

———. 1971. Ecosystems of national parks. *Science* 172:642–51.

———. 1973. Wildfires in northern Yellowstone National Park. *Ecology* 54:1111–17.

———. 1982. *The northern Yellowstone elk: Ecology and management.* New York: Macmillan.

———. 1987. Willow-moose relationships in Grand Teton National Park: A continuing evaluation. Report to the superintendent, Grand Teton National Park.

———. 1992. Willow-moose relationships in Grand Teton National Park: A 1992 update. Report to the superintendent, Grand Teton National Park.

Huntly, N., and O. J. Reichman. 1994. Effects of subterranean mammalian herbivores on vegetation. *J. Mammal.* 75:852–59.

Jackson, C. S. 1947. *Picture maker of the Old West: William H. Jackson.* New York: Charles Scribner's Sons.

Janetski, J. C. 1993. Ethnohistory and human ecology in the Greater Yellowstone Area. Abstract. Jackson, Wyo.: Rocky Mountain Anthro. Conference.

Jakubos, B., and W. H. Romme. 1993. Invasion of subalpine meadows by lodgepole pine in Yellowstone National Park, Wyoming, U.S.A. *Arctic Alpine Res.* 25:382–90.

Johnson, K. L. 1987. *Rangeland through time.* Misc. Publ. 50. Agric. Exper. Sta., University of Wyoming, Laramie.

Jonas, R. J. 1955. A population and ecological study of the beaver (*Castor canadensis*) of Yellowstone National Park. M.S. thesis, University of Idaho, Moscow.

Jones, W. A. 1875. *Report upon the reconnaissance of Wyoming, including Yellowstone National Park, made in the summer of 1873.* Washington, D.C.: U.S. Government Printing Office.

Kay, C. E. 1990. Yellowstone's northern elk herd: A critical evaluation of the natural regulation paradigm. Ph.D. diss., Utah State University, Logan.

———. 1993. Aspen seedlings in recently burned areas of Grand Teton and Yellowstone National Parks. *Northw. Sci.* 67:94–104.

———. 1994. Aboriginal overkill: The role of Native Americans in structuring western ecosystems. *Human Nature* 5:359–98.

Keefer, W. R. 1971. *The geologic story of Yellowstone National Park.* U.S. Geological Survey Bull. 1347.

Klein, S. 1989. The fate of lead in Lewis Lake, Yellowstone National Park. Ph.D. diss., University of Colorado, Boulder.

Knight, D. H. 1994. *Mountains and plains: The ecology of Wyoming landscapes.* New Haven, Conn.: Yale University Press.

Lack, D. 1954. *The natural regulation of animal numbers.* Oxford: Oxford University Press.

Laycock, W. A. 1958. The initial pattern of revegetation of pocket gopher mounds. *Ecology* 39:346–51.

Lemke, T. G., J. A. Mack, and D. B. Houston. 1998. Winter range expansion of the northern Yellowstone elk. *Intermountain Journal of Sciences.* In press.

Lewin, R. 1986. In ecology, change brings stability. *Science* 234:1071–73.

Lime, D. W., B. A. Koth, and J. C. Vlaming. 1993. Effects of restoring wolves on Yellowstone area big game and grizzly bears: Opinions of scientists. In *Ecological issues on reintroducing wolves into Yellowstone National Park*, ed. R. S. Cook, 306–26. National Park Service Sci. Monogr. NPS/NRYell/NRSM-93-22.

Locke, W. W. and G. A. Meyer. 1994. A 10,000-year record of vertical deformation across the Yellowstone Caldera margin: The shorelines of Yellowstone Lake. *J. Geophysical Res.* 99:20,079–94.

Lovering, T. S. 1930. The New World or Cooke City mining district, Park County, Mont. In *Contributions to economic geology* (1929). Part 1: Metals and nonmetals except fuels. Geologists in charge G. F. Loughlin, G. R. Mansfield, and E. F. Burchard, 1–87. U.S. Geological Survey Bull. 811.

Lyon, L. J. 1971. *Vegetal development following prescribed burning of Douglas-fir in south central Idaho.* U.S. Forest Service Res. Paper INT-105. Logan, Utah: Intermountain Forest and Range Exper. Sta.

Mack, J. A. and F. J. Singer. 1992. Population models for elk, mule deer, and moose on Yellowstone's northern winter range. In *Wolves for Yellowstone? A report to the United States Congress.* Vol. 4. Research and analysis, ed. J. D. Varley and W. G. Brewster, 4-5 through 4-41. Yellowstone National Park, Wyo.: National Park Service.

———. 1993a. Population models for elk, deer, and moose on Yellowstone's northern winter range. In *Ecological issues on reintroducing wolves into Yellowstone National Park*, ed. R. S. Cook, 270–305. National Park Service Sci. Monogr. NPS/NRYell/NRSM-93-22.

———. 1993*b*. Using Pop-II models to predict the effects of wolf predation and hunter harvests on elk, mule deer, and moose on the northern range. In *Ecological issues on reintroducing wolves into Yellowstone National Park*, ed. R. S. Cook, 49–74. National Park Service Sci. Monogr. NPS/NPYell/NRSM-93-22.

Macnab, J. 1985. Carrying capacity and related slippery shibboleths. *Wildl. Soc. Bull.* 13:403–10.

Mahaney, W. C., and J. R. Spence. 1990. Neoglacial chronology and floristics in the Middle Teton area, central Teton Range, western Wyoming. *J. Quaternary Sci.* 5:53–66.

Mattson, D. J. 1990. Human impacts on bear habitat use. *Int. Conf. Bear Res. Manage.* 8:33–56.

May, R. M. 1979. Arctic animals and climatic changes. *Nature* 281:177–78.

McInnes, P. A., R. J. Naiman, J. Pastor, and Y. Cohen. 1992. Effects of moose browsing on vegetation and litter of the boreal forest, Isle Royale, Michigan, USA. *Ecology* 73:2059–75.

McNaughton, S. J. 1985. Ecology of a grazing system: The Serengeti. *Ecol. Monogr.* 55:259–94.

Meagher, M. 1973. *The bison of Yellowstone National Park*. National Park Service Sci. Monogr. no. 1.

———. 1989. Range expansion by bison of Yellowstone National Park. *J. Mammal.* 70:670–75.

———. 1993. Winter recreation–induced changes in bison numbers and distribution in Yellowstone National Park. Draft unpub. rept.

Meagher, M., W. J. Quinn, and L. Stackhouse. 1992. Chlamydial-caused infectious keratoconjunctivitis in bighorn sheep of Yellowstone National Park. *J. Wildl. Dis.* 28:171–76.

Merrill, E. H., N. L. Stanton, and J. C. Hak. 1994. Responses of bluebunch wheatgrass, Idaho fescue, and nematodes to ungulate grazing in Yellowstone National Park. *Oikos* 69:231–40.

Meyer, G. A. 1993. Holocene and modern geomorphic response to forest fires and climate change in Yellowstone National Park. Ph.D. diss., University of New Mexico, Albuquerque.

Meyer, G. A., S. G. Wells, and A. J. T. Jull. 1995. Fire and alluvial chronology in Yellowstone National Park: Climatic and intrinsic controls on Holocene geomorphic processes. *Geological Soc. Amer. Bull.* 107:1211–230.

Millspaugh, S. H. 1994. Postglacial fire history of the Cygnet Lake region, Central Plateau. In *Postglacial fire frequency and its relation to long-term vegetational and climatic changes in Yellowstone National Park*, comp. C. Whitlock, S. H. Millspaugh, P. J. Bartlein, and S. L. Shafer, 54–68. Draft final report, University of Wyoming-NPS Research Center.

Millspaugh, S. H., and C. Whitlock. 1995. A 750-yr fire history based on lake sediment records in Central Yellowstone National Park. *The Holocene* 5:283–92.

Morris, R. F., ed. 1963. *The dynamics of epidemic spruce budworm populations*. Memoirs of the Entomological Soc. of Canada no. 31.

Murphy, K. 1998. Ecology of the cougar (*Puma concolor*) in the northern Yellowstone ecosystem. Ph.D. diss., University of Idaho, Moscow.

Myers, N. 1993. The question of linkages in environment and development. *Bioscience* 43:302–10.

Naiman, R. J., C. A. Johnston, and J. C. Kelley. 1988. Alteration of North American streams by beaver. *Bioscience* 38:753–62.

National Research Council. 1992. *Science and the national parks*. Washington, D.C.: National Academy Press.

Norris, P. W. 1881. *Annual report of the Superintendent of the Yellowstone National Park to the Secretary of the Interior for the year 1880*. Washington, D.C.: Government Printing Office.

Owen-Smith, R. N. 1988. *Megaherbivores: The influence of very large body size on ecology*. Cambridge, Eng.: Cambridge University Press.

Pastor, J., R. J. Naiman, B. Dewey, and P. McInnes. 1988. Moose, microbes and the boreal forest. *Bioscience* 38:770–77.

Pearson, S. M., M. G. Turner, L. L. Wallace, and W. H. Romme. 1995. Winter habitat use by large ungulates following fire in northern Yellowstone National Park. *Ecol. Appl.* 5:744–55.

Picton, H. D. 1979. A climate index and mule deer fawn survival in Montana. *Int. J. Biometeorology* 23:115–22.

Pielou, E. C. 1991. *After the Ice Age: The return of life to glaciated North America*. Chicago: University of Chicago Press.

Pierce, K. L. 1979. *History and dynamics of glaciation in the northern Yellowstone National Park area*. U.S. Geological Survey Prof. Paper 729-F.

Pierce, K. L., and J. D. Good. 1992. *Field guide to the Quaternary geology of Jackson Hole, Wyoming*. U.S. Geological Survey Open File Rept. 92-504.

Pierce, K. L., and L. A. Morgan. 1992. The track of the Yellowstone hotspot: Volcanism, faulting, and uplift. *Geol. Soc. Amer. Memoir* 179:1–53.

Porter, S. C., K. L. Pierce, and T. D. Hamilton. 1983. Late Wisconsin mountain glaciation in the western United States. In *Late-Quaternary environments of the United States*, vol. 1, ed. S. C. Porter, 71–111. Minneapolis: University of Minnesota Press.

Precht, H., J. Christopherson, H. Hensel, and W. Larcher, eds. 1973. *Temperature and light*. New York: Springer-Verlag.

Prostka, H. J., H. R. Blank, R. L. Christiansen, and E. L. Ruppel. 1975. *Geologic map of the Tower area, Yellowstone National Park*. U.S. Geological Survey GQ 1247.

Renkin, R. A., and D. G. Despain. 1992. Fuel moisture, forest type, and lightning-caused fire in Yellowstone National Park. *Can. J. Forest Res.* 22:37–45.

Riney, T. 1964. The impact of introductions of large herbivores on the tropical environment. *Int. Union Cons. Nat.*, New Series (4):261–73.

Rochefort, R. M., R. L. Little, A. Woodward, and D. L. Peterson. 1994. Changes in subalpine tree distribution in western North America: A review of climate and other causal factors. *The Holocene* 4:89–100.

Rogers, G. F., H. E. Malde, and R. M. Turner. 1984. *Bibliography of repeat photography for evaluating landscape change*. Salt Lake City: University of Utah Press.

Rolston, H. 1989. Biology and philosophy in Yellowstone. *Biology and Philosophy* 4:1–18.

———. 1994. *Conserving natural value*. New York: Columbia University Press.

Romme, W. H. 1982. Fire and landscape diversity in subalpine forests in Yellowstone National Park. *Ecol. Monogr.* 52:199–221.

Romme, W. H., and D. G. Despain. 1989. Historical perspective on the Yellowstone fires of 1988. *Bioscience* 39:695–700.

Romme, W. H., and D. H. Knight. 1982. Landscape diversity: The concept applied to Yellowstone Park. *Bioscience* 32:664–70.

Romme, W. H., D. H. Knight, and J. B. Yavitt. 1986. Mountain pine beetle outbreaks in the Rocky Mountains: Regulators of primary productivity? *Amer. Naturalist* 127:484–94.

Romme, W. H., and M. G. Turner. 1991. Implications of global climatic change for biogeographic patterns in the greater Yellowstone ecosystem. *Cons. Biology* 5:373–86.

Romme, W. H., M. G. Turner, L. Wallace, and J. Walker. 1995. Aspen, elk,

and fire in northern Yellowstone National Park. *Ecology* 76: 2097–106.

Romme, W. H., M. G. Turner, R. H. Gardner, W. W. Hargrove, G. Tuskan, D. G. Despain, and R. Renkin. 1995. A rare episode of sexual reproduction in aspen (Populus tremuloides) following the 1988 fires. Unpubl. manuscript.

Schreiner, E. G., M. B. Gracz, A. Woodward, and N. M. Buckingham. 1994. Mountain goat herbivory IV: Rare plants and synthesis. In *Mountain goats in Olympic National Park: biology and management of an introduced species*, comp. D. B. Houston, E. G. Schreiner, and B. B. Moorhead, 173–85. National Park Service Sci. Monogr. NPS/NROlym/NRSM-94-25.

Schullery, P. 1989. The fires and fire policy. *Bioscience* 39:686–94.

Sellars, R. W. 1997. *Illusions of primitive America: History of nature preservation in the national parks*. New Haven, Conn.: Yale University Press.

Shepard, N., and G. Caughley. 1987. Options for management of kangaroos. In *Kangaroos, their ecology and management in the sheep rangelands of Australia*, ed. G. Caughley, N. Shepherd, and J. Short, 189–219. Cambridge, Eng.: Cambridge University Press.

Shovic, H., J. Mohrman, and R. Ewing. 1988. Major erosive lands in the upper Yellowstone River drainage basin from Livingston, Montana, to Yellowstone Lake outlet, Yellowstone National Park. Interagency Coop. Report to the National Park Service. May 20, 1988. Yellowstone National Park, Wyo.

Sinclair, A. R. E. 1989. Population regulation in animals. In *Ecological concepts: The contribution of ecology to an understanding of the natural world*, ed. J. M. Cherrett, 197–241. Blackwell, Eng.: 29th Symp. of the British Ecol. Soc.

———. 1995. Equilibria in plant-herbivore interactions. In *Serengeti II: Dynamics, management, and conservation of an ecosystem*, ed. A. R. E. Sinclair and P. Arcese, 91–113. Chicago: University of Chicago Press.

Sinclair, A. R. E., and P. Arcese. 1995. Population consequences of predation-sensitive foraging: The Serengeti wildebeest. *Ecology* 76: 882–91.

Sinclair, A. R. E., and M. Norton-Griffiths, eds. 1979. *Serengeti: Dynamics of an ecosystem*. Chicago: University of Chicago Press.

Singer, F. J. 1991. The ungulate prey base for wolves in Yellowstone National Park. In *The greater Yellowstone ecosystem: Redefining America's wilderness heritage*, ed. R. B. Keiter and M. S. Boyce, 323–49. New Haven, Conn.: Yale University Press.

Singer, F. J., and J. A. Mack. 1993. Potential ungulate prey base for grey wolves. In *Ecological Issues on reintroducing wolves into Yellowstone National Park*, ed. R. S. Cook, 75–102. National Park Service Sci. Monogr. NPS/NRYell/NRSM-93-22.

Singer, F. J., and J. E. Norland. 1994. Niche relationships within a guild of ungulate species in Yellowstone National Park, Wyoming, following release from artificial controls. *Can. J. Zoology* 72:1383–94.

Singer, F. J., and R. Renkin. 1995. Effects of browsing by native ungulates on the shrubs in big sagebrush communities in Yellowstone National Park. *Great Basin Nat.* 55:201–12.

Singer, F. J., L. Mack, and R. Cates. 1994. Ungulate herbivory of willows on Yellowstone's northern winter range. *J. Range Manage.* 47: 435–44.

Smith, R. B., and L. W. Braile. 1984. Crustal structure and evolution of an explosive silicic volcanic system at Yellowstone National Park. In *Explosive volcanism: Inception, evolution, and hazards*. Studies in geophysics, 96–109. Washington, D.C.: National Academy Press.

———. 1993. Topographic signature, space-time evolution and physical properties of the Yellowstone–Snake River Plain volcanic system: The Yellowstone hotspot. In *Geology of Wyoming*, ed. A. W. Snoke, J. R. Steidmann, and S. M. Roberts, 694–754. Geological Survey of Wyo. Memoir No. 5.

Soule, M. E. 1990. The onslaught of alien species and other challenges in the coming decades. *Cons. Biol.* 4:233–39.

Stanford, D. J., and J. S. Day, eds. 1991. *Ice age hunters of the Rockies*. Niwot: University Press of Colorado.

Streubel, D. 1989. *Small mammals of the Yellowstone ecosystem*. Boulder, Colo.: Roberts Rinehart, Inc.

Strong, W. E. 1876. *A trip to the Yellowstone National Park in July, August, and September, 1875*. Washington, D.C.: Published by author. (Reprint, Norman: University of Oklahoma Press.)

Swenson, J. E., K. L. Alt, and R. L. Eng. 1986. Ecology of bald eagles in the Greater Yellowstone Ecosystem. *Wildl. Monogr.* 95:1–46.

Tilden, F. 1964. *Following the frontier with F. Jay Haynes: Pioneer photographer of the Old West*. New York: Knopf.

Turner, C. G. 1992. New World origins: new research from the Americas and the Soviet Union. In *Ice age hunters of the Rockies*, ed. D. J. Stanford and J. S. Day, 7–50. Niwot: University Press of Colorado.

Turner, M. G., Y. Wu, W. H. Romme, and L. L. Wallace. 1993. A landscape simulation model of winter foraging by large ungulates. *Ecol. Modeling* 69:163–84.

Turner, M. G., Y. Wu, W. H. Romme, L. L. Wallace, and A. Brenkert. 1994. Simulating interactions between ungulates, vegetation, and fire in northern Yellowstone National Park during winter. *Ecol. Appl.* 4:472–96.

Tweedy, F. 1886. *Flora of the Yellowstone National Park*. Washington, D.C.: Published by the author.

Tyers, D. 1993. Winter ecology of moose on the northern Yellowstone winter range. Draft report to the Northern Yellowstone Cooperative Working Group.

Varley, J. D. 1981. *A history of fish stocking activities in Yellowstone National Park between 1881 and 1980*. Information Paper no. 35. Yellowstone National Park, Wyo.: U.S. Fish and Wildlife Service.

Varley, J. D., and P. Schullery. 1983. *Freshwater wilderness*. Yellowstone National Park, Wyo.: Yellowstone Library and Museum Association.

Varley, N. 1994. Summer-fall habitat use and fall diets of mountain goats and bighorn sheep in the Absaroka Range, Montana. *Biennial Symp. Northern Sheep and Goat Council* 9:131–38.

———. 1995. Ecology of mountain goats in the Absaroka Range, south-central Montana. M.S. thesis, Montana State University, Bozeman.

Vavra, M., W. A. Laycock, and R. D. Pieper. 1994. *Ecological implications for livestock herbivory in the West*. Denver, Colo.: Society for Range Management.

Veblen, T. T., and D. C. Lorenz. 1991. *The Colorado Front Range: A century of ecological change. Salt Lake City*: University of Utah Press.

Vohs, P., ed. 1996. Report to Congress on ungulate grazing on Yellowstone's northern winter range. In preparation.

Walker, D. N. 1993. Late Pleistocene and Holocene mammalian faunas of the Greater Yellowstone Ecosystem and surrounding regions. Abstract. Jackson, Wyo.: Rocky Mountain Anthr. Conference.

Wallace, L. L. 1990. Epilogue: A search for paradigms. In *Fire in North American tallgrass prairies*, ed. S. L. Collins and L. L. Wallace, 147–51. Norman: University of Oklahoma Press.

Wallace, L. L., M. G. Turner, W. H. Romme, R. V. O'Neill, and Y. Wu. 1993. Bison and fire: Landscape analysis of ungulate response to Yellowstone's fires. In *Proc. North American Bison Public Herds Symp.*, comp. R. Walker, 79–120. Custer, S. Dak.: Custer State Park.

———. 1995. Scale of heterogeneity of forage production and winter foraging by elk and bison. *Landscape Ecol.* 10(2):75–83.

Warren, E. R. 1926. *A study of the beaver in the Yancey Region of Yellowstone National Park*. Roosevelt Wildl. Ann. no. 1.

White, C. A. n.d. Banff landscapes: A century of change. Draft manuscript. Alberta, Can.: Banff National Park.

Whitlock, C. 1993. Postglacial vegetation and climate of Grand Teton and southern Yellowstone National Parks. *Ecol. Monogr.* 63:173–78.

Whitlock, C., and P. J. Bartlein. 1993. Spatial variations of Holocene climatic change in the Yellowstone region. *Quaternary Res.* 39:231–38.

Whitlock, C., P. J. Bartlein, and K. J. Van Norman. 1995. Stability of Holocene climate regimes in the Yellowstone region. *Quaternary Res.* 43:433–36.

Whitlock, C., S. C. Fritz, and D. R. Engstrom. 1991. A prehistoric perspective on the northern range. In *The greater Yellowstone ecosystem: Redefining America's wilderness heritage*, ed. R. B. Keiter and M. S. Boyce, 289–305. New Haven, Conn.: Yale University Press.

Whitlock, C., S. H. Millspaugh, P. J. Bartlein, and S. L. Shafer. 1994. Postglacial fire frequency and its relation to long-term vegetational and climatic changes in Yellowstone Park. Draft final report, University of Wyoming–NPS Research Center.

Whittlesey, L. 1988. *Yellowstone place names.* Helena: Montana Historical Society Press.

Woodward, A., E. G. Schreiner, D. B. Houston, and B. B. Moorhead. 1994. Ungulate-forest relationships in Olympic National Park: Retrospective exclosure studies. *Northw. Sci.* 68:97–110.

Wright, R. G. and S. C. Bunting. 1994. *The landscapes of Craters of the Moon National Monument.* Moscow: University of Idaho Press.

Wyoming State Historical Society. 1976. *Re-discovering the Bighorns: A pictorial study of 75 years of ecological change.* Cheyenne: Wyoming State Historical Society.

Yeager, D. G. 1934. *Bob Flame, ranger.* New York: Sears Publishing.

Youmans, C. C. 1979. Characteristics of pocket gopher populations in relation to selected environmental factors in Pelican Valley, Yellowstone National Park. M.S. thesis, Montana State University, Bozeman.

Index

Dashes indicate repetition of previous subentry.